D1452450

VOLUMES IN THIS SERIES

Reports

1. *A Survey of Sardis and the Major Monuments Outside the City Walls* (1975), by George M. A. Hanfmann and Jane C. Waldbaum

Monographs

1. *Byzantine Coins* (1971), by George E. Bates
2. *Ancient Literary Sources* (1972), by John G. Pedley
3. *Neue epichorische Schriftzeugnisse aus Sardis* (1975), by Roberto Gusmani
4. *Byzantine and Turkish Sardis* (1976), by Clive Foss

ARCHAEOLOGICAL EXPLORATION OF SARDIS

Fogg Art Museum of Harvard University - Cornell University
Corning Museum of Glass
Sponsored by the American Schools of Oriental Research

GENERAL EDITORS

George M.A. Hanfmann and Stephen W. Jacobs

MONOGRAPH 4

BYZANTINE AND TURKISH SARDIS

Clive Foss

HARVARD UNIVERSITY PRESS
Cambridge, Massachusetts, and London, England 1976

Copyright © 1976 by the President and Fellows
of Harvard College
All rights reserved
Printed in the United States of America
Publication of this volume has been aided
by grants from the Loeb Classical Library
Foundation and the University of Massachusetts,
Boston

Library of Congress Cataloging in Publication Data

Foss, Clive.
  Byzantine and Turkish Sardis.

  (Monograph - Archaeological Exploration of Sar-
dis; 4)
  Bibliography: p.
  Includes index.
  1. Sardis—History. I. Title. II. Series:
Archaeological Exploration of Sardis. Monograph;
4.
DS156.S3F67   939.2′2   75-14017
ISBN 0-674-08969-3

Editors' Preface

The Archaeological Exploration of Sardis has been carried on since 1958 as a joint effort of the Fogg Art Museum of Harvard University and Cornell University; the Corning Museum of Glass was a participant from 1968-1971. The development of this program was greatly furthered by the sponsorship of the American Schools of Oriental Research. An informal survey of the history of the project from 1957-1972 is found in G. M. A. Hanfmann's *Letters from Sardis* (1972). The results of this collaborative effort are being published in two series of volumes. The final Reports, the first of which appeared in 1975, contain the evidence from the excavations, accounts of major architectural monuments, and certain major categories of excavated objects. The Monographs are devoted to special subjects which supplement the Reports.

In the fourth volume of Sardis Monographs Clive Foss of the University of Massachusetts in Boston presents an account of late antique (284-616), Byzantine, and Turkish Sardis. The volume is thus in a sense a continuation of Sardis Monograph 2, *Ancient Literary Sources on Sardis* by John Griffiths Pedley, which documents the history of the city to A.D. 284. Whereas Pedley gives a narrative of the earlier history of the city separately in his book *Sardis in the Age of Croesus* (1968), Foss has combined a narrative account and a collection of sources in a pioneering study of late antique and post-antique Sardis.

As a frequent visitor to Sardis since 1965, when he contributed important observations on the dating of the Byzantine Main

Avenue, as a staff member since 1969, who has catalogued many of our inscriptions and coins, as an indefatigable explorer of the Sardis region, and as a researcher with a special interest in the Byzantine history and topography of Western Asia Minor, Clive Foss is uniquely qualified to undertake the study of this difficult and hitherto unexplored subject. The Sardis program is indebted to him for his effectiveness and promptness in executing his task.

We take this opportunity to express our profound gratitude to the Government of the Republic of Turkey, especially to the Ministry of National Education, to the Division of Cultural Affairs in the Prime Ministry, and most recently to the Ministry of Culture for the privilege of studying the cultural heritage of Turkey. The constant help and cooperation of the Department of Antiquities and Museums has made this work fruitful and rewarding. The successive Directors General and other officers in Ankara as well as the representatives of the Department attached to the expedition in the field have helped us to solve many problems.

At the Sardis Research and Publications unit at Harvard, work on illustrations and other needs of the manuscript was performed by Elizabeth Wahle.

We acknowledge gratefully the sustained interest of the cooperating American institutions, whose presidents, deans, and other officers have furthered the program. Initial financial support for the Sardis program came from the Bollingen Foundation (1957-1965) and the Old Dominion Foundation (1966-1968). From 1962-1965 a grant made through Harvard University by the Department of State under Public Law 480 greatly increased the effectiveness of field research and the training program. Grateful acknowledgment is also made to the Ford Foundation for a grant for student traineeships through Cornell University from 1968 to 1972, and to the Memorial Foundation for Jewish Culture for a grant toward the publication of the Synagogue. Generous assistance was received from the Loeb Classical Library Foundation and the Billy Rose Foundation. Many individuals and private foundations have sustained the project by their contributions as Supporters of Sardis (through Harvard University), as contributors to the Committee to Preserve the Ancient Synagogue of Sardis, and as donors to the American Schools of Oriental Research.

Our special gratitude goes to a number of friends and foundations who in recent years have participated in the matching grants of the National Endowment for the Humanities. Since 1967 the aid received from the Endowment has been a mainstay of the program; without these grants we could not have proceeded with our research in the field nor with our studies and publication efforts at home. Work on the present Monograph (1969, 1972-1973) benefited by Endowment matching grants H69-0-23, RO-6435-72-264, RO-8359-73-217.

We join Clive Foss in thanking the institutions which have supported his research and thus made this book possible. The Archaeological Exploration of Sardis is happy to acknowledge the welcome aid received toward actual publication costs of this monograph from the Loeb Classical Library Foundation and from the University of Massachusetts.

George M. A. Hanfmann
Harvard University

Stephen W. Jacobs
Cornell University

Author's Preface

Until the beginning of systematic excavation, Sardis was known chiefly from the pages of Herodotus, who described an archaic period when the city was a proverbial center of wealth and luxury. The later history, if it was considered at all, was known only from occasional mentions by poets and historians and from the descriptions of travelers. The excavations, those of the Princeton Expedition from 1910-1914 and of the annual Harvard-Cornell campaigns since 1958, have revealed a great amount of information from all periods of the city's history. Something is now known about the material culture of every period from the Bronze Age through the Ottoman, and sufficient information is at hand that synthesis may be attempted.

Many of the remains belong to the postclassical period, from the late third century until modern times—an obscure age which has generally received as little attention from archaeologists as archaeology itself has from historians of the Byzantine period. This vast period falls into three clearly marked divisions: the late antique, the Byzantine, and the Turkish,[1] each of which has characteristics

---

1. The following terms are used to refer to the periods of time covered in this work: late antique, 284 to 616; Dark Ages, 616 to mid-ninth century; Middle Byzantine, mid-ninth century to 1204; Lascarid, 1204 to 1261; Palaeologue, 1261 to ca.1315; Seljuk, ca.1315 to 1425; Ottoman, 1425 to 1923. Although some of these terms may seem at variance from normal usage, they are capable of accurate definition and are used consistently here. I have used "late antique" because it has closely related noun and adjective forms (unlike "Late Roman" *vel sim.*) and does not imply a continuity with the following period, as does "Early Byzantine." The evidence shows a clear break in the Dark Ages at Sardis as elsewhere. I only use "early Christian" in referring to ecclesiastical history.

and problems of its own. In Late Antiquity, Sardis was a large and flourishing metropolis which maintained many of the traditions of the classical age. Sources, though scarce, are better than those of succeeding periods; both secular and ecclesiastical writers occasionally mention Sardis, while several inscriptions provide information. Much more important, however, is the archaeological record. Although only a small part of the site has been excavated, most sectors have produced late antique remains, and, in the western part of the city, a whole quarter built up in the period has been discovered.

When the city was destroyed in a Persian attack of 616, a new and less happy period of its history began. The seven hundred years of the Byzantine age are obscure, here as elsewhere. The sources are poor: Sardis is hardly mentioned at all until the end of the period and inscriptions are practically nonexistent. The remains show the poverty of the age: the city had ceased to exist and was replaced by a town with a castle and scattered small settlements.

There was no great break in the material culture of the town when the Turks took it around 1315. The fundamental change from a Greek, Christian town to a Turkish, Islamic one is hardly visible in the archaeological record, but Sardis remained a town with a castle. This pattern persisted until the early fifteenth century when Sardis came under Ottoman rule and insensibly declined to a village inhabited, if at all, by nomads. As may be expected from the historical circumstances, the archaeological record of the Turkish period is skimpy. Sources, of the kind used so far, vanish, since the place was too poor and obscure to occupy the attention of historians. New sources, however, become available in the form of Turkish documents and the narratives of European and Turkish visitors to a place whose ancient renown was beginning to draw the attention of scientific travelers. Because Turkish Sardis aid not sink into complete oblivion, it is possible to trace the history of the city, town, or village fairly continuously down to the present.

In this volume, I have attempted to provide such a history, based on all available sources, both written and archaeological. The two kinds of sources tend to complement one another: the excavations, for example, have shown that the city was destroyed in 616, a fact not mentioned by historians of the time; similarly, the Arab attack of a century later, which appears in the sources, has left little trace in the remains. Thus, by combining the two types of evidence, a more complete picture may be obtained. Gaps which persist can be readily understood from the nature of the sources; some will be filled by future excavation, which will no doubt alter interpretations and conclusions presented here. I hope, however, to provide a framework into which future discoveries may be fitted.

A city does not live in isolation. Ideally, a history of Sardis or any comparable city would place it in the context of its surrounding region and its age. Only some of that may be attempted here, since the regional and urban history of Asia Minor in postclassical periods is still in its infancy. Archaeologists have until recently tended to ignore the unattractive and banal remains of later ages which obstruct their investigation of the classical, while often historians seem unacquainted with the archaeological evidence. In a recent (and unpublished) doctoral dissertation, I sketched the urban history of western Asia Minor from Diocletian to the Turkish conquest.[2] The present work on Sardis is expanded from part of that thesis; other material presented there will be drawn upon to compare the development of Sardis with that of other contemporary cities. Regional history, on the other hand, will hardly be considered; a brief sketch of it appears in another volume of this series.[3] For the period under consideration, the history of the region would have to be pieced together from sources even more exiguous than those about the city; such work cannot be undertaken here. I have, however, occasionally used sources which deal with the province, Lydia, in order to provide a background for events at Sardis.

Chapter four of the text is a selection from the written sources which presents some idea of the evidence upon which this study is based. Reference to the sources is made in the text by means of numbers in parentheses. The text is accompanied by two appendices. The first is a tabulation of the known archbishops of Sardis from the beginning to the suppression of the diocese in 1369, and

2. Clive Foss, "Byzantine Cities of Western Asia Minor" (Diss. Harvard, 1972).
3. For the region of Sardis, see C. Foss and G. M. A. Hanfmann, "Regional Setting and Urban Development," in G. M. A. Hanfmann and J. Waldbaum, *A Survey of Sardis and the Major Monuments Outside the City Walls*, Sardis Report 1 (Cambridge, Mass. 1975).

the second discusses the long-prevalent notion that the city was destroyed by Tamerlane in 1402.

All photographs, unless otherwise indicated, have been provided by the Archaeological Exploration of Sardis.

It is a great pleasure to record the help I have received at all stages of the composition of this work and to express my thanks to the friends and colleagues who have so generously offered such help. Professor John Kroll suggested this topic to me and proposed my name to the Sardis Expedition. Professor G. M. A. Hanfmann, director of the expedition, kindly invited me to undertake this work, generously made me a member of the expedition, and granted me free access to its findings. Research on the site was partially financed by grants from the American Research Institute in Turkey, the University of Massachusetts, and the Archaeological Exploration of Sardis. Publication of this work was materially assisted by the University of Massachusetts, Boston, which has my sincere thanks, and by the Department of Classics, Harvard University, whose successive chairmen, Professors G. W. Bowersock and Wendell Clausen, generously extended their interest and help.

Professors Ernst Kitzinger, G. M. A. Hanfmann, Mason Hammond, and Cyril Mango, members of the committee which supervised my dissertation, offered generous help, advice, and correction in an early stage of this work. Professor Hammond in particular went through individual chapters with painstaking care to improve their style, organization, and thought. His corrections, like those of the others, were always accompanied by the most thoughtful encouragement.

My colleague, Professor Eric Robinson, put his great knowledge of the history of technology at my disposal, and Mr. Jacob Tulchin aided me in the translation of difficult passages in the sources. Mr. Rudi Lindner of the University of California, Berkeley, read the sections on Turkish Sardis and suggested several valuable additions and alterations. In addition numerous friends at Sardis contributed their time to advise me on specific sectors and problems.

No one who studies Asia Minor can fail to profit from the profound and monumental scholarship of Professor Louis Robert, whose works have been a constant inspiration. He has freely granted me assistance in person and in correspondence and has kindly allowed me to print among the sources new inscriptions which will be properly published in a forthcoming volume of this series.

Finally, I owe a special debt to my mother, to whom this book is gratefully dedicated.

CF

Contents

CONTENTS

BYZANTINE AND TURKISH SARDIS

B	Building B, the Gymnasium
CG	Building CG, Roman baths
HOB	House of Bronzes
IN	Unpublished Sardis inscription
L	Building complex southwest of Artemis Temple
MTW	West Middle Terrace, trench south of HOB
PC	Pactolus Cliff
PN	Pactolus North

I. Late Antique Sardis

Historical Outline

Sardis was founded at the foot of Mount Tmolus by the banks of the gold-bearing Pactolus in the Bronze Age or earlier. The site on which the city grew was easily defensible—a high, isolated hill with streams on the east and west, a steep face to the plain of the Hermus on the north, and the massive range of Tmolus on the south—and in a strategic location. Several natural routes, which later became highways, intersected in the immediate vicinity, connecting the Hellespont and the Aegean with central and southern Asia Minor and ultimately with the lands of the Fertile Crescent. In addition, the site was in the center of a rich and highly fertile region; the plain of the Hermus produced a variety of agricultural products, and the mountain behind it was rich in minerals. Among those was the gold washed down by the Pactolus stream, a copious source of wealth which was to bring to the city great renown.

The town established there soon flourished, and by the time the historical record begins it had become the capital of the Lydian kingdom. Sardis had its most glorious days under the Lydians but continued to prosper as part of the Persian Empire, when it became the seat of a satrapy and the terminus of the great Royal Road which led a three months' journey inland to Susa. When Alexander arrived in 334 B.C., the city became a provincial capital in a Greek kingdom and was soon Hellenized. It was to remain a center of Greek life until the fourteenth century.

1

In these early ages, Sardis grew beside the Pactolus. In 213, however, Antiochus III captured the city after a long siege and moved it to a new site about a kilometer to the east. There, civic buildings typical of a Greek city were erected and a Hellenized metropolis developed through the Hellenistic and Roman ages. Under the empire, the city, rebuilding after the disastrous earthquake of A.D. 17, spread back towards its old location on the Pactolus, an area by then occupied by tombs and monuments. Like the other cities of Asia Minor, Sardis reached the height of its prosperity in the second century, when it flourished as a metropolis of perhaps 100,000 inhabitants, adorned with imposing public buildings.[1]

For the period to be discussed here, historical and literary sources provide relatively little information. Writers of the time were naturally more concerned with the emperor, the army, and the church, and had little occasion to consider the undramatic prosperity of the cities. The paucity of sources, however, does not reflect the importance of Sardis: other great cities receive no more attention from contemporary writers. As in the classical period, written sources may be supplemented by inscriptions, but these are less common in Late Antiquity than earlier. Although they can provide information of considerable interest, they are usually short, often difficult to interpret, and rarely dated. In spite of their limitations, such sources are adequate to suggest the reasons for the prosperity of Sardis in Late Antiquity, and by their very silence attest to the relative tranquility of these three centuries. They illustrate the importance of Sardis as a provincial capital and a military and industrial center; they show the city as the seat of a philosophical school and indicate the variety of occupations and religions of its inhabitants. For a more complete picture, the archaeological record must be consulted, where some indication of the appearance and size of the city, of its houses and monumental buildings, and of its growth and prosperity may be found. Combination of all the sources, which largely complement each other, produces a survey of conditions in an important metropolis of Asia Minor in Late Antiquity.

The cities of Asia Minor flourished during the first two centuries of the Roman Empire. That Sardis was no exception is attested by considerable building activity, numerous inscriptions, and an abundant coinage. This happy state continued through the age of the Severi, but thereafter the country was not spared the disasters which afflicted the empire during the middle and second half of the third century. As Asia Minor was ravaged by civil war, invasion, and the plague, the appearance of its cities came to reflect the troubles of the times. Under the empire, cities of the interior were generally not fortified; their walls were the legions and castles of the frontiers. When this bulwark was broken, new defenses had to be created. The great wall of Rome built by Aurelian around a city whose most recent ramparts were popularly attributed to Servius Tullius is perhaps the most notable example in the empire.

Construction of city walls was a common feature of life in third century Asia Minor. Walls at Nicaea, Miletus, Pergamum, Didyma, and many other places were built or reconstructed in the dark days of the Gothic invasions.[2] Sardis, too, received a new wall, which was probably erected in this period; it has not been dated precisely (fig. 1). This rampart, four kilometers long, descended from the inaccessible slopes of the Acropolis to surround the city on three sides. It had towers and a gate by the Pactolus where the main highway entered the city. The wall stood some seven meters high and was constructed of regular courses of rough stones with almost no use of spoils. The large area which it enclosed—roughly 1800 by 700 meters—seems to represent almost all of Roman Sardis; only one major building, a bath at the eastern edge of the city, was left outside its circuit. This suggests that Sardis suffered no major disaster at the time the wall was built, but the sources and the archaeological record are silent about the city in the late third century.[3]

The reign of Diocletian marks a period of great change for the whole Roman Empire. The highly centralized, bureaucratic, and despotic form of government he and his successors established shows a clear break with the traditions of the early empire. After Constantine had adopted Christianity and implicitly become head of the one religion all the subjects of the empire were soon expected to follow, a political structure was created which was destined to last until the Byzantine Empire fell to the Turks. Among the most fundamental reforms of Diocletian and his successors were those which concerned provincial administration and the army.The provinces were divided into smaller units, subordi-

nated to the complicated hierarchy of the central government, and
the army was reorganized. These reforms directly affected Sardis
and did much to ensure its importance during Late Antiquity.

When Diocletian revised the provincial structure of the Roman
Empire, Sardis became the capital of the province of Lydia and the
seat of its governor. It retained this distinction throughout Late
Antiquity until the empire was reorganized into military districts
called "themes" in the Dark Ages. The new province appears in
contemporary lists from the time of Constantine to that of Justinian. Hierocles, who wrote in the sixth century, mentions Sardis
as the capital, and enumerates twenty-one cities under its jurisdiction.[4] This large number attests to the extent of urbanization in
Lydia and the importance of its capital. As civil organization was
soon imitated by the Church, the bishop of Sardis became the metropolitan of the ecclesiastical province of Lydia, with the bishops
of the other cities subject to him. The organization of the church
proved more stable and more conservative than that of the state
and it long outlived the system which had inspired it. As long as
Christianity was predominant in the area, Sardis remained the
metropolis of the province of Lydia.[5]

Although the governor of the civil province enjoyed the relatively distinguished title of *consularis* (which showed that he was
of the second rank, below proconsuls, but ahead of the great
majority of his colleagues who were mere *praesides*), history has
preserved the memory of very few. Hilarius, a pagan, administered Lydia in the late fourth century; Panhellenius in 382
received a law about slaves who informed against their masters;
Basiliscus erected a fountain in the Gymnasium in the fourth or
fifth century; and Severus Simplicius and a governor whose name
ended in "-nonius" made repairs to that building somewhat later.
Of these, only Panhellenius is otherwise known. He was a native
of the province of Asia who had been educated in Athens. In 388,
he visited Antioch, where he was acquainted with the great sophist
Libanius, and subsequently returned to his native land. When he
was settled there, he was evidently still a person of considerable
influence, for the new vicar of Asia, Domnio, was given a letter of
introduction to him by Libanius.[6]

The obscurity of these office holders is hardly surprising in an
age for which sources are mediocre and inscriptions relatively
scarce. Nor was the office of a kind to confer much fame on its

holder; provincial governorships were not high positions, but merely stepping-stones to some more powerful or lucrative dignity. Tenure was short and marked by great corruption.[7] A good example is provided by the career of Euthalius of Laodicea, who governed Lydia while Rufinus was praetorian prefect (392-395). He plundered the provincials so excessively that he was fined fifteen pounds of gold by Rufinus, a sum which he managed successfully to embezzle. With the fortune he had accumulated in his governorship, he became a rich man and was able to progress to a distinguished career.[8] Similar cases were no doubt numerous. It is therefore hardly surprising that Claudian mentions Lydia as one of the governorships sold in 399 by Eutropius, the notorious praetorian prefect under Arcadius. The invective of the poet condemns the eunuch minister for a practice which by his day was far from unusual.[9]

In the complex organization of the late antique government, provincial governors were in some ways subordinated to vicars who had jurisdiction over larger areas called dioceses. Lydia was included in the diocese of Asiana, which consisted of western Asia Minor from the Hellespont to Lycaonia. The vicar had financial and judicial duties in his diocese—he collected and remitted taxes and presided as judge of appeals from the governors' courts—but his powers were limited, for a governor was not completely his subordinate and could deal directly with the central government. The office eventually came to be felt unnecessary, and was in most cases suppressed by Justinian in 536. Vicars are generally more obscure figures than governors; only two are known whose activity may be associated with Sardis. Musonius, vicar in 367-368, used Sardis as the base from which he set out on a campaign against the Isaurians (source 4). Acholius, of uncertain date, was honored by a verse inscription which praised his justice and buildings in obscure language (source 20). Much more important to the life of the city were the governor and the municipal officials.

In its municipal institutions, Sardis, like the other cities of Asia Minor, preserved the relics of an ancient autonomy which the despotism of the day had long since robbed of any meaning. The main organ of local government was the Council (*boulē*) which under the early empire had cared for the finances, public works, and public services of the city. In Late Antiquity, the councils, which continued to have some responsibility for municipal finances, played an active though diminishing role. The number of their members constantly declined, and their functions effectively ceased with the reforms of Anastasius which transferred management of the finances of the cities to the agents of the central government. Responsibility for public works and services had already been taken over by the provincial governors.[10]

The Council of Sardis continued to exist late into the fifth century; inscriptions mentioning it were carved in the ceremonial entrance of the Gymnasium on a floor laid at that time (fig. 2). Nothing is revealed about the history or functions of the Sardian Council, but the nature of the inscriptions suggests that its members engaged in some kind of ceremonial activity in the area of the Gymnasium. Another inscription in the same place mentions the Elders (*gerousia*) of the city. It is extremely doubtful that this organization, also known from earlier inscriptions, had any real political function; in all probability it was an association of citizens who would have great influence from the dignity of age and office. The *gerousia*, too, apparently had its place in the municipal ceremonial of an age in which such activities presented the facade, without the reality, of power.[11]

The actual administration of the city was entrusted to various executive officers. In the fifth century the most important of these was the *defensor civitatis*, who combined the functions of judge with those of chief municipal magistrate.[12] An important inscription (source 14) illustrates his eminence at Sardis in 459, when he presided over the settlement of a strike of the building artisans of the city. The inscription records the settlement of a dispute between workers and employers, both of whom swore to Aurelianus, *defensor* of Sardis, that they would abide by the terms of the settlement.

Diocletian and his successors did not limit their concern to the organization of the government. The immediate needs of defense were paramount, but the financial well-being of the provinces was also necessary to maintain the stability of the state. A functioning system of highways was essential for both prosperity and defense, but the highway network had been allowed to fall into decay during the anarchy and chaos of the third century. The efforts of Diocletian and Constantine to restore it are particularly evident in Lydia. The highways which led from Sardis to Smyrna, to Pergamum via Thyateira, to Daldis, and to the Anatolian plateau via

Bagis and Phrygia (with a branch to Silandus) were all repaired,[13] an activity reflecting the extensive building programs of the period and the major military reforms these emperors carried out. The army was the most important user of the highways, and, since Sardis had by now become a military center, it was imperative to secure its communications with the rest of the region.

Among its major military reforms the government of Diocletian created a system of state-operated armaments factories, the product of financial and military developments alike. Equipment had formerly been sold to the soldiers by means of deductions from their pay; now, with the great depreciation of the currency, this financial transaction was avoided and the government supplied weapons and armor of its own manufacture. This ensured the regular supply of equipment and is typical of an age which had experienced the partial collapse of a money economy. At the same time the cavalry, which had become the most important branch of the army, was adopting much heavier armor, and the factories (*fabricae*) were presumably built to standardize and to supply this equipment.[14] One of Diocletian's main concerns was the security of the eastern frontier against the renascent power of Sassanid Persia. The *fabricae*, most of which were established along the frontier, are to be seen as part of the military and economic reforms which characterize his whole reign.[15]

In Asia Minor, only three of these factories were located within the frontiers and only one in the whole diocese of Asia. The *Notitia Dignitatum*, written about 400, lists a *fabrica scutaria et armorum*, a shield and weapon factory, at Sardis (source 1). Although other evidence is lacking, it is reasonable to associate the construction of this factory with the reforms of Diocletian since the *fabricae* at Nicomedia, Antioch, Edessa, and Damascus were built during his reign.[16] The factory at Sardis might equally have been established in the time of Constantine, in connection with other military reforms, notably the creation of the *comitatenses*, the field army of the interior which was stationed all over the empire and used to garrison cities.[17]

Although the location of the *fabrica* of Sardis remains uncertain, the tombstone of one of its officials provides further confirmation of its existence. The inscription records the memory of one Panion, *fabricensis* and *ducenarius*—member of the guild of factory employees, with a salary of 200,000 sesterces (source 2).

His title and salary show that he was a member of the equestrian order and a high official of the empire and further illustrate the importance of the *fabrica*. The stone is inscribed in a crude and careless hand, which could be appropriate to any part of the period; two inscriptions in similar lettering, however, have been dated to the fourth century.

The location of Sardis on the highways connecting the Hellespont, the Aegean, and the plateau of Anatolia and the presence of the only weapons factory in the whole area would have made the city a major military center. Its importance is attested by texts of the fourth century. During the revolt of Procopius in 365, the emperor Valens made Sardis his base for a time (source 3). Three years later, it was from Sardis that Musonius, vicar of Asia, set out on the campaign against the Isaurians which was to prove fatal to him and his army (source 4). In 396, Timasius, *magister militum* under Theodosius, used Sardis as his headquarters; here he made the acquaintance of Bargus, the Syrian sausage seller, who was to be responsible for his fall (source 5).

Late fourth century repairs of the highways which led to Sardis from Smyrna, Thyateira, and Daldis probably also reflect the military importance of the city. There is, however, no clear evidence that any large body of troops was stationed there nor is any special military commander of the district mentioned. Tombstones of soldiers from the period have been found, but they are too few to indicate which or how many troops were based at Sardis.[18]

During the long period from Diocletian to Heraclius, Sardis rarely had to function as a military center, for the age was one of almost uninterrupted peace for the city and the province; wars against internal or external foes were almost entirely fought in other parts of the empire. Such losses as the city suffered came as the result of imperial policy. When Constantinople was founded in 330, Sardis was one of the cities which Constantine looted to decorate his new capital; its antique treasures were still visible in the Hippodrome of Constantinople centuries later (source 6). There were a few serious disturbances in the late fourth and early fifth centuries, but none of them involved the city in disaster.

In September 365, Procopius, a relative of the emperor Julian, revolted against Valens who had recently been proclaimed. At first he met with some success, for his general Marcellus took

Cyzicus and then followed the imperial commander Serenianus into Lydia where he defeated and killed him. However, the following spring the usurper, who had gained control of much of Asia Minor, met Valens and the imperial forces at Thyateira in Lydia, and Procopius lost this battle when most of his troops deserted to the emperor. After his victory, Valens sojourned in Sardis and eventually advanced to Nacoleia in Phrygia where he finally defeated and killed the rebel.[19]

If the revolt of Procopius did little damage in Lydia, that of the Ostrogoths under Tribigild was far more serious. The Goths had been settled in Phrygia by Theodosius in 386 to serve as cavalry in the imperial army. Under the leadership of their commander, Tribigild, they broke into revolt in the spring of 399 and began to devastate the peaceful provinces of western Asia Minor. As they proceeded, they were joined by runaway slaves and peasants and attacked every place that lay on their route. Lydia in particular was placed in great danger. Many of its inhabitants fled to the coast and the islands, while the people of the coast expected a greater disaster than they had experienced to strike them. The rebels, however, turned southwards from Phrygia to ravage Pisidia and Pamphylia. Everywhere they went, the Goths attacked cities, plundered the countryside, and slaughtered the inhabitants.

At this time, the Roman army was commanded by another German, Gainas, *magister militum in praesenti* under the feeble regime of Arcadius. Instead of impeding the disastrous progress of Tribigild, he secretly supported him, hoping thus to gain an ally in his own plans to overthrow the government. Gainas and Tribigild, therefore, after an initial appearance of fighting, came to an agreement, and both marched in the direction of the capital. Tribigild followed behind through upper Lydia, along a route which avoided Sardis, presumably the direct road from Philadelphia to Thyateira. When the two met in Thyateira, they regretted not having attacked Sardis, which could have been taken easily since no relief was available. They turned back with the intention of storming the city, but Sardis was saved by a providential rainstorm which caused the Hermus to rise so much that the barbarians were unable to cross (source 7). After abandoning their attempt on Sardis, the Goths marched off towards the capital and soon left Asia.[20] Although the destruction caused by this revolt was severe, it was an isolated incident in a long period of peace. The provinces eventually recovered, and Sardis, itself untouched, remained undisturbed until the disastrous days of Heraclius.

The obscurity of the following century and a half at Sardis probably reflects the peace of the times as much as the lack of sources. The city does, however, appear in the literature of the age.[21] Nonnus, who wrote a long and tedious epic on Dionysus in the fifth century, commemorated the antiquity of the city, drawing on local traditions and histories (source 8). Since Dionysus is supposed to have been born on Mount Tmolus, the poet had frequent occasion to mention Lydia. In the reign of Justinian, Macedonius Consul wrote an epigram in which Sardis itself spoke and described its own antiquity and traditions (source 9). The rather wistful tone of the poem seems appropriate to an age which so often looked to a glorious past.

Although Sardis suffered no further from invasion or civil war, there is evidence that the sixth century was not a happy time for the inhabitants of the area. The reign of Justinian is generally considered the most magnificent in all of Byzantine history, and few who visit Istanbul, read Procopius, or consult the law codes would have reason to question this opinion. During his reign great effort and expense were devoted to the defense of the frontiers and the construction of magnificent buildings in the capital and a few other places. But on closer inspection this work seems to resemble a glorious facade built onto a crumbling edifice. There is little evidence of any corresponding prosperity in the provinces of Asia Minor but rather hints that their situation had seriously deteriorated.

The adulatory work of Procopius, *On the Buildings*, spares no opportunity to praise Justinian by describing the great projects carried out in the capital, on the frontiers, at Ephesus, and in Bithynia, but it is almost completely silent about any such work done in the rest of Asia Minor. Other sources of the period have little to say about the provinces of Anatolia: Lydia is rarely mentioned and Sardis not at all. One of the problems which plagued all the governments of Late Antiquity was manifest in Lydia on the eve of the reign of Justinian. Since the third century, proprietors had been deserting their land, sometimes because of a shortage of manpower, but more often as a result of the increasing burden of taxation. The government found some solution in assigning the deserted lands to neighboring proprietors who would be responsible for the taxes on them. A law of 521-523 addressed to Ortalinus, the governor of Lydia, dealing with a rather complicated case of such assignment shows that the province was not free of this trouble, and the epilogue, in which the governor and his staff are threatened with a stiff fine if they failed to comply with the provisions of the decree, may be taken to indicate that such unpopular measures would bring resistance and perhaps collusion between the governor and influential local landowners.[22] The situation of the province and the empire in the time of Justinian could only have exacerbated such problems.

John the Lydian, a native of Philadelphia, presents an angry narrative which is of great value in illustrating local conditions. The praetorian prefect John of Cappadocia (531-541) used all possible means to raise revenues to avert the financial disaster which threatened the state as a result of the extravagant programs of public works and even more expensive wars of reconquest in the West. His ruthlessness made itself particularly felt in Lydia, where he was assisted by the vicar of Asia, John Maxilloplumacius, "Pillow-jaw," a nickname reflecting his gross obesity. According to the indignant account of John the Lydian, Maxilloplumacius came to Philadelphia and released a horde of wild beasts and Cappadocians (both terms referring to tax collectors) on the country, and so bled it that Philadelphia was stripped of its money and people and left without the resources to recover. In addition, no wife, maiden, or young boy was spared from the lust of the vicar, nor did family, rank, or service provide any protection from his ravages. A certain Petronius of Philadelphia, a good speaker and a man of a distinguished family, owned a stone of great value. In order to get the stone, Maxilloplumacius had Petronius tortured and imprisoned in a stable. The whole city was filled with pity and indignation: the bishop appealed to the vicar, who ignored all pleas and was only content when Petronius finally surrendered all his property and valuables. In a similar instance, a veteran named Proclus was forced to pay twenty pieces of gold, a sum greater than he possessed. He too was tortured but finally escaped by committing suicide. Maxilloplumacius plundered Lydia for a whole year before turning his activities to the rest of Asia, where, in a move to economize, he suppressed the public post by which farmers had transported their goods to market. As a result, crops

were not sold but rotted and the farmers, deprived of their liveli-
hood, were unable to pay their taxes and fled from the land.[23]

Because he came from Philadelphia, John the Lydian might be
accused of partiality and exaggeration, but there is no reason to
doubt that the provincial population suffered tremendously from
the exactions of the treasury.[24] Although John writes only about
his native town, it is evident that the whole region, including Sardis, was similarly ravaged. The tax collector was not the only
agent of the government to inflict trouble on Lydia; the strictly
orthodox regime of Justinian also carried out a vigorous persecution of the pagan population which still survived at Sardis and in
the countryside.[25] But the greatest disasters were produced not by
man but by nature. The bubonic plague ravaged the empire in
542-543, with recurrences for the next fifty years. Although Lydia
is not specifically mentioned, it is hardly likely to have escaped
this calamity which is known to have reached central and northwestern Asia Minor. The death toll was enormous and the
resources of manpower available for labor and the army were
severely diminished; the plague was so serious that its effects have
been compared with those of the Black Death of the Middle
Ages.[26]

This series of catastrophes naturally provoked a reaction from
the population, and the province seems to have fallen into a
chaotic state. For decades, the people of the provinces had been
paying a high price for the extravagances of the government; the
burden finally became intolerable and uncontrollable violence
broke out in the diocese of Asia. To deal with the widespread
revolts and brigandage, the government apppointed a special officer, a *biokolytes* or suppresser of violence, to rule Lydia with full
military powers. Similar officers were installed in neighboring
provinces where the civil governors had also proved incapable of
dealing with the problems. Typically of the age, the cure proved as
bad as the disease: a law of 553 ordered the *biokolytes* suppressed
in Phrygia and Pisidia in response to an appeal of the inhabitants.
They had reported that civil disturbance had ended, but that the
biokolytes and his men continued to harass the province, arresting
and punishing unjustly, so that the whole place had become unin-
habitable. Justinian relieved these districts, but maintained the
biokolytes in Lydia, where the situation was apparently not yet

under control.[27] Since the subsequent history of the province in the sixth century is unknown, it is not possible to determine whether the disturbances were successfully repressed or persisted until the country succumbed to the great invasions of the seventh century.

These fragmentary events should be seen against the background of conditions in Asia Minor under Justinian. Although not usually discussed in general works, the troubles of Anatolia are known from a remarkable inscription of 527 and from various laws. The inscription, from western Pisidia, contains the petition of the priests of a certain oratory of Saint John for protection from the emperors. Their lands and peasants were being harassed by imperial officials, police, and troops stationed in the vicinity; some lands had been seized on one pretext or another. In their reply Justin and Justinian ordered that an investigation take place and that the governor of the province have the lands restored to the church.[28] The tone and content are strikingly reminiscent of similar petitions addressed to the emperors of the third century by the suffering peasantry of Asia Minor, which have been used to illustrate the anarchy and misery of that time.[29] Further consideration of the evidence shows that the comparison between the third century and the time of Justinian is not altogether unjust.

Amid the vast bulk of Justinian's legislation, the Novels in particular provide some insight into internal conditions and show clearly that, in Asia Minor at least, the empire was undergoing a severe crisis. Governors were looting the provinces; large landowners kept private armies, attacked the lands of others, and seized their peasants, and the exactions of the military were dreadful. Brigandage prevailed over many provinces, and the officials appointed to suppress it usually turned out to be more of a plague than the bandits.[30] The government made extensive efforts to correct the situation by fundamental reforms in the administrative system, but the general inefficacy of the work is revealed by the continuing series of laws which extend throughout most of the reign of Justinian. Because of the obscurity of the following period, the situation cannot be traced further. It is only certain that the troubles, whether or not successfully repressed, soon yielded to a far worse period: the age of invasions in the seventh century which marked the beginning of the Middle Ages.

Industry and Commerce

With the exception of the gold of the Pactolus, all the natural resources which had made Sardis a major center of trade and industry in earlier times were available in Late Antiquity.[31] Sardis doubtless benefited from its role as provincial capital and military center, and, although the sources provide much less abundant information for Late Antiquity than for previous centuries, it is clear that the city continued to flourish in commerce and industry.

The greatest single industry of late antique Sardis was probably the imperial arms factory. Since this provided armor and weapons for the whole diocese of Asia, it was presumably a very large establishment. The employees of the *fabricae* formed an important element in the population of the cities in which they were located and were a force to be reckoned with in civic affairs; they were prominent, for example, in riots in Hadrianopolis and Caesarea.[32] Although none of the factory buildings have been located, comparison may be made with the legionary *fabrica* at Corstopitum in England, which has been excavated and seems to have employed a force of several hundred; the imperial factories would have been much larger.[33]

After 396 the arms factories were run by the state, under the direction of the *magister officiorum;* they had been previously administered by the praetorian prefects. Private armorers were allowed to operate until the reign of Justinian, when weapon-making was made a state monopoly and the factories became completely responsible for supplying the army. The workers (*fabricenses*) were free men who formed a hereditary corporation; they were bound to their jobs and their sons were expected to succeed them. Slaves aided them in their work. There were severe penalties for *fabricenses* who attempted to leave the service, significantly described as *militia*, a term which was applied to most forms of government service in the period. The service, however, was not without distinction. Laws of the period prohibit municipal decurions from trying to enter the corporation, indicating that the position of *fabricensis* was a desirable one, and the chief of staff of the *fabrica* was given the high rank of an imperial bodyguard on his retirement.[34] The importance of the *fabricenses* to the state is shown by the words of the emperor Theodosius II: "the harsh necessity of war has invented the guild of armorers which guards the decrees of the emperors with a kind of immortality . . . for this guild arms, this guild equips our army."[35]

The metal working industry of Sardis produced more than weapons and armor. Most industry in the ancient world, as in many parts of Turkey today, was carried out on a small scale and the craftsman was often the retailer of his own products. The excavations of a series of shops along the southern facade of the great Gymnasium complex at Sardis has revealed a variety of metal objects which were presumably produced in the same shops. Iron and bronze locks, various tools of both metals, bronze vessels, balances, and utensils have been found.[36] Since the cost of transport was notoriously high in antiquity and since Sardis is known to have been a center of metalwork, with all the necessary raw materials easily available, it is reasonable to conclude that such objects were of local manufacture.

The ancient textile industry also continued to be important in late antique Sardis. The state operated weaving mills for wool and linen, as well as dyeworks for the production of uniforms for the army and civil service. The list of these factories in the *Notitia Dignitatum* has not survived for the eastern part of the empire, but it is probable that there was at least one of them at Sardis. Inscriptions which refer to the guilds of clothes sellers and pantsmakers or tailors attest to the large-scale production of clothing in the fourth century,[37] and the excavations have revealed small establishments of textile production. One of the shops contained hearths, sulfur, pounders, mortars, and pestles, to suggest that it was a paint or dye works.[38] Another aspect of the industry is indicated by the remains found in the basement of the House of Bronzes, a large late antique house south of the Gymnasium. A vat, sulfur, and heating equipment found here were probably used for bleaching wool.[39] Considering the scale of industry at the time, this may have been a commercial establishment.

Many other industries and crafts flourished, among which the most important was probably the manufacture of glass, carried out in one or possibly two factories. Remains of the workshops or factories have not been discovered, but the vast quantity of glass objects excavated is sufficient to posit their existence. The objects, probably datable to the fifth and sixth centuries, consist of fragments of vessels as well as a remarkably extensive collection of window glass. Windows and vessels alike are of the same thin fabric, apparently the production of the same factory. Most of the glass was found at sectors HOB and the Byzantine Shops, the latter being particularly rich in window panes.[40] The gems found in the excavations of the Synagogue and the shops were probably the work of local craftsmen. Semi-precious stones were common in the neighborhood, and the quality of the craftsmanship is comparable with that of other products of the city.[41]

The fifth century, when many buildings were being erected in Sardis, was a particularly active time for the trades and crafts associated with construction. The intensity of this activity is witnessed by a famous inscription, the agreement of 459 which settled a strike of the building artisans of the city.[42] Stoneworkers, mosaicists, and marblecutters would have been important in the economy to judge by the large numbers of their high quality products which have survived. Particularly notable are the mosaics of a villa at Pactolus North with naturalistic representations of animals, and those of the Synagogue in geometric and floral patterns (figs. 15, 16, 18, 25, 26). The portrait sculpture of Sardis, also of fine quality, probably indicates that a school of portraiture existed there (fig. 3).[43]

The commercial life of the city has been illustrated by the excavation of the Byzantine Shops on the main highway adjacent to the Gymnasium, where Christian and Jewish proprietors manufactured and sold a variety of goods including metal tools and utensils, glass vessels (or their contents), and possibly jewelery. Such shops represent a phenomenon typical of the age: commercial centers of the cities shifted from open squares, the ancient agoras, to rows of shops located behind colonnades on main thoroughfares.[44] Less is known of trade: some of the products manufactured from the natural resources of the area were presumably used widely, but it has not yet been determined whether objects found at Sardis include imports from other centers or whether specific classes of manufactures were exported.

A late antique inscription of Sardis raises important questions about the economic and technological life of the age (source 10). This inscription is on the tombstone of one Euchromius, also called Leontius, a water mill engineer, and has been dated to the fourth or fifth century. Since this Leontius was a mechanical engineer who constructed water mills as a profession, the inscription may be considered as evidence for the widespread use of water mills in the region. If Leontius was a native or resident of Sardis, the implication follows that one or more such mills were operating in the city.[45] The history of technology may be divided into periods according to the available means of producing energy; the introduction of the water mill, which could do the work of at least three horses, was a major advance in the production of energy for manufacturing. Although known as early as the first century B.C., it seems only to have come into widespread use in Late Antiquity, when it is duly listed, as a rather expensive object, in the Price Edict of Diocletian. The only representation of a water mill in Roman art appears in the mosaics of the Great Palace of Constantinople, dated to the early fifth century, but it shows that attention was paid to such technology in the highest circles. A well-preserved example from the Athenian Agora, set up c.470, has been investigated in detail. This was of the efficient overshot type. Others are known from Rome and Arles, where a series of them constituted a "factory" for the production of flour. Most of the mills known were used for this purpose, but their possible applications were extensive. Mills, for example, apparently provided power for cutting marble in northern Gaul in the late fourth century.[46]

The water mill at Sardis may be seen in the context of the industrial advances of the time, which have not yet been sufficiently studied. It has been supposed that such mechanization was a consequence of shortage of labor,[47] and if this is true, the whole question would have important implications for the history of Late Antiquity. In Sardis and many other cities there is considerable evidence of widespread prosperity in the fourth and particularly the fifth century which has generally been attributed to the natural recovery accompanying the restoration of peace and settled conditions wherein trade and manufacturing could flourish. To these factors should perhaps be added a technological advance which might have enabled a relatively small population to produce as much as the larger populations of earlier centuries. Such questions are obviously beyond the scope of the present discussion; it is adequate here to note that Sardis participated in the technological advances of the time and may have owed some of its prosperity to that fact. Whatever the level of technology, the economy of the city depended on a skilled work force, and surviving documents give an idea of the variety of trades and professions practiced in late antique Sardis, such as bakers, tailors, clothing sellers, and building artisans, in addition to those already considered.

The tombstone of one Aurelius Zoticus, member of the *gerousia* and municipal baker, was found near the Temple of Artemis and dated to the third or fourth century (source 11). Zoticus, as a member of the *gerousia*, the Elders of the city, would have been a prominent and wealthy citizen, not a humble baker or retailer of bread. In Late Antiquity, governors and councilors took pains to guarantee an adequate supply of bread at a reasonable price for the city populations. Because compulsion was the typical solution of the age, most bakers were bound to their trades by the fourth century and obliged to provide a certain quantity of bread at a fixed price. In addition they were obliged to grind flour and bake bread for the army on campaign. In normal times, these obligations could be borne, but during a scarcity or in wartime, the burdens could become intolerable, especially for smaller operators. A series of laws of the fourth century reflects the difficulties of the situation and the constant efforts of the imperial government to ensure that there would always be enough bakers to keep the citizens supplied.[48] Some bakeries, of course, were large and successful establishments and their proprietors could become wealthy and hope to rise to high positions; some even became senators. Zoticus of Sardis was evidently a successful man. His title of municipal baker suggests that he may have been responsible for providing a distribution of free bread (*artos politikos*) to the people of the city. The bread dole of Rome, imitated in Constantinople when that became the capital of the empire, is famous, but there is less evidence for such practices in the provinces. A similar system apparently operated in Alexandria, Carthage and Antioch. The inscription of Sardis may indicate that the practice was more widespread than has been generally supposed.[49]

A Hellenistic stele found near the Temple of Artemis had been appropriated in the fourth century to provide the tombstone of one Julianus, a *bracarius* (source 12). This term, which originally meant "maker of trousers," had become generalized as a result of changing fashions to denote the maker of any kind of clothes—a tailor. Although the classical Roman, who prided himself on belonging to the *gens togata*, had regarded trousers as a dress appropriate only to barbarians, the militarization of the empire caused the fashion to spread to the highest circles and the term to take on a far broader meaning. The new dress met resistance, however, and two laws of Honorius in 399 prohibited the wearing of trousers in the city of Rome. If this prohibition was extended to the other cities of the empire, and if it was obeyed, it would be possible to consider Julianus as a manufacturer of trousers for the army.[50]

In Late Antiquity tradesmen and craftsmen were members of guilds called *collegia*. These originally free associations had become transformed so that membership in them was now compulsory, for they served a useful function for the state. Through them, the government could impose taxes and forced labor as well as control trade and labor practices. Two inscriptions of Sardis refer to these guilds: one is the marker of the collective tomb of the assistants of the clothes dealers' guild (source 13), and the other deals with a strike of the guild of building workers (source 14).

The latter inscription, dated to 459, is of considerable interest. It shows that strikes had been frequent; workers had left their tasks unfinished and obstructed others from accomplishing theirs. Most of the document consists of the agreement made between the guild of builders and artisans and their employers, as sworn on oath to the *defensor* of Sardis. The guild promised that all work would be completed provided that the agreed wages were paid and determined a course of action to be followed in the case of several contingencies. If a worker declined to complete his job, the union would replace him with another of its own members; if he, too, failed to work, the union would pay a fine to be used for the city's public works and the artisan himself would be liable to prosecution. If a worker should obstruct the employer during construction, the union would pay an indemnity. With the consent of the employer, a worker might be excused for seven days and be guaranteed the same job upon his return. In case of a worker's illness the employer would wait twenty days; if the worker had not reappeared by then, the union would provide another in his place.

This document provides the most detailed evidence available for working conditions in Late Antiquity. Strikes, perhaps for higher wages, were common and could be settled by mutual arrangement between the guilds and the employers. Such settlements would be enforced by the guild, which was in turn responsible to the municipal government if the terms were not carried out. By this time the guilds evidently had effective control over their members, could bargain for them, and could reach a settlement which would be binding upon the individual workers.[51]

In all this, the increasing rigidity and regimentation generally considered characteristic of the age is evident. At the same time, a considerable amount of flexibility survived: the agreement recognized the fact that workers might leave their jobs for any reason. The guild did not prevent that, but only promised to provide a substitute. Collective bargaining apparently did not exist; wages were to be settled between employer and worker. Strikes were seemingly an individual matter: in this document, complaints had been made against various artisans who had obstructed the work, not against the whole guild.

The document is illustrative of the age. Late Antiquity in many ways presented an apparently rigid and orderly facade, but behind it lay a far more flexible and complex system. Labor disputes were not settled entirely by the monolithic acts of government and guild; the workers still preserved a good deal of freedom of action. Similarly, the government of the time consisted not merely of a rigid hierarchical order of emperor, prefect, vicar, and governor, but was complicated and highly corrupt. Many offices overlapped others and constant change was provided by a series of expedients attempting to solve problems which arose. The propaganda of the day aimed to make everything appear simple and orderly, but one must seek a different truth behind the appearances.[52]

Public Works and Public Services

Because of the relative scarcity of inscriptions, the nature and finances of the public works and public services of Sardis in Late Antiquity are not very well known. There is sufficient material, however, to indicate that many of the facilities available to the population in Antiquity continued into this period, and that Sardis was in this respect comparable to other great centers of the empire.

The excavations have revealed some of the public buildings constructed and maintained in Late Antiquity. Notable among them is the Gymnasium at the western edge of the city (figs. 4-6). This complex, which included an open colonnaded exercise ground (the Palaestra), an elaborate entrance portal called the Marble Court, baths, and rooms for meetings or lectures, was restored on the orders of local governors. The restorations, which cannot be precisely dated, seem to have been largely decorative and concerned the Marble Court, the rooms adjacent to it, and the Palaestra. They were carried out by Severus Simplicius (source 15) and another governor whose name ended in "-nonius" (source 16). A third governor, Basiliscus, erected beside the swimming pool an elaborate fountain which poured forth water from the mouths of serpents (source 17). It is typical of the age that governors were responsible for such works.[53]

The functions of the Gymnasium in Late Antiquity are not entirely certain. In other cities, gymnasia were abandoned because of both the disapproval of the church and the decline in civic revenues, which made the burden of providing heat and free olive oil intolerable.[54] The Gymnasium of Sardis, however, contained baths, and it is probably as a bath that it continued to function. There is some indication that it may also have played an important role as the site of municipal ceremonial; the inscriptions of the Council and Elders already discussed were found on the floor of the Marble Court. One part of the complex was transformed to quite different uses: the long hall on the south side of the Palaestra became a synagogue, apparently in the second half of the third century.

Improvements of considerable public utility were carried out along the south side of the Gymnasium complex, where a long row of shops was added and the street in front of them paved with marble and adorned with colonnades and sidewalks covered with mosaics. A similar project was carried out south of the Gymnasium in a quarter which was largely built up in Late Antiquity. Across the highway from the eastern end of the Gymnasium, a Tetrapylon was erected and a street, also colonnaded and apparently lined with shops, was constructed to continue to the southwest. In these cases, new commercial centers were being provided for the people of Sardis.

The building inscription of the Tetrapylon and street (source 18) provides important information about the topography of the area, but nowhere states who was responsible for the construction. This omission would at least suggest that the governor did not supervise the work, for governors of the time were notoriously unembarrassed to put their names on public works. Another inscription (source 19) found on the same spot notes that the area was cleared out, presumably before the street was built, without the expense of city funds, but does not indicate how the project was financed.

A marble base immured in the fortifications of the Acropolis bears the praises, as it once bore the statue, of a vicar of Asia, Acholius (source 20). The verses inscribed on it laud the justice and excellence of his rule and state that "by laying a foundation of courses of stone, he wrought for the inhabitants a precinct of freedom." Although the meaning of those lines remains enigmatic, they seem to refer to a construction or benefaction granted to the city by the vicar, whose role in such matters was generally much less prominent than that of the governors.

In Sardis, as in other cities, the Church came to take on increasing responsibility for public services in Late Antiquity. The development is probably due as much to the wealth of the Church in a period when civic revenues were declining as to the Christian obligation to provide charity for the poor and the sick. An inscription of the time of Justinian provides an indication of ecclesiastical beneficence at Sardis (source 21). This mentions a hospice (*xenon*) of the sick, probably a combination of an inn and a hospital, a type of charity which the Church was then providing in many parts of the empire.[55]

Among its varied public services, the late antique city offered higher education, primarily in rhetoric and philosophy. The state took an increasing interest in education to provide a supply of trained men to the large bureaucracies of the central and provincial administrations. The government supported chairs in Rome and Constantinople and subsidized professors in cities like Sardis which had the rank of metropolis. Important cities thus had teachers of rhetoric and grammar on the public payroll and were anxious to attract the best available. A successful municipality might hope to attract a famous teacher who would found a school, which might bring renown to the city and train men qualified to serve either as teachers or government officials.[56] In many cases the careers were closely connected; a teacher might be rewarded with some nominal administrative post, or leave his profession and rise to high rank in government service.

In the fourth century, teaching of rhetoric and philosophy flourished in Asia Minor. The most famous school was that of

Pergamum, where the emperor Julian studied, but Sardis also became an important intellectual center, as shown by the *Lives of the Sophists* written around 400 by Eunapius, the most illustrious Sardian of the age. His works, though rich in information, are written in a complex and diffuse style with little attention to chronology, so that many details of the functioning of the school, such as the official position of the teachers he mentions, remain unknown. Likewise, it is impossible to determine where in the city the school functioned, though a central location, as in some part of the Gymnasium complex, would not be improbable.

The school at Pergamum, of which that of Sardis was an offshoot, was founded in the early fourth century by Aedesius, a pupil of Iamblichus. It could thus trace its philosophical origins to the Neoplatonic teachings of Plotinus, and to their elaboration by Iamblichus, for whom philosophy was closely linked with magic and the supernatural. Aedesius and his followers at Sardis belonged to the school of theurgists, "those who perform the divine," that is, men who used magic for a religious purpose. Their greatest claim to distinction lay not in original thought or in development of philosophic doctrine but in the miracles they performed—causing statues to move or speak, for example—and in their powers of divination, by which they could gain a clear knowledge of the future. Their practices were those of magicians, and in many ways bore a striking resemblance to modern spiritualism.[57] At the same time, they studied and passed on the learning of the great philosophers, practiced and taught rhetoric, and studied the healing arts. Their activities are to be regarded not as merely the mystical practices of charlatans, an impression which comes naturally to any reader of Eunapius, but as a reflection of the mentality of the age, in which superstition and magic played a predominant role.[58]

Chrysanthius, the founder of the local school and the greatest of its "sophists," was a native of Sardis from a family of senatorial rank. His grandfather, Innocentius, was a rich and distinguished man whom the emperors (apparently Diocletian and his colleagues) had entrusted with the duty of compiling the laws.[59] When he was a young man, Chrysanthius went to Pergamum to study with Aedesius, and his education there clearly reflects the nature of the school. He first studied Plato and Aristotle thoroughly, then devoted himself to oratory, in which he became particularly proficient.[60] He next turned to the study of the gods and the more mystical teachings of Pythagoras and Apollonius of Tyana. Theurgy was the culminating stage of the training, and Chrysanthius was soon initiated into the greatest sacrament of the theurgists, the "immortalization" of the soul, by which the soul was separated from the body and united with the divinity, a ritual which guaranteed the initiate a place in a celestial paradise.[61] Thereafter, he became skilled in every kind of divination and saw the future as clearly as if he were present with the gods.

Like many of the "philosophers" of the time, Chrysanthius made his fame as much by foretelling the future as by practicing more mundane subjects. At Pergamum, he attracted the attention and admiration of the young Julian, later known as "the Apostate," who came there to study in 351. The superstitious prince eventually left for Ephesus to learn from the most illustrious miracle worker of the age, Maximus. There he was also instructed by Chrysanthius, whom he persuaded to continue as his teacher. Julian studied with the two theurgists until he was made Caesar and sent to the West in 354.

After this, Chrysanthius returned to Sardis, where he taught for the rest of his long life. When Julian became emperor, he remembered his old teacher, and summoned him to the capital. Chrysanthius declined the invitation because he could see the future so clearly, and remained at Sardis where he was made high priest of Lydia. In this office, he did not persecute the Christians and perhaps because of this remained undisturbed as a teacher at Sardis, where, he gave instruction in religion and philosophy and lived the life of a philosopher. He never wavered in his devotion to the gods, affected poverty, rarely bathed, ate no pork and little other meat, and continued to write books (none of which has survived) until an advanced age. Eunapius has described his fearsome magnetism as a teacher: whenever he entered into a discussion, all others would become silent, knowing that they could not compete with his brilliance. When he became involved in a debate, his eyes would glow and his hair stand on end. His career at Sardis, known only from a diffuse biography by his student Eunapius, continued until his death at the age of 80 in about 390.[62]

Chrysanthius had some famous colleagues at Sardis, and trained many distinguished pupils. Among the former was the

Phrygian rhetorician Eunapius. When Julian came to the throne in 361, Eunapius led a delegation from Lydia to present a golden crown to the emperor and to request some unspecified favor. He spoke so well that he not only gained for the Lydians more than they had expected, but so impressed the emperor that he was ordered to speak in a particularly difficult legal case, which he proceeded to win. Eunapius' position as head of the embassy suggests that he was the professor of rhetoric at Sardis, but his career was not confined to teaching, for he subsequently served in the staff of Musonius, vicar of Asia in 367-368. Nothing more is known of him, but his uncommon name makes it not improbable that he was the father or grandfather of the famous writer.[63]

Musonius, under whom Eunapius served, was an important figure of the fourth century who illustrates the success the study of rhetoric might bring. He studied with the sophist Eusebius at Alexandria and taught rhetoric at Athens, the greatest philosophical school of the time. After a dispute with his colleague, the Christian sophist Prohaeresius, he entered a career of government service, rising to the high positions of vicar of Macedonia in 362 and vicar of Asia in 367-368. In that office, he used Sardis as the military base from which he set out on a fatal campaign against the Isaurians. His relations with the school there are uncertain, but he clearly had friends among the intellectuals of the city. When he left on his campaign, he was seen off by the young Eunapius, then about fifteen, and an otherwise unknown local writer, Theodore, who wrote a poetic lament on his death (source 4).[64]

The most illustrious colleague of Chrysanthius was the medical writer Oribasius, whose voluminous works, composed largely of extracts from Galen, still survive. Oribasius was a sophist and physician, a pupil of Zeno of Cyprus. He was a native of Pergamum and practiced there until he was sent into exile after the death of Julian, with whom he had been closely associated. Later, he was recalled and may have settled at Sardis. At any rate, he was there to treat Chrysanthius in his final illness; the two had presumably been associates at Pergamum when Julian studied there.[65] Oribasius was on close terms with the writer Eunapius whom he encouraged to write the *History*, and for that work prepared a memoir of Julian's eastern campaign in which he himself had participated. He addressed to Eunapius several surviving books on medicine abridged from his more comprehensive work and intended as a manual for use in places or situations where no doctor was available.[66]

Whatever the role of Oribasius in the city, the practice of medicine was well established at Sardis. Ionicus, a friend of Oribasius and like him a pupil of Zeno, was a native of Sardis and son of a famous physician. The few remarks Eunapius makes about him illustrate the nature of much of the medical practice of the day, which was closely connected with philosophy and theurgy. Ionicus thoroughly knew the healing arts, was a competent surgeon, understood the use of drugs, and engaged in research. He was also an expert in philosophy and rhetoric; he composed poetry and, like so many of his colleagues, practiced divination, thus belonging to the school of theurgists. He died towards the end of the fourth century.[67]

The most distinguished product of the school which Chrysanthius founded at Sardis was the sophist Eunapius (346-c.414) whose writings provide virtually all that is known of these teachers and doctors. Eunapius received his early education from Chrysanthius, who had married his cousin, Melite. At the age of 16, he went to Athens to study with the famous sophist Prohaeresius. During his five years' residence there he was initiated into the Eleusinian mysteries and planned to continue his studies in Egypt, the center of medical learning. His parents, however, recalled him to Sardis, where he adopted the calling of sophist and seems to have spent the rest of his life. At Sardis, he taught rhetoric to his own pupils in the morning and devoted the afternoon to study with his old master, Chrysanthius, whom he never ceased to admire. At this stage, he was probably a private teacher, such as existed in all parts of the empire. Official encouragement of public education did not preclude the work of individuals, who were free to set up their own schools and find pupils wherever they chose. It is not certain whether Eunapius later filled an official chair at Sardis, for all that is known of his life comes from casual references in his own writings. Like many of his colleagues, he also practiced medicine and used his knowledge to treat Chrysanthius in his final illness.

Eunapius is best known for two works, the *Universal History*, which continued the history of Dexippus from 270 to the early fifth century, and the *Lives of the Philosophers and Sophists*, composed at the end of the fourth century at the suggestion of Chrysanthius. The work is written in obscure and pretentious style, with almost more digression than organization. Its faults and virtues reflect the nature of the school which inspired it.[68]

Other students of Chrysanthius are hardly more than names. Hellespontius, a sophist of Galatia who had traveled the whole world in his quest for learning, came to Sardis as an old man. He studied with Chrysanthius for some time, but left the city when his teacher was very ill. When Hellespontius died shortly after in Bithynia, his last instructions were to his pupil Procopius, that he should return to Sardis and admire Chrysanthius alone.[69] Chrysanthius left behind two successors in philosophy, perhaps to occupy official chairs at Sardis. These were Epigonus of Lacedaemon and Veronicianus of Sardis; the latter was apparently a friend of Eunapius.[70]

The *Lives* of Eunapius ends with the mention of Epigonus and Veronicianus; the subsequent fate of the Sardian school is therefore unknown. Although its teachers were all pagans, the school survived the triumph of Christianity until the early fourth century at least. In other places, pagans continued to teach until the sixth century as they may have done in Sardis, where paganism survived until the time of Justinian. The intolerant orthodoxy of that emperor, however, caused severe persecutions of pagan teachers and doctors, and it is hardly likely that the school of Sardis, if it still existed, survived his reign.[71]

With the exception of the works of Eunapius, none of the writings of Chrysanthius and his successors has survived. It is thus difficult to assess their work and influence. That most of them were famed as magicians and miracle workers is evident, but at the same time their teachings had a firm foundation in the philosophy, rhetoric, and science of the day. There can be little doubt that a higher education of some practical value was available at Sardis in the fourth and fifth centuries, and that the city, for part of Late Antiquity at least, was a center of learning of some importance.

Pagans, Jews, and Christians

The religious history of late antique Sardis illustrates the transition from paganism to Christianity characteristic of the time and provides abundant documentation for the existence of a large, Hellenized Jewish community in the city.

The pagan cults which had been such an important part of municipal life in the classical period received a mortal blow when Constantine adopted Christianity. Officially revived for a brief moment by Julian, they survived through the fourth century but entered upon a precipitous decline when Theodosius established intolerance and persecution as imperial policy. At Sardis the greatest cult had been that of the goddess Artemis, whose temple was apparently abandoned in the troubles of the third century to be covered with alluvium from the neighboring streams by the middle of the next century—the clearest indication of the demise of paganism in the archaeological record. The circumstances are obscure; it is possible that Christianity had already become the dominant force in the city by the beginning of the fourth century so that resources were no longer available for restoring the temple.

Paganism, however, was by no means dead at Sardis. The philosophical school which flourished there in the fourth century was entirely pagan and the prominence of some of its members assured that Sardis was effected by the brief restoration of paganism under Julian. That emperor appointed his friend and teacher Chrysanthius, high priest of Lydia, as part of his program of revitalizing paganism by strengthening its organization in imitation of the Church. Although Chrysanthius did not persecute the Christians or build new temples, existing temples apparently were restored throughout Lydia under his administration. No trace of this work had survived at Sardis.[72] Later, while Chrysanthius was still alive, two pagans, Justus, the vicar of Asia, and Hilarius, the governor of Lydia, attempted to restore altars and temples at Sardis (source 22). By this time Christianity seems to have triumphed completely, for the two officials found no altars standing in the city. Their work met with a cold reception and proved abortive. It, too, has left no trace.

There were still pagans in Lydia and at Sardis in the time of Justinian.[73] When John of Ephesus was appointed in 542 to rid the country of paganism, he found many devotees of the old religion. He claimed with pride to have converted 80,000 pagans and to have built 98 churches and 12 monasteries in the provinces of Lydia, Asia, Caria and Phrygia.[74] Whether or not these numbers are exaggerated, his work seems to have been effective, for there is no further mention of pagans in the area. By the sixth century, most pagans who survived lived in remote and mountainous districts, but an inscription of Sardis shows that some of them still inhabited an important provincial capital. The document, datable after 539, records that the remaining pagans were banished and that one of them was incarcerated in the *xenon* (source 21). This may be taken as confirmation of the effectiveness of John of Ephesus in carrying out his charge to eliminate paganism.

A Jewish community existed at Sardis among the pagans as early as the fifth century B.C. The prophet Obadiah attests that this consisted of, or included, exiles from Jerusalem. It received considerable reinforcement when Antiochus III (223-187) transplanted some two thousand Jewish families to Lydia and Phrygia to pacify their rebellious inhabitants. The Jews flourished in the Hellenistic and Early Roman periods, and by the first century B.C. they could demonstrate to a Roman official that for a long time they had had at Sardis their own assembly and their own place where they decided their affairs and controversies. In the time of Augustus, they were specifically allowed to remit the temple tax to Jerusalem. They seem to have been a substantial community, which preserved its own religion and customs while adopting the language and civic institutions of the Greeks.[75]

The material remains of the Sardian Jews are well known from the third century and later, when the community seems to have been at the height of its prominence and prosperity. Their greatest monument was the magnificent Synagogue built on the main street of the city, adjacent to the Gymnasium (figs. 13-18). The Synagogue was converted from the earlier building, which perhaps had been intended as an adjunct to the Gymnasium. Its central location strikingly illustrates the influence of the Jews in the third century, when their temple was built, and throughout Late Antiquity, when it was maintained in some splendor. Surviving inscriptions show that the mosaic floors, the marble incrustations on the walls, and the paintings on the ceiling were contributed as offerings by pious members of the community.[76] This elaborate interior decor must have produced a powerful impression on the beholder, not unlike that of the basilical churches of the period which it closely resembles in plan.[77] The Synagogue existed for more than worship and for displaying the glory of God. There was also a school attached to it, as attested by the fourth century inscription of a *hiereus* and *sophodidaskalos*, a priest and "teacher of wisdom." The school apparently functioned in the main hall of the Synagogue building, and would have been an important force in maintaining the traditions of the Jews.[78] This inscription, like almost all the others found at Sardis, was written in Greek, the language in common use by the Jews of Asia Minor.

Inscriptions from the Synagogue and the neighboring shops give some indication of the professions and distinctions of the Jews of Sardis. Some of them were shopkeepers, trading side-by-side with their Christian colleagues. Others were goldsmiths and glassmakers. Several rose to high rank in the municipal and imperial governments, a phenomenon which shows the extent of their Hellenization and integration into municipal life. Nine of those mentioned in the Synagogue inscriptions were members of the city Council, a position requiring considerable wealth and bringing great honor. One even attained the high dignity of *comes*, an honorary title which implies that the holder had progressed to an elevated rank in imperial service.[79] The donations which the congregations made to the Synagogue are ample witness of its wealth, while the continuing repairs and restorations of the building show that the Jews prospered until the destruction of the city in 616. Their subsequent fate is unknown.[80]

Sardis, one of the largest and richest cities of Asia, the seat of an important Jewish community, became a major center of early Christianity in Asia Minor. The origins of the Christian community are uncertain, but a dim tradition of the Greek church may preserve the name of its founder. One calendar names a certain Clement, the first Gentile to believe in Christ, who became bishop of Sardis. He has sometimes been identified with Clement, the fellow laborer of Saint Paul mentioned in the Epistle to the Philippians. In other calendars, however, he appears as bishop of Sardica (the modern Sofia); his identity has never been clearly established.[81]

Whatever its origins, the church was of sufficient importance to be considered one of the seven churches of Asia to which Saint John the Divine addressed letters in the Book of Revelation. The obscure language of the Evangelist seems to say that the church had lapsed from its earlier state, "thou hast a name that thou livest and art dead," and that only a few had not "defiled their garments," that is, perhaps, had not lapsed into paganism or heresy.[82]

A century later, the church at Sardis was plainly flourishing, for it produced an outstanding apologist and writer, the bishop Melito, who presided in the time of Antoninus Pius and Marcus Aurelius and was the author of numerous works on Christian faith and doctrine. Of most of these, only the titles or fragments survive, among them a quotation from the *Extracts* in which Melito made the earliest known list of the canonical books of the Old Testament. For that, he had travelled to the Holy Land to carry out his researches. Only one of Melito's works survives almost complete, the *Homily on the Passover*. This work not only shows that the bishop of Sardis was well versed in the literary technique of the Second Sophistic (he was also known as a skilled orator), but illuminates the relationship between Christians and Jews at the time. Melito, like many Christians in Asia Minor, was a Quarto-deciman, a group which celebrated Easter on the day of the Passover, regardless of the day of the week, a practice later condemned as a heresy. Despite this Judaizing tendency, Melito was no admirer of "Israel," which he strongly attacks for crucifying Christ. It is quite possible that this hostility to the Jews arose from the presence of a large and influential Jewish community at Sardis, in the face of which the bishop may have felt the need to define the position of his church. The homily is thus to be seen in the context of a conflict between the Christians and Jews, which may have provided the occasion for the composition of the *Apology* for the faith that Melito possibly presented to the emperor Lucius Verus on his visit to Sardis in 166. Melito died before 180, and was buried at Sardis. Apparently he was never canonized.[83]

Sardis did, however, produce two saints, martyrs in the persecutions of the third century. Therapon, a priest of Sardis, was executed at Satala in Lydia under Valerian (source 23), and Apollonius, about whom virtually nothing is known, succumbed to one of the persecutions of the third century (source 24). An inscription found in the village of Sart contains a formula commonly taken to be crypto-Christian and may date from the time of the persecutions.[84]

The ecclesiastical history of Sardis in Late Antiquity is poorly known. Names of several bishops are recorded, but none of them achieved any great distinction. Since the administration of the church imitated that of the state, Sardis was the seat of the metropolitan bishop of Lydia, a situation determined by the time of the Council of Nicaea and prevailing until 1369. The bishop of Sardis enjoyed an exceptionally high position in the hierarchy of the Orthodox Church. Until the early fourteenth century, he ranked sixth in precedence after the patriarchs and consequently appears, especially in the Middle Ages, as an influential figure in ecclesiastical affairs. Individual bishops of later periods will be discussed below.[85]

The history of the Church in Late Antiquity is dominated by the interminable controversies on the nature of Christ and the Trinity which caused widespread confusion and disturbance throughout the eastern empire. Doctrinal strife at Sardis provided the few occasions for the mention of the city by the ecclesiastical historians. In 360 the bishop Heortasius was deposed on the grounds that he had been ordained without the sanction of the Lydian bishops. This may mean that he differed from them, or from the patriarch, in doctrine.[86] Three years later, during the long struggle between the Arian and orthodox parties, Aetius, the leader of the most extreme Arians, appointed a certain Candidus to take charge of the church of Lydia—that is, to be bishop of Sardis. Although Candidus was a relative of the emperor Jovian, he seems not to have been well received, for shortly afterwards Aetius was obliged to go to Lydia himself to ensure the new bishop's successful occupation of his see. The subsequent fate of Arianism at Sardis is unknown, but it is not likely to have outlasted the reign of its partisan, the emperor Valens.[87]

Sardis was not free from heresy, though not a center of it. The Quartodecimans, long established in the city, still had churches in Asia and Lydia, when John Chrysostom confiscated them in about 401. This did not end their activity in the region. The fanatic patriarch Nestorius (428-431) is recorded to have visited calamities upon the Quartodecimans in Asia, Lydia, and Caria, and by so doing to have provoked riots at Sardis in which multitudes perished (source 25). Such factional struggle was common in the cities of Asia Minor at the time and the large number of casualties suggests the strength of the heresy which had received the blessing of Melito.[88]

Heresy was rife in the eastern part of the province of Lydia, probably because of its proximity to Phrygia, the breeding ground of all sorts of Christian aberrations. In the region of Philadelphia, the Quartodecimans had bishops and numerous adherents in the early fifth century. Their abjurations of heresy at the Council of

Ephesus in 431 are preserved, along with those of some local Novatians, intransigent puritans who differed little from the Orthodox in doctrine and only began to be persecuted by Nestorius.[89] Philadelphia also provided a recruiting ground for the Montanists, a primitive sect of a revivalist type, whose spiritual elite was given to speaking in tongues. The tombstone of a local Montanist bishop dated to 514-515 was found in Mendehora, a town of the Cogamus Valley about thirty kilometers east of Sardis.[90] Whether the errors of Novatianism and Montanism spread farther west to infect Sardis, the capital of the province, is uncertain.

The most important of all the heresies was that of the Monophysites, who came to claim the allegiance of the provinces east of Asia Minor. Their belief in the single nature of Christ was developed after the Council of Ephesus in 431 had condemned the opposite view of Nestorius. Monophysite enthusiasts, particularly Eutyches, an abbot of Constantinople, spread the doctrine in the following decades. In 448, Florentius, bishop of Sardis, wrote to the patriarch about the doctrinal differences which had arisen between him and two of his suffragans, the bishops of the neighboring towns of Hyrcanis and Hierocaesarea, who both apparently leaned to Monophysitism. As a result, the patriarch called a synod which condemned Eutyches and his teaching, and the heresy was finally rejected by the Church as a whole at the Council of Chalcedon in 451. There, Florentius, one of the few bishops of the eastern Church to know Latin, functioned as a translator for his colleagues.[91]

After Chalcedon, conflict between the Monophysites and the Orthodox was endemic until the Arab conquests of the seventh century removed the offending provinces from the empire. In 457, when the Monophysite bishop of Alexandria demanded a new council, the emperor Leo wrote to the leaders of the Church for advice, and a synod of the bishops of Lydia was held at Sardis to discuss the question. The bishops answered the emperor with a letter in which the doctrines of Chalcedon were upheld and the actions of the Monophysites deplored.[92]

The controversy was still raging in the mid-sixth century. Justinian and his uncle Justin had endeavored to repress all heresy and tolerate only the Orthodox, but the adherents of the Monophysites were so numerous that a compromise was eventually reached. In this the empress Theodora tacitly supported the Monophysites, who were allowed not only to exist but even to proselytize. When John of Hephaestopolis went on a missionary journey to Lydia around 536, he found many "convents of believers," perhaps survivors from earlier efforts of the Monophysites under the more tolerant reign of their sympathizer Anastasius.[93] The greatest Monophysite missionary was Jacob Baradaeus who ordained numerous bishops in the cities of Asia Minor between 553 and 556. Among them was John of Amida, who became bishop of Ephesus in 558 and is generally known as John of Ephesus. John is famous for his massive conversions of pagans in Lydia and other provinces of western Asia Minor under Justinian, but he also profited from his position to spread the Monophysite faith. Among the bishops he ordained was one Elisaeus of Sardis, who was brought to Constantinople in 571 and imprisoned during a general persecution of Monophysites. Elisaeus had presumably been rival to an Orthodox bishop; there is no evidence that Monophysitism in Sardis survived his arrest.[94]

While the literary sources thus give a fragmentary impression of the progress and problems of Christianity at Sardis, the archaeological record provides visible illustration of the conversion of the city into a Christian metropolis. Crosses were carved on the Temple of Artemis to nullify the power of the demons who, it was believed, dwelt in the material of pagan edifices. Over one corner of the temple, a small church was built in the fourth century, apparently to serve as a local chapel. Religious implements, including a shovel for embers decorated with a cross, were found in a luxurious house south of the Gymnasium, the so-called House of Bronzes, and in one of the Byzantine shops a marble basin with crosses carved on it was built. The greatest church of Sardis, probably the cathedral of the city, stood on the highway east of the Gymnasium. The present structure, which has not been excavated, has been attributed to the time of Justinian. If the church was a product of that time, it illustrates the imperial munificence which could still cause large churches to be erected in an age when there was relatively little major construction. The Christian inscriptions of Sardis, most of them tombstones, offer little information.[95]

The Material Remains:
Sardis in the Time of Diocletian

The Lydian city of Sardis grew up along the stream of the gold-bearing Pactolus, which, according to Herodotus, flowed through its agora. None of the important remains from the Lydian period which the excavations have uncovered lie far from the stream. Persian and Early Hellenistic Sardis occupied the same area, with its Necropolis on the high hill west of the Pactolus. In these times, the construction of the Temple of Artemis was begun, near an area which had already been inhabited by the Lydians. The Pactolus seems to have remained the axis of the city until 215-213, when Antiochus III took Sardis after an especially destructive siege and ordered the city moved to a new site about a kilometer to the east under the foothills of the Acropolis. Since most of the excavations have been carried out in the western parts of Sardis, details about the Hellenistic and Roman city, which centered on the new site, have not been determined. Substantial remains still stand, however, and have been sufficiently well surveyed to make it possible to reconstruct a general picture of Sardis at the beginning of the late antique period.[96]

The main axis of Sardis in the time of Diocletian was the highway which ran east and west along the Hermus Valley. The Pactolus marked the edge of the city; to the west the monuments of the Roman Necropolis stretched along the highway. Near the Pactolus lay numerous graves and monuments from the Hellenistic and Roman periods, interspersed with industrial installations. Somewhat to the south, a group of industrial buildings, including a lamp kiln, stretched along the eastern bank of the Pactolus.

On the north of the highway towered one of the most monumental buildings of Sardis, the Roman Gymnasium, under construction over a long period of time and finally completed in the early third century. This complex was built on an artificial terrace where tombs had previously stood, high over the fertile plain of the Hermus. The highway had been realigned as part of the same plan, and ran along the southern facade of the building. The Gymnasium, a combination gymnasium and bath of a type common in Asia Minor, was the largest such establishment at Sardis (figs. 4, 5). The main covered part of the building contained the bathing establishment, with its hot and cold baths and swimming pool. It was a vast structure about 80 x 120 meters centered on two symmetrical apsed halls. The interior rooms were revetted with marble and paved with mosaic floors; fountains adorned the niches around the swimming pool. The entrance to the building was an imposing high portal decorated with columns and pilasters, with a screen colonnade in front, which is now being restored to its antique state (fig. 6). This so-called Marble Court faced into a colonnaded palaestra about 80 meters square, flanked by two long symmetrical halls, apparently intended for use as dressing rooms, for lectures, and for cult practices. The main entrance to the complex was on the east, where a colonnaded street ran along its facade.

By the beginning of the late antique period, the southern hall flanking the Palaestra had been converted to a new use. Because of considerable rebuilding later, the exact circumstances of the change cannot be determined, but coin finds and inscriptions indicate that the building had become a synagogue in the third century. In this stage, the Synagogue consisted of a long hall with an apse at the west end, mosaic floors, and walls decorated with marble revetment (figs. 13-18).[97]

A road apparently led northeast from the main entrance to the Gymnasium past three or four massive buildings. These are represented now only by huge mounds covered with vineyards, but their size and central location suggest that they may have formed part of the civic center of Roman Sardis. The *praetorium*, a governor's residence or local military headquarters, probably stood in this area. Its existence is mentioned in a saint's life which refers to events of the third century.[98] Beyond the mounds, the road would have continued past the Roman basilica, Building C, a structure whose massive marble piers supported vaults of brick.[99] There may have been other buildings, now represented by rising ground, north and east of the basilica. Beyond them, the terrain drops off to the Hermus plain (fig. 7).

The main east-west highway led to another group of monumental buildings. About 500 meters east of the Gymnasium stands the long wall of an extensive Roman construction built in a style similar to that of the City Wall (fig. 8). Its central location and fortress-like appearance suggest the possibility that it may have been the weapons factory of Sardis, but there is no evidence to support an identification.[100] To the southeast, built into the foothills of the Acropolis and visible from most of the city was the Theater of Sardis, which held some 20,000 people. It was a structure of mortared rubble faced with masonry, as was the Stadium which lay directly in front of it.[101]

Beside a stream at the eastern edge of the city, about a kilometer and a half from the Gymnasium, stood another large Roman bath, Building CG, a masonry structure of the second century A.D. The Gymnasium and the Bath formed the eastern and western extremities of the monumental center of the city. They were located at the edges of the city probably because of the great amount of supplies which had to be brought in to them, and because they were both in convenient proximity to streams.

The central part of the city thus stretched along the highway for almost two kilometers. On the south it was bounded by the steeply rising foothills of the Acropolis and on the north by the broad and fertile plain of the Hermus, the "Sardian" plain of Antiquity. Its greatest extent north and south was about 700 meters. The central part of Sardis thus comprised an area roughly comparable to the old section of Ankara today or to Izmir in the nineteenth century. Residential quarters were presumably scattered throughout this central area; there is no part of it which does not preserve some traces of ancient building, and many houses have been found in the excavated western quarters.

One major building, the Temple of Artemis, was eccentric to the main axis of the city, and far from the center. It lay on the eastern bank of the Pactolus more than a kilometer south of the highway. The road along the Pactolus passed through sector PN, where, in an area largely empty, were Roman tombs and monuments dominated by an artificial mound covered with burials. As it continued southward, the road was lined with tombs which formed an extension of the Roman Necropolis until it reached the temple, a building of the Ionic order which had been begun in the Hellenistic period and was still being worked on in the reign of Antoninus Pius.

The area of the temple changed drastically in Late Antiquity. The evidence is not altogether clear and subject therefore to varying interpretations. By the mid-fourth century, the eastern end of the temple had been buried in over a meter of deposits brought down by the streams which flow to the north and south of it. It is quite likely that the building had been at least partially abandoned, but the extent to which it may have been subsequently dug out is not known.[102] The circumstances under which the temple declined can only be conjectured, since there are no sources for the history of Sardis during the late third century. Conceivably, in that time of anarchy and crisis, the building had been abandoned during some barbarian attack, or because the resources of the city had been insufficient to maintain it. But that is only speculation; it is also possible that the temple was maintained until the advent of Christianity, and that the meter of deposits accumulated in the half-century or so after that.

Whether or not it was functioning, the temple still stood, surrounded by a complex of buildings (fig. 9). These were Roman constructions of mortared rubble, built apparently after the earthquake of A.D. 17; some of them were still in use as late as the fifth century. Their presence suggests considerable activity in the area, at least in the early Roman period. Two streets lined with buildings and monuments can be traced north of the temple, and east of them, a high terrace led northwest up to a stoa. The hillside behind the temple was terraced and covered with small buildings and monuments, and south of the temple lay the large Building L. Several Roman vaulted chamber tombs lay both north and south of the temple.

In the time of Diocletian, Sardis was a metropolis distinguished by major public buildings stretching along the main highway. The western quarters, where the city had originally been located, were largely given over to tombs and monuments, but a road led south through this Necropolis to the Temple of Artemis, which may have still been functioning. Late Antiquity, contrary to the impression given by many modern writers, was a time of prosperity marked by considerable building activity; the excavations have cast a great deal of light on such activity and on the expansion of the city in this period. Since so much has been discovered, and in order not to burden the reader by the very abundance of material, it seems best to present the evidence of the expansion and rebuilding of Sardis in Late Antiquity sector by sector, as the excavations have revealed it.

The Expansion of the City in Late Antiquity

Detailed knowledge of the growth of Sardis and of the various building projects which were planned and executed during Late Antiquity depends on the evidence provided by the excavations. Since the site of the city is enormous, most of these have been confined to its western quarters, which can therefore be considered closely. With one exception, the buildings of the central and eastern parts of the city have not been excavated, but there is sufficient evidence to indicate that these quarters were inhabited and saw considerable activity in Late Antiquity. Municipal life continued on the same scale in this period as in earlier centuries; the civic buildings of the city center were doubtless maintained and even added to as Sardis became a provincial capital and military center.

In the eastern part, the Theater, Odeon, and Stadium would certainly still have functioned, though they are not mentioned in any texts. People of the time were notoriously fond of chariot races and spectacles of all kinds; a sculpture of a charioteer and graffiti representing horses (fig. 10) found by the Synagogue show that the Sardians were no exception.[103] This part of Sardis received at least one major new addition during the period: a large domed basilica, Building D, was built on the northern side of the highway not far east of the agora (fig. 11). This building, which, to judge by its size and commanding central location, was probably the cathedral of Sardis, appears to be of the Justinianic period.[104] At the eastern edge of the city, Bath CG received alterations and additions in the form of brick walls and frescoes in Late Antiquity, but there is evidence to suggest that it may have been abandoned during the period because of flooding and silting.[105]

Little is known about the area to the west of the Pactolus, now covered by the houses of the village of Sart. The city proper seems to have begun at the Pactolus, with the main Roman Necropolis stretching along the highway to the west. The road was lined with monumental tombs, of which the most imposing to have survived until modern times was that of Claudia Antonia Sabina, a work of the early third century. The Necropolis was in use in Late Antiquity. A painted Christian chamber tomb, now destroyed, stood on the northern side of the highway opposite the monument of Sabina. Its interior was covered with frescoes showing peacocks, flowers, other birds, a basket, and a Christogram. The paintings, which closely resemble those of the "Peacock Tomb" on the Pactolus, have been dated to the fourth century.[106]

Much more information is available about the western quarters, which may conveniently be considered by sectors starting at the Gymnasium complex and proceeding south along the Pactolus to the temple.

The Roman Bath and Gymnasium complex was maintained during the period, although it has often been presumed that the disapproval of the Church caused the buildings to fall out of use. Two major inscriptions, as well as the evidence of the excavations, attest to considerable decorative restoration of the Marble Court and the rooms around it. It is not certain how far any of the restorations affected the western part of the building. One of the inscriptions, containing several ornate verses typical of the period, is difficult to interpret accurately (source 16). It mentions a gold-gleaming roof, mosaics, and pavement, which were restored by a certain "-nonius" (the inscription is incomplete). The other commemorates the restoration of the *aleipterion* by Severus Simplicius, governor of Lydia (source 15). Neither inscription can be dated by style or content. The excavations, however, have produced evidence for restorations in the Gymnasium for which some chronology may be determined. Considerable fragments of late antique revetment have been found in the Marble Court, where a new marble floor was laid over the old mosaics of an adjacent room around 500 (fig. 12).[107] New capitals made for a reconstruction of the colonnade of the Palaestra have been dated to the late fifth century,[108] and it may be possible to associate these repairs with the inscriptions. The new revetment and floors in and around the Marble Court could be part of the work of -"nonius" commemorated in verse. The association of the restoration of Severus with the Palaestra, however, is more dubious, though it is possible that both works and both inscriptions are roughly contemporary. Given the short terms of provincial governors and their concern for praising their own works, the two inscriptions could refer to a project which lasted longer than the term of one governor.

One other governor of the period had a hand in decorating the Gymnasium. A verse inscription found adjacent to the swimming pool records that Basiliscus removed a fountain from a road junction and set it up in the Gymnasium (source 17). Cuttings on the block bearing the inscription show that the fountain sat on top of it. The fountain was made in the shape of brazen serpents with gilded heads; the water issued from their mouths. It is thus clear that work was going on in the Gymnasium and that a certain standard of magnificence was being maintained up to the early sixth century.

In Late Antiquity, as the Gymnasium came to function primarily as a bath, the Palaestra, no longer needed as an exercise-ground, was available for new uses. The great open square with its monumental portal appears to have been utilized as the scene for some of the elaborate ceremonial of municipal life, as shown by the inscriptions of the floor of the Marble Court which named the *Boule* and *Gerousia*. On other occasions, it may have served the role of a public park—a place of resort and relaxation in the center of the city. In any case, one corner of the Palaestra shows the activity of some late antique idlers in the form of an elaborate series of graffiti scratched on the plaster wall of a passage which had once led to the apse of the Synagogue (fig. 10). These scribblings provide a curious record of the mentality of the day, but one difficult to interpret. Among the objects which can be recognized, horses, birds, crosses, and crude human figures are prominent. A palm tree incised beside one of the horses might suggest that some of the graffiti have reference to horse racing. Others, however, strike a strongly religious note: in addition to the numerous crosses, some of the birds resemble cherubim, and one figure appears to be a priest or bishop in a robe adorned with a cross. The drawings are accompanied by short inscriptions which consist mostly of invocations to the Deity to protect the writer— an extremely common sentiment at the time. Since the whole consists of casual scratchings, it is not possible to attribute any profound significance to the graffiti. They may be taken as indicative of thoughts in the mind of a late antique public, some of them perhaps inspired by sights or events witnessed in the Gymnasium area.[109]

The Synagogue flourished throughout the period. The elaborate *skoutlosis* decoration and mosaic floors were continually restored, and one major rebuilding took place. In the late fourth century, a colonnaded forecourt with stuccoed walls, mosaic floors, and a central fountain was added, possibly connected with change in Jewish ritual. Later, perhaps during the fifth century, the forecourt was decorated with marble revetment, and some of the mosaics were replaced.

In its final stage, the Synagogue consisted of a long Main Hall, the colonnaded forecourt with its central fountain, and a porch, also colonnaded, facing the street (figs. 13, 14). The Main Hall, used for instruction as well as worship, terminated in an apse at the western end which was adorned with three rows of marble-covered benches for the elders of the congregation. The apse was paved with a mosaic which, like others of the Synagogue, contained no specifically Jewish decoration: it portrayed a crater with vines stretching from it, a common motif of the period (fig. 15). A lectern, a massive table supported by stone eagles, stood before the apse. The whole of the Main Hall was carpeted with mosaics of geometrical design (fig. 16), its walls were covered with elaborate marble revetment with inscriptions commemorating the piety and generosity of the donors, and its ceiling was apparently painted. Two symmetrical shrines, one of them probably intended to contain the Torah, closed the Main Hall off from the forecourt. The forecourt resembled the atrium of a Christian church (fig. 17). It had colonnades on all sides, mosaic floors (fig. 18), walls covered with marble, and a fountain in the shape of a great crater in the center. In general, the resemblance between the Synagogue and contemporary Christian basilicas is striking, and may serve as an illustration of the adaptation of the Sardian Jews to their Greek environment.

The Synagogue continued to be repaired into the sixth and even early seventh century, but this later work, mostly in the forecourt and the adjacent porch, is of a less ambitious nature and lower quality. It may suggest the advent of less happy times, an impression not contradicted by evidence from other parts of the city.[110]

In the area to the south of the Gymnasium complex, the late antique planners made the greatest changes in the appearance of Sardis. The Romans had apparently already laid out the east-west highway along the facade of the Gymnasium, but in the late fourth century it assumed an appearance characteristic of cities in the eastern part of the empire. The street was paved with marble and lined with colonnades; behind the northern colonnade a long row of twenty-nine shops was built against the wall of the Gymnasium (fig. 19). Such colonnaded streets with shops were typical of these times, which saw the shift of retailing and small manufacturing from the agora to the street. In Sardis, the street was about twelve and one half meters wide, with a sidewalk two meters wide along the southern colonnade. The northern colonnade rose on two steps above the highway; behind it, an open space paved with mosaics allowed access to the shops. The colonnade would have supported a wooden roof to provide the shoppers with protection from the elements.[111]

The shops themselves, apparently laid out in the same project as the highway, were two-story structures built of reused marble fragments and brick (fig. 20). The upper story was probably used for storage or living quarters, while the lower contained the retail and manufacturing establishments. To judge by the extensive finds of window panes in the sector, the shops were well lighted with glass windows. The function of several of these shops has been determined: they included a restaurant, a shop for the sale and repair of locks, a tool shop, and a dye works. Christian and Jewish proprietors traded side by side and did most of their business on a small scale. Vast numbers of copper coins, typical "small change" of the time, have been found in the excavations. The dates of the coins and of the objects found in the excavations show continuing activity in the shops down to the early seventh century. These shops probably provided a commercial center for the western part of Sardis.[112]

During the fourth and fifth centuries the formerly desolate area south of the highway was the scene of considerable building activity. A large building of some kind, possibly a house, had already been constructed over the former burial grounds immediately across from the Gymnasium, perhaps in the third century. Few traces of the building survive, as it was soon replaced by the large and elegant House of Bronzes. This house, which occupied an important location, was apparently built in the fourth century. It was set back about twenty meters from the highway and connected with it by an inclined ramp paved with brick leading into the lower floor of the house, a storage and work area which contained numerous traces of industrial activity, including facilities for bleaching. Even this lower level of the house, presumably used by the slaves, was luxurious; the largest rooms were paved with elaborate *opus sectile* of colored marble.

The bronze vessels which gave the house its name were found in a storage chamber on this ground level; they included a wine flagon, heating vessels, censers, and an embers shovel decorated with a cross (fig. 21). These obviously Christian objects suggest that the house may have belonged to some high church dignitary. Straight ahead of the entrance, a flight of steps in a small tile-paved vestibule led up to the main floor. The house seems to have had a second story and covered an area of about 30 x 25 meters; a large enclosed garden apparently lay to the south and southwest of it. The building was used and maintained for some three centuries. Rebuilding or expansion continued into the sixth century, and the house was in use until the Persian invasion of 616.[113]

One of the foothills of the Acropolis rises steeply less than one hundred meters south of the House of Bronzes. During Late Antiquity this slope was covered with houses built on terraces, and was apparently one of the major residential areas of the western part of the city, commanding a fine view over the Gymnasium to the plain of the Hermus and the mountains beyond. Below them, a long colonnaded street stretched for at least two hundred meters from the general area of the highway towards the southwest. On its north side adjacent to the House of Bronzes was the large rectangular Building R which seems to have contained some industry, and to the south of that was a long two-story structure facing onto the street.[114]

The street was some seven meters wide, paved with marble, and lined with colonnades. Statuary was displayed in the colonnades which ran in front of buildings on both sides. Here, as in the case of the marble highway by the Gymnasium, there were probably rows of shops and small industrial establishments, with the street forming the commercial center of the area.[115]

This street is of particular interest because its building inscription has survived to provide important information about the topography of the area and the building projects of the time (source 18). The text, preceded and followed by crosses, states that the colonnaded street (*embolos*) was built from the *tetrapylon* to the *embolos* of Hypaepa after the gate had been cut out and the whole area cleared. It was found at the northern end of the street beside a ruined brick structure (fig. 22) which lay next to the Roman Building R; it presumably deals with work in the immediate vicinity of its find spot.

The *embolos* mentioned is certainly the colonnaded street running through this area (fig. 23). The *embolos* of Hypaepa was presumably a street which led towards Hypaepa or to a Hypaepan gate. Since the road to Hypaepa led up the Pactolus on its way into Mount Tmolus, this street probably ran near the river and is possibly to be identified with the street which passed through the sector PN and along the river bank. The tetrapylon is presumably the ruined structure next to Building R, and the gate may be the Southwest Gate of the City Wall. If the street is projected to the southwest, it could pass through that gate.

The inscription, therefore, deals with a project of monumental proportions: the colonnaded street was built at one time, according to a plan, for a distance of some two hundred meters. The work seems to have taken place in the fifth century. It is not yet possible to determine whether the operation involved widening and improving an already existing street or cutting a completely new one through the area. The mention of the gate being "cut out," however, suggests that the latter is preferable. The whole area was built up in Late Antiquity and may have expanded in a haphazard and congested manner. The new street could have provided improved transit through the area and easier communication with the quarters which lay beyond. It could have introduced order into the quarter and provided it with a regularized commercial center.

The Tetrapylon mentioned was probably an important building, a four-sided monumental arch of a type common in the eastern cities of the empire. The tetrapylon often formed the center for new towns laid out according to the somewhat formal and rigid planning of the time. Such a building could serve a variety of purposes: it could act as a focus for a system of streets, mark a junction between two major arteries, or function as a public building. Whatever the precise nature of the Sardian Tetrapylon, it probably served as the center of the quarter, and its presence suggests that the buildings adjacent to it were of some importance.[116]

The *embolos*, or its continuation, led past the gate to the sector PN, where a great deal of building was carried out in Late Antiquity. The sector had been mostly uninhabited since the Hellenistic period and contained graves and monuments and some industrial establishments. The extent to which it was deserted during the Early Roman period is shown by the subsequent construction of late antique buildings directly over Hellenistic foundations.[117] In the fourth or early fifth century, a small bath was built here to the west of the street, presumably to serve an inhabited area which had grown up in the vicinity. None of these habitations survives, but large numbers of waterpipes from the fourth century suggest the presence of a reservoir or cistern in the area.

In the early fifth century, several large buildings were put up here (fig. 24). One of them, on the west side of the road, was apparently a luxurious villa with long halls paved with mosaic (figs. 25,26). It was so designed as to incorporate the earlier bath. But beside and behind the building numerous tomb monuments remained, some of which were incorporated in later stages of building adjacent to it. An open area to the northwest remained empty or may have been a garden.

On the opposite side of the street stood a large three-aisled basilical church (fig. 27) with narthex and atrium, constructed on a regular plan according to which the length (sixty-three meters) was three times the width (twenty-one). The interior as well as the atrium was paved with a mosaic of floral and geometric designs, and the walls were frescoed or revetted with marble. Coins provide a date of c.350-360 for the construction. Like many churches of the period, this basilica was established in a necropolis, a situation recognized and encouraged by the imperial government. A law of 386 provided for the construction of buildings for the veneration of saints wherever they may be buried. Such seems to have been the purpose of the basilica at PN, for its builders deliberately included an old grave in the north aisle of the church, possibly the tomb of a victim of the great persecution.[118]

The church was expanded and remodeled in Late Antiquity. A chapel consisting of an apsidal hall with a tile floor was added on the north side, west of the atrium. It was subsequently transformed by the addition of an entrance to the street. Another chapel was built further to the west; its walls cover part of the original mosaic of the atrium. Within the church itself, the mosaic of the nave was eventually replaced by a floor of marble *opus sectile*, a phenomenon already observed in the Marble Court. This work may have taken place in the sixth century. A new layer of frescoes in the apse may be contemporary.[119]

The quarter thus contained an important church and a luxurious villa, both built over the earlier graveyard. The buildings exhibit various stages of repair which extend well into the sixth century and indicate the continued prosperity of the area.[120]

At the same time, the graveyards did not disappear: burials were still taking place in the northwestern part of PN in the fourth and fifth centuries, and monumental tombs were built along the river where the Roman Necropolis had been. South of PN in the scarp of the Pactolus, the excavators have uncovered a large chamber tomb with elaborate frescoes of a conventional kind showing garlands, baskets, and peacocks; it was consequently named the "Peacock Tomb" (fig. 28). This Tomb seems to have been built in the fourth or fifth century and was subsequently visited for centuries, as finds of coins on the floor indicate. Traces of other tombs are visible all along the river as far as the temple. The road to Hypaepa presumably ran through this area and was lined with tombs and monuments.[121]

As the city expanded during Late Antiquity, the appearance of the whole area along the river changed. Although tombs continued to be built, many of the earlier ones were abandoned and covered over with new constructions. In most cases, the older graves were completely disregarded, possibly because they were the tombs of pagans while the new inhabitants were Christians but more probably because the passage of time had obliterated the memory of their earlier inhabitants. There are two interesting exceptions, at PN and HOB, where early graves were deliberately preserved by later builders.[122]

Much of the area along the river came to be covered with villas. Traces of one were investigated at the sector PC, about two hundred meters south of PN along the river, where a large house with a mosaic floor of the fifth century was found (fig. 29). Another villa lay back from the road on the foothills of the Acropolis overlooking the river. There, in a ravine north of the temple, a broad entrance passage flanked by columns led through an arched portal into spacious and solidly built rooms. About 400 meters north of the temple, remains of a hypocaust and of a mosaic with geometric designs, perhaps of the fifth century, attest the presence of another villa with a private bath. Other traces of buildings, some of them presumably walls of houses, still project from the scarp of the Pactolus all the way from sector PN to the temple. The whole area was thus built over with villas interspersed among the tombs and monuments of the necropolis, which itself was not entirely abandoned.[123]

The Temple of Artemis and its precinct declined in Late Antiquity from a major cult center of the city to the site of a small church, a graveyard, and a few habitations (fig. 9). Whether the temple was still functioning at the beginning of the period or not, it was definitely abandoned and partly buried in deposits from the nearby streams by the mid-fourth century. Graves had already existed in the temple precinct, but they became much more numerous in the third century and after. Inscriptions show that the whole area was used for burials from the third through the sixth century; there was an extensive cemetery along the southern side of the temple, and tombs continued up the Pactolus in the old Lydian Necropolis.[124]

Coins finds provide a fair picture of the history of the temple area. There are few of the third century, from Caracalla to Diocletian, but they become increasingly numerous subsequently until the time of Arcadius. Significantly, there is no break in the chronological sequence; the precinct was never completely deserted, but there was certainly more activity during the fourth century. The coins become especially abundant in the second half of the century, when the new religion arrived to replace the old, and the small Church M was built over the eastern end of the temple (figs. 30, 31).[125]

The church was constructed over a layer of deposits more than a meter thick in this scene of abandonment and desolation. The building is simple; in its original form, it consisted of a squarish single-aisled nave about 8.5 x 7 meters terminating in an apse with a half-dome. The interior was plastered and covered with frescoes and contained a simple altar consisting of a block of sandstone laid on a marble support. About twenty-five meters away, two small columns stood at the same level as the church and on axis with its entrance; they were perhaps part of an entranceway or served to mark out the church precinct.[126]

This unpretentious building was clearly not designed to serve a large congregation; it was not in the same class with the enormous basilicas which were being constructed all over the empire at the time or with the substantial building at PN. The building was probably intended to be the mortuary chapel for the graveyard, and to answer the spiritual needs of whatever population still lived in the neighborhood. Chapels built in cemeteries outside the city walls are common all over the empire in this period, as already noted.

Another building in the area may also have served a Christian function. A flight of steps led up from a street on the north side of the temple to a rectangular structure which was added in Late Antiquity to enclose a Roman barrel vaulted chamber tomb of the second or third century. The enclosure was probably intended as the mausoleum of some particularly holy man, conceivably the victim of one of the persecutions. Its north-south orientation, however, discourages interpretation as a chapel or *martyrion*.[127]

Architecturally, the church has no connection with the temple; it is not built over the altar or in the cella but next to a corner of the exterior colonnade. It was thus not intended to replace the abandoned temple. Nor need it be supposed that the Christians had to build a church here to exorcise the demons, whose power, they felt, would remain in such a major pagan holy place. The sign of the cross was sufficient for this purpose and had the power to put whole hosts of demons to flight. A well-known law of Theodosius II provided that remaining temples be destroyed and purified by the sign of the cross. The Artemis Temple, though long since disused, was thus well purified; twenty-five crosses, one with the inscription ΦΩΣ ΖΩΗ, were carved on the cella wall opposite the church. Because of their location, they can be considered contemporary with the church. Such crosses and inscriptions are common in the eastern parts of the empire, frequently appearing in association with church buildings, and doubtless all served the same apotropaic function.[128]

The Temple of Artemis suffered a disaster from which it never recovered, and the whole area around it assumed the desolate appearance of the western part of Sardis at the beginning of the late antique period. Graves and mausolea predominated, but there were habitations northwest of the temple. Although Sardis grew in size and prosperity in the succeeding centuries, the rise of Christianity ensured that the temple would never be restored.

The considerable changes which took place around the temple in Late Antiquity were not the result of extravagant building projects or expansion of the city but of a gradual increase of population associated with the continuing work of destruction. The small Church M was enlarged by the addition of a second apse to the east, built apparently to contain a tomb. This has been dated to the sixth century; somewhat earlier, a room was added to the north side of the church. The function of this room, which is almost as large as the main building, is not known; it may have been a pastophory or diaconicon, perhaps representing the expansion of the church to serve a more numerous congregation.[129]

The population of the temple area seems to have increased. Though evidence of habitation is confined to Building L south of the temple and to the quarter to the northwest, it is important to remember that there are many buildings in the temple precinct which cannot be dated, and that large numbers of late foundations were removed by the earlier excavators as they cleaned out the temple.

Much industrial activity was also going on. The temple had become a quarry and a good deal of the western and central part was broken up to be used for building materials or made into lime. The work was so thorough that the marble-breakers actually excavated and removed the foundations when the remains which stood above ground had been exhausted. Coins found with deposits of marble chips show that this work of destruction, which may have begun in the fourth century, was continuing actively in the sixth and early seventh centuries, and ended only with the abandonment of the whole area in 616. A coin hoard datable to that year was discovered under two marble blocks of the north wall of the temple which were in the process of being broken up. Limekilns found on the same level indicate the fate of large parts of the building. Such activity took place on a large scale, and most of the temple was probably destroyed by the seventh century.[130]

Operations on this scale would have required a large number of workers, who may have lived in the area. The enlargement of the church may thus be connected with the destruction of the temple. The temple area seems not to have been reintegrated into the city; it was remote from the center and had little importance once the temple was closed. But the temple had been built on a grand scale and provided vast quantities of building materials for the inhabitants of those western quarters of the city which were being built up in Late Antiquity.

Sardis changed considerably during the late antique period, which ended with the devastation of the Persian attack of 616. The great official building projects of the time as well as private construction on a large scale had left their mark on every part of the city. These changes are now most evident in the excavated western quarters but were certainly not confined to them. In the center of the city, the great "Justinianic" basilica was built, probably as the cathedral church of the city, and at the eastern edge of Sardis Bath CG had been restored and enlarged.

The importance of Sardis and the evidence of considerable repairs in the Gymnasium complex suggest that the major civic buildings of the central and eastern parts of the city were at least maintained. In this prosperous age, there was a great deal of building all over the eastern parts of the empire. Provincial governors particularly were anxious to put up some monument of their administration to help their progress to more exalted offices. Evidence of changes throughout the city might therefore be expected, but for the moment only those in the western quarters can be considered in detail.

The three centuries of the period completely altered the appearance of the western part of Sardis. Whole new quarters had sprung up where there had only been tombs and monuments with scattered industry in 284. Colonnaded streets, commercial buildings, houses, and luxurious villas covered this formerly rather desolate area. The Gymnasium complex remained more or less unchanged on the interior because successive restorations had maintained its former splendor; the Synagogue had been remodeled by the addition of the colonnaded forecourt, and it too had been carefully maintained and repaired. The southern facade of the complex, however, had changed considerably. A long row of shops had been built with a mosaic pavement extending before them to the colonnaded marble street.

Across that street, the former graveyard had yielded to the rich House of Bronzes, and the area behind it was full of buildings. Houses on terraces covered the slopes of the hills, and a colonnaded street with attached commercial buildings ran beneath them from the monumental Tetrapylon to the city gate. Continuing from there, the street (no longer colonnaded) led past the church and villa of PN towards the river. The Pactolus was lined with monuments and villas which continued in the direction of the temple and up into the hills. The whole quarter south of the

Gymnasium and along the river as far as the temple must have given an impression of comfort and opulence, a "garden of luxury" in the words of a later patriarch.

Only the temple area failed to share in this embellishment. The once great Temple of Artemis was in ruins and on its way to complete destruction. It had been succeeded by a small church, several monuments, and a graveyard. The sanctuary, once one of the glories of the city, now found itself practically abandoned in a remote and inconvenient location by the citizens of the new Christian Sardis, which, though it stretched out in the direction of the temple, was spiritually far removed from it.

It is impossible to make any definitive statement about the growth or decline of the population of Sardis in Late Antiquity. The new western quarter may represent an absolute increase in the size and population of the city, or it may have been accompanied by a corresponding, or greater, decline of other sections. Examples ancient and modern would suggest that the latter is the more likely alternative. Late antique Ephesus has produced clear instances of rebuilding and decay in the same age: new buildings were erected and old ones restored throughout the city while a large area in the center was allowed to lie in ruins for a century or more.[131] Similarly, the abundant legislation of the fourth century about public works complains incessantly about the decay of the cities which the governors neglected while putting up ostentatious and often useless monuments of their munificence in vain pursuit of glory.[132] An accurate appraisal of the situation at Sardis must necessarily await future excavation; for the moment, it is only possible to note that the western part of the city was expanding, while the central and eastern areas at least saw some repair and new construction.

II. Byzantine Sardis

The Dark Ages

In the spring of 616, the peace and prosperity and, in a sense, the very existence of late antique Sardis came to a sudden and violent end. The metropolis of Lydia was reduced to such a "field of desolation and destruction" that it ceased to resemble a city for a considerable period and was never to regain the splendor which had distinguished it under the Lydians, Persians, Greeks and Romans. The excavations have provided clear evidence for the date and nature of the disaster. The western quarters of the city from the Gymnasium to the Temple were destroyed and abandoned at a date which large finds of coins show to have been early in 616. The circumstances were violent. Traces of burning have been found in the Gymnasium, and especially in the House of Bronzes, where an iron sword in a context datable to this time bears witness to the events of the fall of Sardis. The unexcavated parts of the city, of course, provide no such specific evidence. The Roman Bath CG was certainly abandoned for several centuries, perhaps beginning before 616, but for the rest there is no certain evidence. Nothing, however, has been found to contradict the impression of general destruction and abandonment.[1]

Coin finds are especially numerous in the Byzantine Shops, where small change was extensively used. Their sequence stops suddenly with the issues of 615/616. At Pactolus North there are no clear signs of violent destruction, but, to judge from the lack of coins, all activity ceased until the ninth century. If that sector was not destroyed, it was probably because of its location outside of the City Wall; in time of attack, it would have been abandoned as the population sought refuge behind the walls, where the heaviest fighting would have taken place. The temple presents a similar picture: no clear evidence of destruction, but sudden abandonment witnessed by a hoard of coins, the latest of 615. This had been hidden in a sack under a block of marble, apparently by one of the workers excavating for lime.[2] All the evidence points to a large-scale violent destruction, by human means, presumably in a war. The excavations reveal what happened and when, but tell nothing of the circumstances. For these the mediocre historical sources of the period must be consulted.

The history of the Byzantine Empire in the seventh century is obscure: most of the historians whose works survive lived long after the events they describe, and there are major historical problems associated with the period. It is hardly surprising that the siege and destruction of Sardis is nowhere mentioned, especially considering the circumstances of the time. The seventh century was an age of war and crisis, when the empire was struggling for its very existence; there was little leisure for writing history.

The provinces of Asia Minor had enjoyed almost uninterrupted peace since the time of Diocletian, but it came to an abrupt end in the war between the Byzantine and Persian empires, the last great world war of Antiquity, which lasted without interruption from the accession of Focas in 602 until the victory won by Heraclius in 628. In the course of this war campaigns were fought from Azerbaijan and Iraq in the east to Constantinople in the west, from the Caucasus in the north to the frontiers of Ethiopia in the south, and Asia Minor suffered tremendously. At the same time, invasions of Slavs and Avars devastated the Balkans; no part of the empire was spared. Early in the war, the defenses of the eastern frontier collapsed, and the victorious armies of the Persian king Chosroes II overran the eastern provinces. Mesopotamia, Syria, Palestine, and Egypt were taken, and Asia Minor was subject to constant and often successful attack in every quarter.

A detailed reconstruction of events in Asia Minor during this critical period is not possible, but the combination of the historical sources with the archaeological and numismatic evidence provides a general outline. During the reign of Focas, the Persian forces advanced into Armenia and Mesopotamia and established their control of the approaches to Asia Minor. In 611 they made their first conquest within the peninsula; Caesarea in Cappadocia was seized and held for over a year. After inflicting tremendous defeats on the Byzantines in Syria and Palestine, the armies of Chosroes were free to ravage all of Asia Minor. In 615, they penetrated as far as Chalcedon, and during the following decade were free to attack at will. The sketchy literary sources mention only Ancyra and Rhodes specifically as falling to the Persians, but finds of coin hoards and other buried treasure of these years and the evidence of destruction in various sites show that the flames of war were carried as far as the Aegean, and probably on several occasions. A series of bold campaigns which Heraclius led deep into enemy territory beginning in 623, however, turned the tide and ensured a Byzantine victory. After a last spectacular attack on the capital in 626, the Persians withdrew from Asia Minor forever, and the devastated country returned to Byzantine rule.[3]

Although the narrative of these campaigns is fragmentary and often unclear, it is not hard to imagine the situation which prevailed at the time. The frontier defenses had collapsed, Byzantine resistance was sporadic, and the central government, oppressed by disasters on all sides, was in no position to defend every city. The major Persian attacks were primarily intended to secure the northern highway which led through Caesarea and Ancyra to the capital, but other raids, even considerable expeditions, were sent to different parts of Anatolia to crush local resistance or plunder the rich and peaceful cities. There is no evidence that the Persians planned or accomplished the occupation of much of Asia Minor.

The destruction of Sardis is to be attributed to an otherwise unknown Persian raid in the spring campaigning season of 616. The circumstances are obscure, but the attack must have been on a large scale to effect such destruction on a great and fortified center like Sardis. Although the details may remain unknown, there can be little doubt that Sardis was destroyed by the armies of the Persian king Chosroes II in 616.

The two centuries after this calamity are the most obscure period of the history of Sardis: The sources are uninformative, and the excavations have revealed little that can be dated to the time. The effects of the disaster of 616 were far-reaching, and Sardis never recovered. The great late antique city ceased to exist and was replaced by a settlement or settlements on a much smaller scale. Nothing is certain for the decades after 616; the excavated western parts of the city seem to have been abandoned completely, and it is not possible to determine whether city life of any kind continued on the site of Sardis. By the ninth century, when more information is available, the late antique city, with its classical appearance, had vanished, to be replaced by a more typically medieval town with a fortress on the Acropolis and settlements in the plain below. The settlements were eventually to expand, but Sardis remained a town settlement dominated by a fortress until it disappeared altogether.

The history of Sardis is a microcosm of the history of the empire: the Roman state survived, at least in its late antique form, until the beginning of the seventh century, but by the ninth century it had assumed a quite different "Byzantine" form. The crucial period of transition was the seventh century, which remains almost completely unknown. It seems that at Sardis late antique traditions and city life were brutally destroyed; they may, of course, have already been in decline. Little or nothing survived the Persian war and the Arab invasions which soon followed. The population of the whole area was drastically reduced, and resources were simply not available to maintain the urban culture which had characterised the Greek and Roman states. A new beginning was made, and something called a city in the language of the time grew up at Sardis, but it never came to bear the least resemblance to the great city among whose ruins it was built.

The seventh century was an age of continual crisis: The Persians were no sooner defeated than a newer and more persistent enemy appeared in the Arabs, who began to conquer the eastern provinces of the empire within a decade of Heraclius' epic victories. The empire, exhausted from its struggles, could not defeat them, and the losses were permanent. Syria, Palestine, and Egypt became part of the Caliphate; a new frontier was established at the Taurus. In the east only Anatolia remained to become the heartland of the medieval empire. But the frontier was by no means secure. Arab raids penetrated annually into the provinces for a century while the empire was on the defensive, even fighting for survival. The enemy twice devastated the whole of Asia Minor on their way to besiege Constantinople, in 674-678 and in 716. On other occasions raids reached every corner of the peninsula, as they had during the war with the Persians. In this wretched time the population suffered tremendously, as their crops and animals were seized and the fortified towns in which they took refuge were attacked. Although Sardis is not mentioned for the century after 616, the excavations reveal the extent of destruction and show the new kind of settlement which was developing there in response to circumstances so drastically different from the calm prosperity of Late Antiquity.

A half century of almost constant warfare came to an end in 656 when the caliph Othman was assassinated and the Arabs became embroiled in civil war. During this lull in the fighting, the Byzantine government was able to undertake some reconstruction in the badly damaged provinces. Traces of this work at Sardis reveal the extent of the destruction which had taken place and the nature of the measures which the empire took to provide some security for its inhabitants. The work was military: road and castle building. There seems to have been no question of repairing or reconstructing major buildings which had fallen into ruin and been abandoned since the Persian attack. The needs of defense were the most pressing and all evidence suggests that the population was so reduced that it no longer had any need for the civic services which had previously been provided on such a large scale.

The imperial forces arrived about 660 and built a new road past the Gymnasium complex, parallel to the old marble highway. They occupied some rooms of the now deserted Gymnasium during the work, where numerous coins of Constans II, of which the latest date to about 660, were found in association with traces of the road building. The new road was wide (about fifteen meters) and cobbled. It apparently represents a major rebuilding of the highway up the Hermus Valley, which, in Sardis at least, had been in disrepair for some forty years. This new road was built directly over the remains of the Byzantine Shops and the colonnades in front of them (fig. 32). The ruins were leveled and cemented and then paved over with cobblestones. This provides a striking illustration of conditions at the time: the Gymnasium complex was abandoned and in ruins, and no effort was made to restore it.[4]

The fortification walls, whose impressive remains are still visible along the southern edge of the Acropolis, were probably built at the same time as the new road and as part of the same program of restoration and defense. The present remains consist of a wall about two hundred meters long built along the steep southern side of the Acropolis, following the contours of the hill (fig. 33). A gate with a tower beside it is preserved in the center, and the eastern walls are covered with an elaborate brick gallery with large openings commanding the southern approaches through the valley between the Acropolis hill and the foothills of Mount Tmolus. An isolated fragment of a double wall with a gate survives on the westernmost hill of the Acropolis, about four hundred meters to the west of the main wall (fig. 34). The wall possibly once made a circuit around the whole Acropolis, but if so most of it has been lost through erosion of the soft conglomerate of which the whole system of foothills of Tmolus is composed.

The walls stand about ten meters high and are some three meters thick. They consist of a core of rubble completely faced with neatly cut reused fragments; very little brick was employed in the construction. The facing, which covers the wall inside and out above the foundations, includes thousands of architectural fragments robbed from buildings of all periods from the fifth century B.C. to the fourth century A.D. The isolated tower to the west, however, employs a somewhat different technique: its facing is interrupted by regular bands of brick courses, somewhat reminiscent of the walls of Constantinople. Great effort was put into the construction of the fortification walls: all traces of previous building were removed, and in places the hill was scraped down to bedrock; the foundations of the wall rest in a trench dug a meter deep into the conglomerate. Judging by the lack of clear traces of later repairs, the walls were carefully and soundly built and performed their functions well into the fifteenth century.[5]

The walls themselves provide little evidence for the date of their construction; there is no building inscription, and parallels from other sites offer little precision. In their style of construction the walls at Sardis resemble the so-called "Gate of Persecutions" at Ephesus and the walls of Magnesia on the Maeander; the former is dated to the reign of Justinian, the latter very tentatively to the time of the Persian wars.[6] The fragments in the walls of Sardis contain numerous inscriptions, the latest that can be dated is from the reign of Justinian, after 539 (source 21). It is immured into the lower part of the tower west of the gate which provides the present entrance and shows no indication of being part of a later repair.

The walls should, therefore, be later than the reign of Justinian and constructed at a time when numerous spoils from the city were available for their construction. The large number and variety of these spoils makes it highly unlikely that they could have come from buildings already standing on the Acropolis; there is, in fact, no evidence that the Acropolis was in use during the Roman period.[7] It would be most reasonable to assume that the walls were built when much of the city lay in ruins and spoils were readily available, that is, after 616.

Remains of buildings inside the fortifications help to confirm this dating and to indicate the extent of reconstruction which took place. Several trenches have been dug on the Acropolis and a large part of the area inside the wall has been cleared. Remains of buildings found there fall into three major periods, of which the first was apparently contemporary with the construction of the walls. Remains from the first period, which consist of floor levels and traces of fairly substantial buildings mostly obliterated by later construction, were destroyed by violence and burning. The few coins found at that level fall into the period 590-711, with most dating from the reign of Constans II (641-668). This suggests that the walls and the buildings within them were built at the same time that the highway was reconstructed and a major program of defense was being carried out.[8]

There is no certain explanation for the difference in technique of the isolated wall to the west, which employs brick courses. Possibly it is a fragment of an earlier fortification which has left no other traces anywhere on the Acropolis. A natural catastrophe may account for this. Sometime in the seventh century the eastern end of the Artemis Temple was overwhelmed and the small Church M was buried, probably by a major earthquake, a common phenomenon in the Hermus Valley. This could have shaken the loose conglomerate of the Acropolis, precipitating whatever constructions were there down the slope and overthrowing the colonnades of the Byzantine Shops where the road was built. No more satisfactory explanation is presently available.[9]

The seventh century, therefore, saw the construction of the highway and citadel, with the buildings inside it, some of which were probably habitations. But there is no certain evidence anywhere else in the site for habitation or continuity from Late Antiquity. All the excavated sectors seem to have been abandoned;

there are no remains which can be dated to the two centuries after
the Persian attack, and practically no coins. Only five coins have
been found in all sectors for the period 668-815, compared to the
eighty-nine coins of Constans II (641-668) or the four hundred ten
of Heraclius (602-641).[10]

This does not mean that Sardis disappeared completely in 616.
There were habitations on the Acropolis after the mid-seventh
century; a bishop of Sardis attended the Council of Constantinople in 680; and the evidence of the coins is not as decisive
as it may appear. Byzantine bronze coins from the late seventh to the early ninth century are rare everywhere except in
Constantinople; they are notably absent from other excavated
sites, and were probably minted in very small quantities. The
severe disturbances of the time would hardly leave the economy
untouched: in a period when the population was reduced, cities
destroyed, and the trade disrupted, the monetary economy was
probably replaced to a large extent by a natural one, and few
bronze coins were issued to appear at Sardis or anywhere else.

It is also important to remember in this context that much of the
site has not been excavated. Settlements of some size could have
existed in the central and western parts of the city, where the area
known as the Byzantine Fortress is of potentially great interest for
the history of the period. This is a hill projecting from the north
slope of the Acropolis which seems to contain a Byzantine fortification. Building A in the center of the city may also have functioned as a defense. Remains of its last phase of construction,
dated to the period after 616, suggest that the building was turned
into a fortress.[11] Evidence might also be expected from Church D
beside the highway, apparently the cathedral of Byzantine Sardis.

The Arab invasions, interrupted by the short period of civil
war, soon resumed and remained a serious threat to the empire
until the great victory of Leo III as Acroenus in 740, after which the
empire gradually began to recover and assume a less defensive
position. Before then, however, Arab armies had once again
besieged Constantinople, devastating the provinces on the way.
Maslama, brother of the caliph Suleyman, led an expedition
overland in 716 which first attacked Amorium in Phrygia then
descended into Asia, where the troops wintered before moving on
to the capital. In their progress, the Arabs followed the route
through Lydia and took both Sardis and Pergamum as well as

numerous unspecified fortresses. Once again, the capture of Sardis appears in no Byzantine source,[12] but oriental writers mention it specifically (source 26). In these sources Sardis is called a "city" in contrast to the various fortresses. This may suggest that the place was still of considerable importance and consisted of more than the fortifications on the Acropolis.

Presumably, some part of the lower city was still inhabited, but the evidence now available relates only to the Acropolis, where there was "a sudden and violent destruction followed by a period of desertion during which fill and earth gradually accumulated." Destruction and burning were evident in each of the sectors excavated within the fortification wall, and the first period of the Byzantine Acropolis, dating to the seventh century, came to an end. The date of the destruction is not well established, but it was certainly before the eleventh century, for a plaque dated to c.1000-1050 was found in a grave which disrupted the earlier level of building. Coin finds allow a little more precision; they show that reconstruction in the eastern sector within the wall began in the tenth century. The sequence of coins from the first period of building ends in 711. The earth and debris above the destruction level presumably took some time to accumulate, so it is reasonable to associate the end of the first period with the Arab invasion under Maslama. For the next two centuries the buildings of the Acropolis were in ruins and the place almost abandoned, though several graves dug in the fill over the ruins and below the later buildings indicate there was some habitation.[13] It is possible that squatters lived there and the fortress fell into disuse, or that only a small garrison was maintained.

For the century following the Arab attack the excavated sectors reveal nothing that could be called a city or even a settlement, but occasional mentions in the sources indicate that the place continued to exist. Whatever settlements constituted eighth century Sardis were presumably in the unexcavated areas. Their defense may have been the Byzantine Fortress or Building A. Nothing certain is known, except that a battle was fought at Sardis in 743 between Constantine V and his father-in-law Artavasdus, who led an unsuccessful revolt against him, and that bishop Euthymius of Sardis, who will be discussed below, was one of the leaders of the church in the late eighth and early ninth centuries.[14]

Among the other problems of a dismal age, the region of Sardis seems not to have been spared the effects of the bubonic plague which devastated the empire from 744-747. According to an oriental source, Lydia was one of the provinces of Asia Minor where the plague raged with especial severity. "In these regions" writes Dionysius of Tell-Mahre, a Syriac chronicler of the ninth century, "numerous towns and villages suddenly became deserted, without anyone living in them or passing through." Although the narrative is somewhat rhetorical, Greek sources confirm the severity of the pestilence, which can only have had a debilitating effect on the already ravaged and weakened provinces of Anatolia.[15]

The Dark Ages were a time of continuing changes for the empire as the Arab attacks continued, though with diminishing tempo. As late as 799 raids still reached Lydia; security was far from established.[16] Urban life everywhere in Asia Minor decayed, and most of the population lived in heavily fortified towns or in the countryside near castles where they could take refuge as needed. Centers which had been important in Late Antiquity declined as the interest of the government was shifted from the old trade routes to the great military highways across the peninsula from Constantinople to the east. Consequently, cities along these routes, such as Dorylaeum, Cotyaeum, Amorium, and Ancyra, assumed greater importance, and little is heard of places like Sardis.

Alteration of routes, decay of urban life, and extension of a network of fortresses throughout the threatened territories were only part of the changes brought about by the long period of invasions. The whole administrative organization of the empire was modified and militarized as the needs of defense became paramount. The system of Diocletian, in which small provinces had a separate civil and military administration, yielded to one in which a general exercised supreme authority over a large area. The details are obscure and the subject of acrid controversy, but the new "theme" system, called after the new circumscriptions ruled by a general, came into existence gradually during the seventh and eighth centuries.

At first, the old provinces continued to exist as subdivisions of the themes, but they were eventually replaced by purely military administrative districts. As originally conceived, the themes were extremely large; only four embraced the whole of Asia Minor.

Sardis was in the Anatolic theme, which included most of central Asia Minor with Lydia and Ionia. Later, probably in the time of Leo III (716-740), the themes were divided, and Sardis became one of the cities of the Thracesian theme, consisting of the Diocletianic provinces of Asia, Lydia, and parts of Phrygia. In the fully developed militarized system, Sardis lost its role as provincial capital and was ruled from Ephesus, the seat of the general of the Thracesians.[17] These administrative changes, along with the alterations of trade and military routes, diminished the importance of Sardis as a city of the Byzantine Empire for centuries to come.

The city did, however, continue to function as the headquarters of some government officials. Although the general of the theme had considerable powers, tax assessment and collection was reserved to the officers of the central treasury, called *dioiketai*. The *dioiketes* of Lydia, known from seals of the eighth and ninth century, presumably had his office at Sardis. Financial officials with the same title had jurisdiction over individual cities; one George, *dioiketes* of Sardis is attested in the ninth century.[18]

The incessant struggle against foreign enemies was accompanied by serious internal strife in the empire in the eighth and ninth centuries. The iconoclastic controversy which raged through these years divided the population and caused widespread persecution, suffering, and sedition throughout the empire. The people of the more Hellenized western provinces seem to have favored orthodoxy, while the inhabitants of central and eastern Anatolia were more inclined towards iconoclasm. The first period of the controversy, from the edict of Leo III in 723 to the Council of Nicaea which restored orthodoxy in 787, was distinguished by the severe persecutions which the iconoclastic emperors carried out in the orthodox provinces.

Sardis was at this time included in the Thracesian theme, the scene of the infamous activities of Michael Lachanodracon, general from c.766 to c.782. A strong supporter of the fervent iconoclast Constantine V, Lachanodracon zealously persecuted the monks of his province. In 770, for example, all the monks and nuns of the theme were assembled in Ephesus and offered the choice of marriage or martyrdom. In the following year Lachanodracon had all the monasteries and nunneries under his administration sold, along with their holy vessels, books, and possessions. Many monks were executed, tortured, blinded, or exiled.

His activities were reportedly so successful that no monk was left in the province.[19]

Although the exploits of Lachanodracon may have been magnified by the malice of monkish chronicles, the sources may be taken to reveal the extent of monasticism in the region in the eighth century. No monasteries have been located in or around Sardis, whch is not specifically mentioned. The province of Lydia, however, did contribute two martyrs to the orthodox cause. Hypatius and Andreas, monks "from the province of Lydia in the land of the Thracesians," became respectively bishop and priest. When the persecutions raged, they succumbed to the cruelty of the heretic and were made martyrs, probably in the time of Constantine V. Despite the lack of details, the martyrdom of Hypatius and Andreas illustrates the resistance to iconoclasm in Lydia and the persecutions which were carried out there.[20]

A far more important figure in the iconoclastic controversy was a bishop of Sardis, Saint Euthymius, who became a martyr for his devotion to the orthodox cause. When iconoclasm was revived and again became official government policy from 815-843, Euthymius was one of the chief leaders of the opposition. Like many prelates of the time, he began his career as a monk and was made bishop of Sardis before the council of 787. He found Sardis full of iconoclasts, probably as a result of the persecutions of Lachanodracon, but soon persuaded them to change their ways and return to orthodoxy (source 22.) He was also prominent in the capital, for the emperors Constantine VI and Irene sent him on an embassy to negotiate peace with the Arabs. Under their successor, Nicephorus I, however, Euthymius fell from favor and was sent into exile because of suspected complicity in a revolt. Although he was soon recalled and the emperor's efforts to have him deposed were unsuccessful, Euthymius never returned to his see in Sardis. The most glorious part of his career—when he was one of the leaders of the iconodule party, resisted the attempts of successive emperors to make him swerve from his faith, and was finally exiled and martyred—took place outside Sardis and Lydia. Euthymius was also a writer; a short treatise on the election of bishops attributed to him has survived.[21]

Euthymius' place at Sardis was filled by John, who showed himself a worthy successor. His life, unfortunately, is very obscure; he is only known from letters written him by the great orthodox champion Theodore of Studium. These reveal that John, a "noble witness of the truth," attended the Synod of 815 and apparently spoke there in defense of the icons, for he suffered imprisonment and exile.[22] One of John's close successors was apparently Antonius, who had previously been a monk. He is known only from a seal which gives him the titles of monk and metropolitan, which would be appropriate to the period after the restoration of icons in 787, when monks rose to considerable prominence.[23]

During the second period of iconoclasm, in which Euthymius and John suffered, persecution once more oppressed the population of Lydia. The life of Saint Peter of Atroa (773-837) provides vivid details of conditions in the province, though it does not mention Sardis specifically. Much of the saint's holy work took place in northern Lydia; it was there that he cured two paralytics after they had recanted their heretical iconoclast beliefs, and from there that he sent an angel to rescue from prison an official who had prayed for his help.[24] Such pious activities, however, were carried out with great risk, for the officers of church and state were watchful for those who deviated from accepted belief. When Peter was passing through northern Lydia with some monks, their party was approached by two iconoclast bishops; the saint was only saved from their embarrassing queries by miraculously becoming invisible. On another occasion he and his brother were stopped on the highway by a general and interrogated. When their iconodule beliefs became known, they were imprisoned, first in a church and later in a castle from which they were only released when their oppressor was suddenly struck down by a fatal disease. Similarly, the abbot of the Lydian monastery of Chareus had been arrested by the iconoclasts and forced to sign a declaration of adhesion to their faith.[25]

The misery of the provincial populations was exacerbated at the same time by a destructive civil war, the revolt of Thomas the Slav, which lasted from 821 to 823 and almost succeeded in dethroning the emperor Michael II. During its course, all of Asia Minor was disturbed. The life of Peter of Atroa again provides detail. A nunnery in Lydia under the jurisdiction of Saint Peter was attacked during the "days of confusion, civil war, and plunder"; the nuns were only saved from the lusts of their assailants by a miraculous appearance of the saint.[26] The official mentioned above whom Peter rescued from captivity was an adherent of

Thomas the Slav, who had been captured by a general loyal to the emperor and imprisoned at Phygela near Ephesus; this too suggests that there were battles in the region.[27] Other sources add no further information about Lydia.

John the victim of the iconoclasts is apparently to be distinguished from another bishop of Sardis by the same name who is known for his literary efforts. This John, who presided in the middle or late ninth century, wrote commentaries on two of the most popular schoolbooks of the time, the *Progymnasmata* of Aphthonius, a textbook of elementary exercises in rhetoric and composition written in the fourth century, and the *de Inventione* of Hermogenes, a second century handbook of rhetoric.[28] John's works need not be taken to indicate any high level of literary achievement or originality, but they do at least illustrate the continuity or revival of basic learning among the higher clergy and in the provinces. One of the functions of a bishop was to provide for public education. The organization of the metropolitan churches was based on that of the patriarchate, to which famous schools were attached. Although practically nothing is known about provincial schools in this period, it is a possibility that John's commentaries were intended for use in such a school at Sardis.[29] It is probable that John was also the author of some saints' lives written in the late ninth century by one John, bishop of Sardis.[30]

Middle Byzantine Sardis

The reforms made in the Dark Ages began to show their effects in the ninth century, when the empire, making use of the great human and natural resources of Asia Minor, began a period of recovery precedent to the expansion and real prosperity of the Macedonian dynasty (867-1025). Although the Arab attacks continued for a time, and the Byzantines suffered a severe defeat in the capture of Amorium in 838, there were no further territorial losses. After the middle of the ninth century, the empire moved to the offensive and a long period of triumphs began which culminated in the reign of Basil II (976-1025). The restoration of peace and settled conditions within the empire provided the background for victories abroad. Trade and urban life revived, and a period of prosperity began which lasted, with one interruption, through the twelfth century. A saint's life dealing with events of the early eleventh century suggests that Lydia shared in the general prosperity. A monk from the monastery of Galesion near Ephesus went to Lydia on one occasion to buy grain, which may imply that the area was producing a surplus.[31]

Conditions in the empire as a whole are reflected at Sardis by a period of recovery and growth which began early in the ninth century. Life returned to the city, though never on the level of Late Antiquity. Instead, a town of medieval appearance developed, with settlements in the plain dominated by the fortress on the Acropolis. The evidence for the Middle Byzantine period at Sardis (c.850-1204) depends almost entirely upon the results of the excavations. The city is only twice mentioned by the secular historians of the period, and that in most cursory and uninformative fashion. In the work *On the Themes* by the emperor Constantine Porphyrogenitus, composed about 933 (source 28), Sardis appears as the third of the twenty cities of Asia (actually those of the Thrascesian Theme). Although this list almost certainly does not reflect the contemporary situation, it suggests that Sardis was still considered as a major center of western Asia Minor. The recapture of the city from the Turks in 1098 is also mentioned (source 29); otherwise historical writers are silent.

Ecclesiastical sources, on the other hand, have frequent occasion to mention the bishops of Sardis in the ninth and tenth centuries. Because of the high rank of the see in the hierarchy of the church, many of these were figures of considerable prominence, but their careers reveal little about conditions at Sardis. Most of the bishops, as shall be seen, seem to have spent as much time as possible in the capital.

Peter, bishop of Miletus, had been deposed by the patriarch Methodius (843-847). As a partisan of Photius in the ecclesiastical controversies of the day, he was rewarded by his patron soon after he became patriarch with the see of Sardis in 859. He seems, however, never to have set foot in his bishopric during his decade of tenure. Instead he played a major role in church politics as a devoted supporter of Photius and apparently was always present in the capital. His learning must have been as great as his loyalty; he is described as *disertissima pars Photii*—no mean compliment considering the great intellectual achievements of the patriarch. In 869, he was sent on an embassy to the Pope, but drowned on the way there when his ship was wrecked in the Adriatic.[32]

In 877, another bishop of the same name owed his succession to Photius. He is only known from a hostile source which relates that he was the private secretary of Photius and did such signal service for the patriarch that he was rewarded with the see of Sardis. The service consisted of forging the seals of all the metropolitans onto a letter which Photius addressed to the Pope to announce his second succession to the patriarchate.[33] This worthy is apparently not to be confused with a third bishop called Peter who had fled from Constantinople in 912 when the imperial officials charged with deposing the current patriarch were seeking him. The only text which mentions him seems to imply that he was ordained by the patriarch Euthymius (907-912).[34]

There is no certain evidence that any of these bishops ever went to Sardis. It is, therefore, almost a surprise to note that Antonius, bishop around 920, actually did set out for his see. He was the recipient of two letters from the patriarch Nicholas Mysticus (912-925) which mention this curious fact. A lead seal bearing his name is also preserved.[35] His two known successors in the tenth century, both named Leo, are only heard of at Constantinople. The former received in abut 945 a plaintive letter from the exiled bishop Alexander of Nicaea asking him to use his influence on his behalf; Leo was evidently in a strong position in the ecclesiastical hierarchy of the capital. Another letter was addressed to him by an anonymous scholar and scribe of Constantinople whom he had apparently consulted about finding a copyist. Whether he wished to have manuscripts copied for his own use or for the church at Sardis is unknown; he seems at least to have been a man of literary tastes, like many of his colleagues. A letter of Leo written in the typically complex style of the period has survived. The other Leo, who attended a synod in Constantinople in 997, was the recipient in the same year of the letter from his namesake, the bishop of Synnada, describing an embassy to Rome and the events which took place there. The whole tone of the letter suggests that Leo was in the capital and privy to the inner workings of ecclesiastical politics.[36]

The bishops of Sardis of the ninth and tenth centuries thus appear to have spent little time in their metropolis. Consequently, little information is available about their activities there. One source, however, gives a few hints. The life of the patriarch Euthymius relates that Euthymius' successor, Nicholas Mysticus, suggested to the emperor a novel way to raise needed revenue. He proposed that certain metropolitans who had been partisans of Euthymius should be taken to their sees in chains and an inventory be carried out of church goods there. It is thus implied that the metropolitans would be forced to reveal the money they had embezzled or goods they had stolen during the patriarchate of Euthymius. Fortunately for the bishops, the investigating commission could find no money, for it had all been given to the poor, as various of the poor themselves testified. In this context, the sudden disappearance of Peter III of Sardis before the arrest of the other bishops may be significant, and the question may be raised whether embezzlement or charity were the more active practice of such bishops.[37]

The notorious reluctance of Byzantine bishops to spend time in their sees was not confined to this period. Even Saint Euthymius is best known for his activity at Nicaea or in the capital, though he does appear to have gone to Sardis. His successor, John, is only known for his actions at Constantinople during the iconoclastic persecutions. Of the six bishops discussed above, only one certainly visited Sardis. The problem became more severe later, under the Palaeologi, when the patriarch was frequently obliged to denounce bishops who refused to leave the capital. The reasons are not far to seek: a metropolitan, especially of such a high ranking see as Sardis, was a man of considerable power and influence in the Church. He had probably worked hard to gain his position, and could best secure the benefits of it by staying in the capital and participating in its intrigues. These bishops were not local worthies who had worked their way up through the ranks from parish priest or monk, but were educated men, often of distinguished family, and frequently of a secular background. For them, only the capital could provide the amenities of life.[38]

Although the position of metropolitan was desirable for the prestige and profits it would bring, the bishops were naturally reluctant to fulfill their obligations to their flocks in person. Nothing could persuade them that the brilliant life of Constantinople was less desirable than a long sojourn in the dusty and ramshackle towns and villages of Anatolia which passed under the name of metropolis.[39] In their absence ecclesiastical business was carried on by the large bureaucracies which formed part of the church structure in a metropolis.[40] To understand the nature of the kind of town a metropolitan was reluctant to visit, the archaeological evidence from Sardis may be consulted with profit.

The excavations show that the Acropolis was reoccupied and that settlements grew up in several sectors of the western part of the city. On the Acropolis, the first period of construction and habitation (seventh-eighth century) had ended in violent destruction and been followed by a period of desertion. The area within the walls began to be built up once again in the tenth century; the construction became quite dense by the eleventh century, indicating large-scale occupation.

Numerous small houses were built close together along the southern fortification wall and in terraces within and above it. The ruins now visible suggest a cluster of houses built like a theater, according to the contours of the land, behind the present entrance to the citadel. The pattern of streets is not clear, but there was a graveyard behind the buildings of the central sector, and a chapel was excavated into the rock under the highest peak of the Acropolis and covered with frescoes. Many of the buildings were built over the earlier graveyard, which in turn had intruded into the buildings of the first period. The Middle Byzantine graves were poorly built and crowded together, but the density of construction and contours of the land left little room for burials, so there is no need to suppose they had been dug in time of some emergency or siege. The main water supply for the settlement came from cisterns; the largest, a well-built barrel-vaulted construction, lay just behind the central terraced buildings.

Most of the buildings were houses consisting of one or more rooms about five meters square, many of which contained a semicircular brick hearth. One building has been interpreted as a manufactory of glazed pottery. The settlement was small and crowded, with houses covering all available land; it had its own water supply, chapel, graveyard, and some facilities for the production of necessities. The relation between this settlement and those which were growing contemporaneously at the temple and in the plain is not clear.[41]

The buildings on the Acropolis continued to be occupied until the late eleventh century, when a long break in the sequence of coins found there extends from 1059-1185. The remains also show an interruption, for there is a later stage of construction in which some units were divided and rebuilt, often on a smaller and less impressive scale than before. That stage of building then continues, without further disturbance, down to the early Ottoman period.[42]

Historical circumstances may explain the break in continuity. After the middle of the eleventh century, at a time when the stability of the Byzantine government was threatened by corruption, neglect of the army, and a continuing conflict between the civil and military aristocracies, the Turks became a serious threat on the eastern frontier. The empire was forced to make a great effort to repel their attacks, which constantly grew more serious. The defeat of the great expedition of the emperor Romanus Diogenes at Manzikert in 1071 was catastrophic for the empire, whose frontier defenses collapsed completely. Turkish hordes soon swept over the whole of Anatolia, much of which was permanently lost to Byzantium. After Manzikert, when the empire was convulsed by civil war for a decade, the progress of the Seljuk Turks was rapid. By the time Alexius Comnenus (1081-1118) came to the throne and began to restore some kind of stability, most of Asia Minor had been incorporated into a Sultanate with its capital at Nicaea.

Smaller Turkish states also sprang up on what had been Byzantine soil: the most important of these was the emirate of Chaka Bey, with its headquarters at Smyrna.[43] Chaka built a navy, established control over the whole Aegean coast with the major islands, and maintained himself in a position to constitute a grave threat to the empire until his murder in 1092. Sardis was apparently part of his domains and remained in Turkish hands until, in 1098, the Byzantine general Ducas recaptured it and Philadelphia after Turkish power in western Asia Minor had been broken by the armies of the First Crusade (source 29).

The two cities were turned over to the general Michael Cecaumenus to administer. His headquarters were probably not at Sardis but at Philadelphia which from this time became the major military and administrative center of the region because of its strategic location on the new frontier with the Turks. In the troubled period of reconquest and reorganization, such small military districts were set up to establish order; others were at Smyrna,

Ephesus, and Lampe.[44] When central control was restored in western Asia Minor, the old system of large provinces governed by a general came back into force, with some changes. Sardis once again became part of the Thracesian theme, probably late in the reign of Alexius Comnenus, but this was now governed from Philadelphia. This situation prevailed through the twelfth century, and possibly later; the administrative history of the region in the last period of Byzantine rule is unclear.[45] Ecclesiastical organization, however, never recognized present realities, and Sardis remained the metropolis of Lydia as long as it was a Christian city.

Conquest of Sardis by the Turks of Chaka probably explains the break in continuity at the Acropolis in the late eleventh century, though no evidence is forthcoming to account for the long gap in the coin sequence. Once Sardis was recaptured by the Byzantines, it entered into a period of peace and recovery which lasted through the twelfth and thirteenth centuries. There were other Turkish attacks in the area—one was defeated near Sardis in 1113—but they were not serious enough to disrupt the life of the city until the late thirteenth century.[46]

The ruins of the Temple of Artemis became the site of considerable activity in the Middle Byzantine period; an important village was established there and continued without interruption down to Ottoman times. This settlement centered on a large cistern built into the ruined temple. The cella of the temple was cleared out, a wall was built into the bank of debris from the earthquake of the seventh century, and the whole cistern was lined with pink waterproof cement. Coins found in the bottom of the cistern, which has been completely removed, show that it was in use from the late ninth century until about 1400.[47] Great numbers of terracotta waterpipes with settling pots to purify the water supply led throughout the whole temple area and indicate a sizable settlement.

The water supply of Roman Sardis presumably had depended on the aqueduct which had brought water down from the slopes of Mount Tmolus. This system had been disrupted by the devastation of 616 and the subsequent landslide; thereafter, no city life could exist until a new water supply was established. Hence, the excavated remains at the temple were in two distinct levels, one datable to the time before 616, the other after the mid-ninth century; there were no remains between these nor were any coins of the period 668-867 found.[48] As at the Acropolis, however, there is slight evidence that the place was not completely abandoned. A tombstone found on the hillside north of the temple uses a peculiar form of the letter *beta* most often found in the late seventh and eighth centuries,[49] which may show there was some habitation near the temple. But there was certainly no substantial settlement there between 616 and the construction of the cistern in the mid-ninth century.

The cistern was surrounded by houses (fig. 35). Numerous walls of undressed stones laid in mud were excavated along the north side of the temple and dated by finds of pottery and coins to the tenth-twelfth centuries. North of these, many unidentified and undated foundations of small buildings along two streets are still visible; these could well date from the Middle Byzantine period and represent the extent of the settlement on that side of the cistern. On the south lay a large cemetery whose church has not been discovered; the earlier Church M had been overwhelmed by the landslide of the seventh century. In the same area the late antique Building L was now reoccupied. Traces of limekilns found in the area show that the industry of Late Antiquity was still being carried on; the temple continued to provide an important quarry for building materials. Here, then, was settlement similar to that on the Acropolis. It was however, much more substantial, containing a large cistern, numerous houses and some industrial activity.[50]

The land stretching about half a kilometer along the Pactolus north of the temple and occupied by villas and tombs in Late Antiquity was apparently abandoned in 616 and never reoccupied. Here, because the slopes of the Acropolis reach almost down to the stream, there was no cultivable land to support the kind of settlement typical of the Dark Ages. The sector of Pactolus Cliff contains more land and some evidence of Middle Byzantine occupation. The villa which had stood there in Late Antiquity was filled with rubble and its walls levelled. Pottery found in association with this work suggests a Middle Byzantine date, but no substantial remains survive. Perhaps a few houses stood here, or the place was simply leveled and the walls trimmed down to clear the land for cultivation.

The nearby sector of Pactolus North contains evidence of more activity, attested both by coin finds and the remains. The sequence of coins, interrupted in the early seventh century, resumes in the ninth and continues through the late eleventh. The late antique villa may have been reoccupied: modification of its walls and damage to its mosaics seems to be dated by Middle Byzantine pottery. A fragmentary inscription in a cursive hand of the twelfth century or later comes from the sector,[51] but more important is the evidence from the basilical church. Its fate in 616 is uncertain: it seems not to have been destroyed, but decline, perhaps accompanied by a temporary abandonment, had set in. In about the ninth century, a solid wall with piers was built over the colonnades, apparently to provide support for a new roof, and the church continued in use, though in a state of constant decay only partially hindered by makeshift measures. By the eleventh century the atrium became a burying ground, while the narthex seems to have been turned into a dwelling or eating room. Graves in the nave have been dated to the eleventh and twelfth centuries. Coins of Constantine X (1059-1067) and Romanus IV (1067-1071) found in graves in the narthex and atrium suggest that the church may have been abandoned, and perhaps partially destroyed, as a result of the Seljuk invasion of Asia Minor after the battle of Manzikert. The church would appear to have been a ruin when the new smaller Church E was constructed on the same spot in the thirteenth century.[52]

The large area between Pactolus North and the highway, densely built up in Late Antiquity, apparently lay abandoned (or cultivated) in this period. No remains and only two coins have been found.[53]

The Gymnasium complex, on the other hand, was the scene of considerable activity, probably because of its location on a still important highway. Coin finds there show continuity from the late eighth century through the fourteenth, with a major gap from 1081-1185 such as was observed at the Acropolis though not the temple. Much of the building apparently remained standing until it was knocked down by an earthquake in the twelfth century, providing an area for limited occupation and some industry. Strata suggesting habitation have been excavated, but no substantial foundations were uncovered. Remains of limekilns of the tenth century show that the Gymnasium, with its abundance of marble decoration, was being used as a quarry for building materials; several columns were found near the kilns, where they had been dragged for conversion into lime. That was not the only kind of industrial activity in the Gymnasium area. Large brick furnaces built into the long building north of the former palaestra were suitable for the manufacture of glazed pottery (fig. 36). The inhabitants of the area seem to have lived to the west of the Gymnasium towards the Pactolus. Remains of buildings from the eleventh century on a street branching diagonally from the highway were found in the sector called "West of West B." The settlement apparently lay around the Gymnasium and along the highway. Like the other inhabited areas, except that on the Acropolis, it was unfortified. Since its exposed location on the highway would have made it especially vulnerable to attack, the gap in the coin sequence here may be associated with the disturbances of the Turkish invasion of the 1080s.[54]

The fate of the unexcavated central part of the city in the Middle Byzantine period is unknown. The only evidence is an inscription of the ninth-tenth centuries which is said to have been found south of Church D. It is apparently a tombstone and invokes the curse of the 318 fathers of the Council of Nicaea on whoever disturbs the site.[55] It is probable that this area of the city, which has fertile soil, supported a village settlement under the Byzantines as it later did in the Ottoman period. Its inhabitants could have sought refuge in the Byzantine Fortress or in Building A in time of invasion. In any case, it is clear that there was no major construction in the area after 616. The many standing ruins and fragments of buildings between the Gymnasium and the eastern end of the city may all be dated to Late Antiquity or earlier.

There was another settlement with some industry at the eastern end of the city at the former Roman Bath CG outside the City Wall. By the tenth century this heavily constructed building was half buried in silt brought down by the stream which runs beside it. Its upper story, all that remained above ground, was then reoccupied and altered; brick walls and arches were built in the bath, and furnaces constructed. Residue in and around the furnaces suggests that the manufacture of glazed pottery and the roasting of iron ores were carried on. Industrial activity may also have included the production of glass, as suggested by the numerous glass bracelets found in the sector datable to the tenth-thirteenth centuries. No trace of houses has yet been discovered, but the presence of several Byzantine graves indicates that the settlement was somewhere in the vicinity.[56]

Middle Byzantine Sardis was considered to be a city, indeed one of the more important cities of the area. But investigation of the remains reveals nothing remotely resembling the great city of Late Antiquity. Instead, a large fortress was maintained and inhabited, and numerous settlements resembling villages were scattered throughout the territory formerly occupied by the city. Between them lay open spaces, presumably cultivated. The remains suggest that each settlement was to some degree self-sufficient: each had its own water supply in the form of cisterns or proximity to streams and some workshops to produce goods necessary for daily life, such as pottery and building materials. With the possible exception of the iron working at Bath CG, there is no evidence for production of goods useful for trade. The connection between the different settlements cannot be determined, though it is plausible to assume that they were collectively known as Sardis and formed part of one whole, all looking to the Acropolis for defense and centering on the one which contained the cathedral, for Sardis was still the ecclesiastical metropolis of Lydia.

Further excavation, especially around Church D, might make the picture much clearer, but one point can be made with certainty: the break with the late antique past was quite complete, and the medieval city was a very different organism from the classical one. The centralization and extensive public services which had characterized the classical city had disappeared, and the loosely connected settlements which made up the medieval city were concerned primarily with self-sufficiency and defense. Because of developments which took place after 616, Sardis had ceased to be a significant commercial and industrial center: its population lived clustered in small and undistinguished villages scattered among the imposing ruins of the antique city, much as it does at the present day.

Sardis in the Empire of Nicaea
and the Last Byzantine Phase

The disastrous defeat of Emperor Manuel Comnenus by the Turks at Myriokephalon in 1176 marked the beginning of the final disintegration of the Byzantine Empire. In the period which followed independent dynasts set themselves up in various western parts of Asia Minor, and their rule was only terminated by the successful Ottoman expansion of the mid-fifteenth century, which once more reunited the whole country. The outstanding skill and diligence of the emperors of Nicaea provided a respite of fifty years (1211-1261) from the chaotic conditions of the times, but the recapture of Constantinople directed the attention of the Byzantine government elsewhere, and Lydia with the rest of Asia Minor soon fell to the constant pressure of the Turkish tribes.

The Comneni (1081-1185) had striven to maintain and strengthen the frontier defenses, but after Myriokephalon the system broke down and Turkish bands penetrated into western Asia Minor. Since the weak and corrupt government of the late twelfth century could provide no security for the provinces, the inhabitants began to take measures for their own protection, and a series of revolts broke out which eventually led to the establishment of independent states on imperial territory.

In 1182 John Comnenus Vatatzes, general of the Thracesian theme, led a rebellion in Philadelphia against the new emperor Andronicus Comnenus. He soon gained the adherence of Sardis and Lydia, and the revolt spread to the neighboring provinces, where the cities were filled with sedition and civil war. Although he succeeded in defeating an imperial force, Vatatzes died at the height of his success and the Philadelphians, bewailing their lost leader, surrendered to the emperor.[57] Seven years later Philadelphia was the seat of another revolt, this one led by a local magnate, Theodore Mangaphas. He assumed the imperial title and brought all of Lydia and the neighboring provinces under his control, an act considered to be so serious that the emperor Isaac Angelus personally led an army to beseige Philadelphia. A compromise was reached by which Mangaphas resumed the role of a private citizen, and imperial control was reestablished. The rebel subsequently escaped to the Turks and led attacks against the Maeander Valley. When the Third Crusade under Frederick Barbarossa passed through Sardis and Philadelphia in 1190, they found the area in imperial hands, though the whole territory to the east had been overrun by the Turks.[58]

Lydia did not long remain reunited with the empire; in 1204 Constantinople was captured by the Fourth Crusade, and centralized control of Asia Minor disintegrated. Independent states sprung up in Trebizond, Heraclea Pontica, Bithynia, Philadelphia, Priene, and the Maeander Valley. Once again, Lydia came under the domination of Mangaphas of Philadelphia. Within a few

years, however, all these principalities except Trebizond fell to
Theodore Lascaris, who organized a state at Nicaea that claimed
to be the successor to the decapitated empire.

Lascaris (1204-1222) and his able son-in-law John Vatatzes
(1222-1254) founded and ruled over a prosperous and successful
state, the so-called Empire of Nicaea, which originally included
most of Bithynia, Mysia, Lydia, and Ionia. Its capital was nominally at Nicaea, the seat of its patriarch, but the emperors, especially Vatatzes, preferred to spend most of their time at two
favorite residences in Lydia, Nymphaeum and Magnesia ad
Sipylum. Strategically and economically, Magnesia, where the
emperors had their treasury and mint, was the most important city
in the state.[59] It lay at a major highway junction with roads leading north to the Hellespont and Bithynia, west to Smyrna and
Ephesus, and east to Philadelphia and the Turkish domains. The
ancient road through Lydia, the main highway between the Greek
and Turkish states, was the axis of the kingdom, and Sardis experienced a time of considerable prosperity because it lay on this
route, halfway between Magnesia and Philadelphia.

The half century between Lascaris' major victory over the Turks
in 1211 and the recapture of Constantinople in 1261 was a flourishing time for Byzantine Lydia, the last that it was to experience.
The wise administration of the Nicene emperors attended to the
needs of defense by building fortresses throughout its territories
and ensured the prosperity of the provinces by encouraging economic self-sufficiency. Their extensive building program attests to
the success of these policies.[60] Fortunately for the stability and
prosperity of the provinces, peace was generally maintained on
the eastern frontier. The Turks had been defeated and the threat
posed by their state at Konya vanished after the Mongol invasion
of 1243 reduced them to impotence and anarchy. In the troubled
years after that defeat, the Seljuk Sultan Kaikaus Izzeddin fled to
Vatatzes, who came to meet him at Sardis in 1257 (source 30); the
emperor conducted the Sultan back to Magnesia, where discussions were held and a treaty highly advantageous to the empire
was signed.[61]

This flourishing period of peace did not last long; the fortunes of
the Asiatic provinces began a precipitous decline after the reconquest of Constantinople in 1261. The imperial government became
preoccupied with adventures in the west, neglected frontier

defense, and alienated the people of the provinces. The situation rapidly became serious: in the reign of Michael Palaeologus (1259-1282), the Turks were reported to be ravaging Lydia and Asia like pirates, making incursions as far as Sardis and Magnesia (source 31). Byzantine resistance was ineffective. By 1313, Magnesia, the most important city of the region, had fallen, the whole Hermus Valley was in the hands of the Turks, and their emirate of Saruhan had been established in Lydia. To understand this rapid transformation, it is necessary briefly to consider the history of Turkish Anatolia in the period.[62]

In the early thirteenth century numerous tribes of Turcoman nomads had arrived in Anatolia, largely as an effect of the Mongol invasions. The Seljuk sultanate of Rum, which provided a stable government with its capital at Konya, had kept these tribes in control and settled many of them on the frontiers. In 1243 at the battle of Kösedağ, however, the Seljuk army was obliterated by the Mongols and the state began to disintegrate, a process that gained momentum after a second defeat in 1256. The severely weakened central authority never recovered under Mongol governors, whose authority in the west was ineffectual, and the Turcoman tribes assumed an increasing degree of independence.

A vivid indication of conditions of the Byzantine frontier in these times is given by the narrative of the flight of Michael Palaeologus from Nicaea in 1256. Suspecting the hostile intentions of the emperor Theodore Lascaris, Palaeologus escaped from Bithynia and arrived at the dwellings of the Turcomans. The chronicler describes them as a race living on the borders, who hated the Romans and rejoiced in plundering them, especially since the Seljuk government was then weakened. They fell on Palaeologus "as a windfall," robbed him of his possessions—gold, silver and clothing—and seized all his followers as slaves. Palaeologus somehow managed to escape and took refuge with the Sultan, who sent letters in vain to recover his lost goods.[63] This illustrates the chaotic conditions of the times as well as the attitude of the Turcomans towards the Byzantines, whom they could regard as rightful prey since they often considered themselves to be warriors of the faith.[64]

With the increasing decay of the central government, the Turcomans came to form their own political entities, independent states on the frontiers between the Seljuks and Byzantines. The first of these was established in 1261 in the region of Denizli, but was soon suppressed. More important for the fate of Byzantine Lydia was the emirate of Germiyan, a tribe originally settled in eastern Asia Minor which had been transferred to Phrygia by the Seljuks before 1277 to control the Turcomans of the region. By the end of the century they had founded a state with its capital at Kütahya (Cotyaeum) and assumed leadership in the struggle against the Infidel.[65]

As long as the Byzantine state had its headquarters in Asia Minor, the frontiers were defended and stability maintained. In 1261, however, Constantinople was recaptured from the Latins and the attention of the emperors shifted from Asia to Europe. The decline of the Byzantine position in Anatolia was rapid. Attacks, as already mentioned, reached Sardis and Magnesia within a few years of the move to Constantinople and the efforts of the Byzantine government to repel them and restore order were in vain. For Lydia, the most important of these attempts was the expedition of Alexius Philanthropenus in 1293-1295. Philanthropenus, who was entrusted with an extended command in western Asia Minor, made his headquarters at Philadelphia. From there, he achieved great success against the Turks, especially in the Maeander Valley, until he revolted against the emperor. His rebellion was soon suppressed by the general of a neighboring province who had Sardis under his administration. With the successful and popular general Philanthropenus removed from the scene, Byzantine power in Anatolia rapidly dwindled. By the end of the century disaster was at hand.[66]

The Turkish advance had been inexorable. The most important frontier fortress in northern Lydia was Magidion, near Saittae, which had a warlike population particularly skilled in archery. Though strengthened in 1269, Magidion was seriously threatened by 1278 and fell to the Turks not long after.[67] Before 1304, Kula, an important fortress and market town and center of the fertile volcanic district about 60 kilometers east of Sardis, was in Turkish hands.[68] More serious was the loss of Tripolis on the Maeander, which had been refortified by Vatatzes. This town was the key to the defenses of Lydia, for it controlled the pass over the eastern end of Mount Tmolus which provided access from the upper Maeander, an area which had been Turkish since 1205, to Philadelphia and the Hermus Valley. Around 1300 the people of Tripolis, hard pressed by Turkish attacks, had entered into an agreement to buy supplies from the local Turks and to allow them to trade in the city. Shortly after, the city was taken by a ruse and became a base for the emir of Germiyan.[69]

After that, the Cogamus and Hermus valleys lay open to attack. The situation was so serious that in 1302 the co-emperor Michael IX led an army of Alan troops to Magnesia, which he planned to use as a base against the Turks. On his arrival, the Turks withdrew to fortresses in the nearby hills; they had already penetrated the countryside deeply, leaving the fortified cities isolated. After an abortive advance the Byzantine army retreated to Magnesia, where it was beseiged by the Turks, who overran the Hermus Valley as far as the coast. Much of the local population, abandoned to these attacks, fled the country; many others were killed.[70] When the Catalan Grand Company, mercenaries in Byzantine service, arrived at Philadelphia in the summer of 1304, they had to rescue the city from a siege led by Germiyan.[71] But their spectacular progress, attended by notable successes against the Turks, was ephemeral and marked the last attempt of the Byzantine government to retain control of the area. Ten years after their departure, Philadelphia was paying tribute to Germiyan, and the whole Hermus Valley had become a Turkish country.[72]

It is against this background that the last events in the history of Byzantine Sardis may be considered. By the end of the thirteenth century most of Lydia had fallen to the Turks, leaving only a few strong fortresses, like islands, in the hands of the empire. Sardis was one of these fortresses, a place of refuge for the farmers of the plain, who constantly had to suffer from the inroads of the Turkish bands. The contemporary historian Pachymeres (1242-1310) provides a remarkable account of a Turkish attack in 1304, the first serious attempt to take the city. His narrative is the single most detailed description of any event in the history of Byzantine Sardis; it is also the last (source 32).

At the time of the attack, Andronicus II (1282-1328), the emperor who presided over the dissolution of Byzantine power in Asia Minor, and the Mongols, nominal suzerains of the Turks of Anatolia, had just concluded a treaty. A certain Turcoman chief called Alaeddin, perhaps one of the lieutenants of the Germiyanids, was then plundering the Hermus Valley. Disturbed by the news of the treaty, he decided to seek a safe place for his men and the treasures he had accumulated. He therefore proposed to the occupants of the citadel of Sardis, which had apparently withstood all attacks, that they allow him to move in and share the fortress with them. The Sardians at first rejected this unwelcome proposal: they had held out and been making successful sallies against the Turks, although in their turn they had been cut off from free access to their fields.

When the Turks pressed the siege, the defenders, unable to sow their fields and running short of water, decided to yield since no relief was in sight. The Turks entered the citadel and occupied part of it, which was cut off from the rest by a wall with a small gate for trade between the two parties. According to their agreement, the Sardians were free to till their fields and their guests to plunder others in the vicinity. The unaccustomed neighbors lived side by side for some time until the Turks recovered from their fear of the Mongols and planned to turn on their hosts. Just in time, the Byzantine forces arrived, moved on the Acropolis by night, and slaughtered the Turks.

This narrative reveals a good deal about conditions at Sardis. The Acropolis was still a defensible and important fortification; the Turks wanted to use it because it was especially strong and inaccessible. It was capable of resisting the kind of attack which local bands of raiding tribesmen might undertake, but was not prepared to withstand a long siege. The shortage of water shows that the citadel was temporarily overcrowded: in peacetime the cisterns were probably adequate for the houses inside the walls, but during an emergency, when the population which lived by agriculture in the plain would take refuge there, the supply might run short. In the Middle Ages, most of the small population of Sardis could probably be accommodated within the fortress walls, but the resources of the city were not very substantial, and it could only hope to hold out a short while without support.

Sardis did not long remain in Byzantine hands after the Turks were driven from the Acropolis. The refortification of the castles between Philadelphia and Magnesia by the Catalan Roger de Flor in the same year is the last indication that Sardis was Byzantine.[73] Thereafter, the obscure period of the Turkish conquest follows, and nothing more is heard of the city for sixty-five years.[74]

Evidence from the excavations complements the material in the sources. Sardis experienced a period of activity and prosperity under the Empire of Nicaea, then survived on a reduced scale until the fifteenth century. During the whole time, the fortifications on the Acropolis were maintained and the settlement within them continued to be inhabited. The houses behind the south fortification wall were in use from the eleventh through the fifteenth century, with no evidence of any major interruption. The dating of these poor and unimpressive remains is difficult, but some repairs and rebuildings seem to fall within the Lascarid and Palaeologan periods.

The settlement of 1304 may have left its trace in the remains on the Acropolis. In the southern part of the citadel—a heavily fortified area which could easily be isolated from the rest—a crudely built wall of rubble and mortar was found in association with late pottery. This was constructed perpendicular to the main fortification wall and could have served to close off this part of the Acropolis. It is possibly the wall mentioned by Pachymeres. If so, it confirms the accuracy of his narrative and offers a rare example of coincidence between the archaeological and literary evidence.[75]

The settlement at the temple also continued down to Ottoman times, apparently on the same scale as in the Middle Byzantine period. Until about 1400 the cistern guaranteed an adequate supply of water to the village around it. Detailed description of this sector is impossible, for many of the remains have been removed and those that survive are so poor and undistinguished that nothing can be determined about their chronology. The coins found at the temple indicate a certain amount of activity; they form a continuous sequence through the fifteenth century and are especially abundant from the Nicene period.[76] Finds of Lascarid coins are particularly numerous from Building L on the southern side of the temple precinct, where lime-burning seems to have been a major activity.[77]

For the rest of the city, except for the sector Pactolus North, there is practically no evidence. Remains are hard to distinguish from those of the previous period, and few coins have been found. There are no Late Byzantine coins from PC, the House of Bronzes, or Bath CG, and only a few from the Gymnasium area. These last show continuity in that sector at least down to the Ottoman period, but none of them have been found in association with remains of buildings.[78] The erection of a long wall on the west bank of the Pactolus, opposite the main part of the city, may be a work of the thirteenth century or somewhat earlier. The building or enclosure of which it formed a part has not been excavated.[79]

Much more is known about the sector Pactolus North, where the ruins of the most substantial building of Byzantine Sardis stand. Church E was erected in the thirteenth century on the site of the fourth century basilica which had stood on the east side of the late antique street. The church is a three-aisled basilica with five domes (figs. 37, 38). It measures about 20 x 11 meters and was built on a large platform. The construction is neat and regular with courses of cut marble and brick in a technique reminiscent of the palace of the Nicene emperors at Nymphaeum and of Palae-ologan churches in Constantinople. The church was carefully built; reinforcing timbers for protection against earthquakes run through the walls and foundations.[80] For the period, this is an impressive building, far different from the crude huts and work-shops found elsewhere on the site. It reflects both the prosperity of Sardis at the time and the extensive building activity of the Nicene emperors, who caused churches to be put up throughout their ter-ritories.

A cemetery extended to the north of the church, but there are no remains of habitations in the immediate vicinity. Not far away, however, at the Southwest Gate of the City Wall, a hoard of coins of John Vatatzes was discovered in association with some late walls.[81] It is hardly likely that these constructions represent any continued use of the City Walls which had been built to defend the area to the east, abandoned since 616. They are most probably the remains of a settlement which could have extended towards the church through an area now covered with village houses.

The church itself may have been the cathedral of Sardis in the Nicene period and after: it is close to the inhabited centers, and the earlier cathedral, Church D far to the east, may have been aban-doned by this time. Since some of the bishops of the Lascarid and Palaeologan periods were men of considerable importance, it is conceivable that the influence of one of them was responsible for the construction of the church.

Theodore Galenus was bishop of Sardis at the end of the twelfth century. He is perhaps to be identified with a Theodore of Sardis who signed a synodic document of 1191. Otherwise, he is only known from two poems written in his memory by his nephew and successor. From these it appears that he was a native of Constantinople, was chosen by the synod to be metropolitan of Sardis, and presided over that church for five years until he died of cancer. He was apparently a highly educated man who instructed his nephew in eloquence, grammar, rhetoric, history, and philosophy. Like many dignitaries, he adopted the habit of a monk shortly before his death. The painting on his tomb, which may have been at Sardis or Constantinople, consequently showed him both as archbishop and as monk. He would appear to have been a teacher at the patriarchal school in the capital, and, like many of his predecessors, may never have visited his diocese.[82]

Nicephorus Chrysoberges, nephew and successor of Galenus, is a much better known figure whose name first appears in 1172 when he was deacon and notary of Saint Sophia. Between 1188 and 1204, he delivered several public addresses to the patriarchs and to the emperors Alexius III and Alexius IV. These were given in Nicephorus' capacity as *maistor ton rhetoron*, a high ecclesiastical official appointed by the emperor, whose duties consisted in giving two public orations a year to the emperor and patriarch, and in teaching rhetoric and philosophy in the patriarchal school. As a teacher of rhetoric, Nicephorus, like his ninth century predecessor John, wrote schoolbooks. Some *progymnasmata*, models for rhetorical composition, survive under his name; these consist of short essays on such subjects as "what does a Christian teacher say when he is forbidden by Julian the Apostate to teach from the pagan philosophers?" Here, too, originality is conspicuously lacking; the same tired themes had been belabored by thirty or more generations of schoolboys, but the tradition at least was maintained.[83]

A successful teacher in the patriarchal school could hope for promotion to a bishopric. This might involve the disagreeable necessity of a move to some dreary province, but, as has been seen, many prelates managed to avoid that altogether. Galenus may have succeeded in staying in the capital, but Nicephorus Chrysoberges was not so fortunate. When Constantinople was taken by the Latins in 1204, the patriarchate was transferred to Nicaea, and Chrysoberges quite probably went on to his flock at Sardis. The date of his appointment there is uncertain; it was probably after 1204, and certainly before 1213, when his signature as bishop of Sardis appears on a synodic letter. By 1216, he had been succeeded by a certain Alexius.[84]

At Sardis, it is probable that Nicephorus maintained the traditions of learning in which he had already distinguished himself. During the Lascarid period, when the capital was in the hands of the crusaders, education was decentralized and schools grew up in the cities of Asia Minor. Sardis, the diocese of one of the outstanding rhetoricians of the day, may have been the seat of such a school.[85]

The works of Chrysoberges of the greatest interest for the history of Sardis are the poems he wrote to describe the decoration of a local church. These consist of three short iambic poems on the archangel Michael, Saint John the Evangelist, and the archangel Gabriel, whose figures adorned the entrance to the church (source 33). Gabriel is particularly described as "guardian of the flock of Sardis," which may indicate that he was patron saint of the city (as, for example, was the archangel Michael of the neighboring Philadelphia) and leaves no doubt that the paintings described were at Sardis. The representations were apparently conventional: Saint Michael guarded the entrance with drawn sword, Saint John opened the metaphorical gates of repentance, while Gabriel stood by the entrance holding the book in which were inscribed the names of those who were saved.[86]

Chrysoberges, a particularly mediocre poet, has left behind other verse descriptions of paintings, among them a long *ekphrasis* of the dormition of the Virgin, a short verse on the parable of Christ with the little child, and a description of a certain princess Irene who became a nun; the second epitaph of Galenus which shows that he was represented both as bishop and monk might be included here. These verses may all have been intended to describe the decoration of a single church at Sardis, but such a hypothesis cannot be advanced with confidence, for there is no evidence in the poems or the manuscript to support it. Equally hypothetical is the identification of the church: Church E was apparently built during the Lascarid period, and may well have been new when the paintings described by Chrysoberges were used to decorate it; on the other hand, there is no indication in the poems that the paintings were put in a new church or an old one, or whether he is describing new paintings or already existing ones. Historically, the latter part of the Lascarid period, when the emperors had their headquarters in Lydia, would seem a more favorable time for the erection of a new church at Sardis. For the present, any association between the paintings and Church E must remain speculative.

One of Chrysoberges' successors was also an important figure in the ecclesiastical history of his age. Andronicus, a native of Paphlagonia, became bishop of Sardis before 1250. In 1253 he was entrusted with the exceptionally important duty of participating in an embassy to the Pope to settle terms for reunion of the Greek and Latin churches. Although the negotiations were successful, the agreed terms were never put into force because the emperor Vatatzes, who supported the union, died the same year.[87] A prelate of such importance might have been able to use his influence at court to gain financial support for construction of a new church at Sardis.

The later career of Andronicus was less brilliant. In 1258 he opposed the coronation of Michael Palaeologus, but was persuaded to accede. In the next year, he fought against the election of Nicephorus of Ephesus as patriarch to replace Arsenius, whose cause, which produced a schism in the church, he proceeded to champion. In 1261 he asked permission to return to his native Paphlagonia. The emperor, who feared he would stir up trouble there, denied this request, saying "you have been ordained metropolitan of Sardis, not of Paphlagonia; you should enjoy dwelling and remaining there, and shepherding the flock."[88] Andronicus was thereupon tonsured as a monk and remained a leader of a schismatic faction which disturbed the church through the reign of Michael Palaeologus.[89]

Palaeologus' rebuke to the bishop of Sardis once again illustrates the perennial problem of the Byzantine church: metropolitans would rather stay in the capital and participate in politics and intrigue than perform the routine duties of their office in the diocese to which they were appointed. The successor of Andronicus provides another example of this phenomenon. Jacob Chalazas, who came from the west, was installed as bishop of Sardis in 1261. Six years later, on his way to Anatolia after "remaining long enough in Constantinople," he transmitted a message from the emperor to persuade the current patriarch Germanus to resign. The implication that he had not yet set foot in Sardis is strong. He next appears in history as an ambassador whom Michael Palaeologus sent to Spain in 1282 to secure an alliance against Charles of Anjou; like many of his predecessors, Chalazas was evidently an important figure in both ecclesiastical and secular politics.[90]

After his old adversary Michael Palaeologus died in 1282,

Andronicus was restored to favor. In 1283 he once again became metropolitan of Sardis and was in addition made father confessor to the new emperor, Andronicus II. With this renewed and strengthened authority, and filled with resentment at his earlier treatment, he presided in the same year over a synod at the Blachernae palace which condemned and persecuted the prelates who had favored union with the Latin church. In 1284, however, he was accused of plotting against the emperor, and deposed from his see; with that, he disappears from history.[91]

The bishopric of Sardis was vacant for a short time after the fall of Andronicus. It was represented at the Council of the Blachernae in 1285 not by its own metropolitan but by Gerasimus the bishop of Corcyra, which had recently been occupied by Charles of Anjou, an inveterate foe of the Byzantines and their church.[92]

Soon after, Sardis once again had its own bishop, Cyril, best known as the recipient of several letters of denunciation from the patriarch Athanasius I. Cyril was bishop in the beginning of the fourteenth century (he was appointed sometime before 1305 and ended his service before 1315), a time when Sardis was suffering from the attacks of the Turks. Such circumstances reinforced a metropolitan's normal desire to stay in the capital. The strict and zealous patriarch had frequent occasion to criticize Cyril and his colleagues who preferred the luxuries of Constantinople to the duty of shepherding their flock, a prospect which at that time would be dangerous as well as unattractive. Perhaps as a result of the patriarch's efforts to oust him from the capital, Cyril became one of his major antagonists. In 1305, however, he received the see of Methymna in Lesbos and was forced to leave Constantinople. The grant of a second diocese, called *kata logon epidoseos* in the ecclesiastical documents, was made frequently during the period of Turkish conquest when church property was being lost, congregations reduced, and dioceses becoming too impoverished to support a metropolitan. In such cases, the bishop would be given the rights to the revenues of a second diocese in a more secure part of the empire. Cyril thus probably never saw his original diocese, which was then reduced to such straits that it could not support him, but went to Lesbos when he was finally forced to leave the delights of the capital.[93]

The last known bishop of Sardis before the metropolitan see was dissolved in 1369 was Gregory, whose signature occurs on synodical acts from 1315 until 1343. His career seems to have resembled that of his predecessor Cyril. The frequent appearance of his name in the acts shows that he was often present in the capital, while the addition of *proedros* of Mytilene to his title after 1329 indicates that he was given that see to administer and for his support. It is not known whether he ever went there, but it is safe to assume that he never spent time in Sardis, which in his day was in the hands of the Turks. In 1350 and 1365 the see was vacant and administered by the bishop of Philadelphia, who was raised to the rank of metropolitan of Lydia when the ecclesiastical metropolis of Sardis was suppressed in 1369.[94]

Although most of the bishops seem to have been absentees, the ecclesiastical history of Sardis in the age of the Lascarids and Palaeologi tends to confirm the impression presented by the historical and archaeological sources. The one period of prosperity which the city enjoyed after the disaster of 616 was the half-century of Lascarid rule when its bishops were particularly prominent. Apart from the fortifications, the only substantial monument of the entire age was the Church E, built in the thirteenth century. In general, Sardis seems otherwise to have continued as it had been in the Middle Byzantine period: a heavily fortified castle on a hilltop containing a village, with other settlements in the plain below. The city, however prosperous, was in no state to undertake such great works as had distinguished it in Late Antiquity. In the last years of its existence as a Byzantine city, Sardis no doubt experienced considerable decline as Turkish attacks drove the inhabitants to take refuge in the citadel. But there was no great break in the life of the city in the Seljuk period, into which the history of the bishops has already carried the narrative. Sardis continued rather as it had been, except for the fundamental change from a Christian to a Turkish town.

III. Turkish Sardis

The Seljuk Period

One of the emirs of Germiyan, a certain Saruhan, became independent in the beginning of the fourteenth century, and, with the conquest of Magnesia in 1313, he established a principality which eventually included all of Lydia with Magidion in the north and the Hermus and Cogamus valleys as far as Philadelphia. That city maintained a precarious and isolated existence under Byzantine rule, while the lands to the east were controlled by Germiyan.[1] The date of the conquest of Sardis is unknown, but it is not likely to have been much later than that of Magnesia or of Nymphaeum (1316).[2] The whole region suffered tremendously during the years of attack and conquest as much of the Christian population fled to the west and large areas became desolate, to be repopulated eventually by the Turcomans.[3] The decline of the Christian community at Sardis during the fourteenth century seems to have been particularly swift.

In 1369, the patriarch of Constantinople issued an edict which ordered the suppression of the metropolis of Sardis, then over 1000 years old (source 34). Jurisdiction over such Christian communities as remained was to be transferred to the metropolitan of Philadelphia, a city which maintained itself independent of the Turks until 1390. The bombastic but sometimes elegant language of the patriarch's letter attests to the demise of Sardis as a Christian center. The patriarch regrets that Sardis, which had been outstanding for so long, had been brought to such a state that "it does not even preserve the appearance and some small character of a city, but has become a field of obliteration and destruction in place of a garden of luxury." He ordered that the whole territory of Sardis, "such as it is," thenceforth be subordinate to the metropolis of Philadelphia, which had not yet been forced to bend its neck to the enemy. Philadelphia was to possess the rank of Sardis for all time, just as "Sardis was once in good state, not yet being given over, God allowing, to the destruction of the enemy." This act, which may have been intended to recognize an already existing situation, may be taken as the epitaph of Byzantine Sardis.

There are no other written sources for Sardis under the Saruhanids, but the excavations have provided evidence which strikingly confirms the decline of the Christian community, and at the same time, in contrast to the sources, reveals a high degree of continuity. Sardis, not a large town under the Lascarids, suffered no spectacular decline during the first century of Turkish rule. The fortifications of the Acropolis and the settlement within them were maintained throughout the Seljuk period. The village at the Temple of Artemis with the large cistern which guaranteed it a supply of water continued to exist until the early fifteenth century at least.[4] Turkish coins found in the Gymnasium suggest that habitation or industrial activity continued there also.[5]

The most extensive and informative excavations for Turkish Sardis have been those of the sector PN, where a Turkish village grew up around the former Church E. The plan of the village cannot now be restored since it was destroyed by fire around 1600 and another village built immediately over it. Its remains, containing some reused column bases and bits of walls, can be dated by finds of coins, however, which show that the village was inhabited from the late fourteenth century through the sixteenth.[6] The archaeological evidence thus casts severe doubt on the accuracy of the literary sources which present a picture of overwhelming devastation and depopulation.

The fate of Church E similarly illustrates the continuity of the settlements at Sardis, but at the same time provides witness to the decline of the Christian community. By the middle of the fourteenth century, the church ceased to function as such, was cut up into compartments, and had a room added at the west end. In the former narthex, on an earth floor above the original floor of the church, which was removed, cooking pots, pithoi, and animal bones were found in a context with Turkish coins of the fourteenth and fifteenth centuries. On the north side of the building, a Lydian sarcophagus was reused as a water container. At the west end of the church a room was added and connected to the narthex. In it, the excavations uncovered a bronze pot and cauldron lying in the midst of charcoal and ashes, as well as a carpenter's plane, a chisel, an iron knife, vases, and lamps. A large burned mass of lime suggested that the building also contained a limekiln.[7]

The church was thus converted into workshops and dwellings not long after the Turkish conquest, a fact which provides tangible confirmation of the patriarch's letter of 1369 and of the decline of Christianity at Sardis. This decline was not the result of a conscious policy of the Turks to extirpate Christianity in the areas where they settled: although many churches were indeed converted to mosques in the cities, others continued in use as Christian buildings as long as there was a congregation to support them. By 1304, when it could be accommodated within the walls of the citadel, the population of Sardis was already small. It is possible that this Christian population may have disappeared by fleeing from the Turkish onslaught as the sources describe; it is also possible that the more prosperous abandoned the country and that those who were left were too few or too poor to maintain the church which, as the most substantial building at Sardis, would have been of obvious utility to the conquerors.

In general, however, the remains show that the sources are not to be taken entirely at their face value. The Christian population may have been severely reduced, but the impression at Sardis is one of continuity between the Byzantine and Seljuk periods rather than of a violent disruption. The settlement pattern of a fortress on the Acropolis containing a village, and of at least two other villages at the temple and sector PN, shows no fundamental change or even notable decline. Except for those of PN, the remains of these villages were not sufficiently extensive to determine whether their inhabitants were Christians or Turks. It is possible that the two communities continued to live in adjacent villages for some time, a phenomenon common in Turkey until 1923.

The emirate of Saruhan lasted less than a century. Like the other small independent states of Asia Minor, it was no match for the growing power of the Ottomans, who had crossed into Europe in the middle of the fourteenth century and established a dominant position in the Balkans as well as in western Asia Minor. In a whirlwind campaign in 1390, the Ottoman sultan Yıldırım Bayezid conquered a vast area in Asia Minor including Saruhan and the last Byzantine possession, Philadelphia. On his way to accept the surrender of the emir of Saruhan, Bayezid crossed Mount Tmolus and descended on Sardis, which was thus incorporated into the Ottoman Empire (source 35).

The triumph of Bayezid, however, was short-lived. By his rapid conquests in Asia Minor, achieved at the expense of fellow Moslems, he brought on himself the unfriendly attention of Tamerlane, who by that time had overrun all the Islamic lands of the east. Urged on by the dispossessed emirs of Asia Minor, the great conqueror resolved on a punitive expedition against Beyazit. The short campaign was decided by one battle. At Ankara on July 28, 1402, the Turkish army was crushed and the sultan led into captivity. Tamerlane then advanced to Kütahya, which became a base for expeditions led by his generals to subdue the rest of Anatolia and capture the surviving sons of Beyazit. He then resolved to restore order in Asia Minor and to transform his campaign into a holy war against the infidel. To establish settled conditions and consolidate his own power in the area, he sent the dispossessed emirs back to their principalities. The emir of Saruhan returned to Manisa before the end of 1402. To crush the infidel, Tamerlane determined to conquer Smyrna, which had been held by the knights of Rhodes since 1344. The city did not long resist. In December 1402, Smyrna was taken and destroyed, its Christian population massacred. His work done, Tamerlane withdrew up the Maeander Valley and slowly made his way back to central Asia.

This short but extremely destructive campaign is described in a rather rhetorical passage of the Greek historian Ducas, who wrote around 1460. According to him, Tamerlane set out from Kütahya, burning cities, enslaving the populations, seizing all the treasures, and advanced to Magnesia. There, "gathering all the gold and silver treasures of Lydia, and heaping up the wealth of Sardis, Philadelphia, and Attalus, he came to Smyrna" (source 36). This confused passage, which seems to imply that Tamerlane himself took Sardis, may be checked against the oriental sources. From them, it becomes apparent that the expedition in question was sent

out by one of the generals of Muhammed Sultan, grandson of
Tamerlane, who had his base at Manisa, while Tamerlane was still
in Kütahya. Since these expeditions destroyed some cities and held
others to ransom, it is not possible to say that Sardis was destroyed,
but rather that it was most probably attacked and bought off its
besiegers.[8] What the "wealth of Sardis" amounted to is impossible
to say; nothing in the physical remains of the city would suggest
that Tamerlane's men found any great treasure. The expression
may be merely rhetorical.

In 1402, Sardis once again became part of the emirate of Saruhan, but the invasion of Tamerlane had caused such devastation
and confusion that none of the restored emirs was very secure in
his position. Under these circumstances, an adventurer arose to
establish himself as the dominant figure in the politics of the region. This was Junayd, the emir of Izmir, who seized power from
the rulers of Aydin and managed to maintain it, with remarkable
changes of fortune, for over twenty years. Having secured his hold
on Aydin by marrying the daughter of the emir, Junayd was left in
sole control of the state when his father-in-law died in 1405. Before
then, he had extended its territory by conquering the lands up to
the Hermus River, including Nymphaeum, Philadelphia, and
Sardis (source 37). He cleverly maintained himself in power during
this period of civil war by submitting to whichever of the sons of
Bayezid seemed to be predominant. After a brief ouster, Junayd
regained his old power in 1411 but was forced two years later to
acknowledge the suzerainty of Mehmet Çelebi, the last of the sons
of Bayezid, and to inscribe the Sultan's name on his own coinage.
Although Mehmet had him expelled from Izmir in 1415, he returned seven years later and resisted the Ottomans until 1425,
when he was finally defeated and executed.[9]

In spite of the confusion of the sources and the period, it is clear
that Sardis was considered a place worth conquering as late as
1405. It was still worth mentioning as a stop on the Hermus highway when Junayd passed through it in 1425.[10] As long as Junayd
was in power, Sardis formed part of the territories under his control and was incorporated into the emirate of Aydin. Because these
emirates became Ottoman provinces with the boundaries which
existed at the time of their annexation, Sardis was included in the
province of Aydin instead of that of Saruhan to which it naturally
belonged, a situation which reflected the conquests of Junayd.[11]

The excavations confirm and supplement the evidence of the literary sources. A group of small silver coins found on the Acropolis, the joint issue of Junayd and Mehmet Çelebi (1413-1415),[12] suggest that the Acropolis was still occupied under Junayd. As long as the Acropolis was maintained, it may be assumed that Sardis had some strategic importance, but after the fortifications were abandoned, there would be nothing to distinguish Sardis, already a place with a small population, from a village.

These coins are the last dated evidence from the Acropolis, which the early travelers unanimously describe as abandoned. Habitation, however, continued for some time after the fortifications fell out of use, as shown by the construction of part of a house over the wall; the remains have not been dated.[13] It is most probable that the necessity of maintaining the fortifications gradually disappeared as settled conditions and a strong central government were restored under Murat II (1421-1451) and his famous son and successor, Mehmet the Conqueror (1451-1481). With the abandonment of the Acropolis fortifications, a new era in the life of Sardis began. The medieval town which had succeeded the flourishing city of antiquity now came to an end, to be succeeded by a small village.[14]

The Ottoman Period

The sources for the history of Sardis in the Ottoman period are considerably different from those of earlier ages. Since the place was reduced to a village, it is not mentioned by historians, nor are inscriptions found,[15] but official documents and narratives of travelers provide much information. The Ottomans kept detailed surveys of the countryside with its villages and farms for tax purposes, and several of these survive; although none has been published in its entirety, summaries are occasionally available to indicate the nature of the local system of administration.[16] Other official documents, published decrees, and judicial decisions illustrate the disturbed condition of the region in the seventeenth and eighteenth centuries, a time of numerous popular revolts and difficulties with nomad tribes.[17] However, none of these official documents provides any detailed information about Sardis itself. For that, the narratives of the travelers who visited the site in increasing numbers from the middle of the fifteenth century are of capital importance. These were mostly European, but two Turks, Evliya Çelebi and Kâtip Çelebi (also known as Haci Kalfa), both writers of the seventeenth century, are among the most valuable. The travelers came primarily to inspect the remains of antiquity at Sardis and only exceptionally devote much attention to the Turkish village which stood on the site. Therefore, little is known of Sardis in the two centuries between the establishment of Otto-man control and the arrival of large numbers of interested travel-ers in the seventeenth century.

According to documents, Sardis was a local administrative center, a *kaza*, in the province of Aydin, which was roughly coter-minous with the former emirate of the same name. It is consistently mentioned as such from the sixteenth century until 1867, when the districts of Alaşehir, Salihli, and Sardis were transferred to the province of Saruhan (now the *vilayet* of Manisa) and Sardis was replaced as an administrative center by Salihli.[18] The area was probably included in the province of Aydin rather than that of Saruhan because it was in the hands of Junayd, emir of Aydin, when it was definitively incorporated into the Ottoman Empire.

Considering the insignificance of the remains, the importance of Sardis seems surprising. The travelers' narratives do not suggest that it was a place of much account after the late seventeenth cen-tury, nor do they hint that it was the residence of a government official. Even though the staff of a *kaza* was negligible—a judge (*kadı*), an officer (*subaşı*), and presumably some assistants or soldiers—it is unlikely that an official of any kind would have escaped the notice of numerous travelers, whom he might natu-rally regard as a potential source of revenue or as objects for har-assment. An explanation is perhaps to be sought in the conserva-tive nature of a bureaucracy. Sardis, an important local center when the Turks took it, was probably allowed to retain its high rank on paper long after it had lost the functions that went with such a distinction. By the beginning of the eighteenth century the nearby town of Salihli was larger than Sardis and became the major market center of the region within the following century.[19] The local administration probably soon moved to the market-town, its natural location. By 1831 that was certainly the case, for a census record of that year refers to the *kaza* of *Sart ma'a Salihli*—Sardis with Salihli—a formula regularly used to indicate that the first place named, though it was still nominally the local capital, had in fact been superseded in its functions by the second.[20] By the late nineteenth century Salihli had officially become the *kaza* of the whole region and Sardis one of its dependent villages, a situation which prevails to the present day.

The earliest description of Ottoman Sardis, that of Evliya Çelebi (1611-1684), shows that it still had some importance in his day (source 38). The castle was abandoned, but the town contained three quarters and 700 houses with earthen roofs. The "quarters" are probably discrete village-type settlements like those revealed by the remains of the Byzantine period. In the town were to be found a mosque, a dervish-lodge, a marketplace, a caravansaray, and a bath. To these should perhaps be added the oil mill of Sardis mentioned in a document of c.1604.[21] Sardis was the site of a weekly market where merchants of the region would gather to buy and sell the local products of grapes, cantelopes, watermelons, and cotton.[22]

Such a description which would be well suited to a county seat, receives some support from the excavations. Remains from PN, the only sector to produce evidence for the period, show that a village existed there from the seventeenth century into the nineteenth. The earlier village on the same site was destroyed by fire, possibly as a result of the great earthquake of 1595, which is recorded to have leveled Sardis, or in consequence of an attack from the popular revolts or robber bands or Turcoman tribes who were infesting the countryside at that time.[23] The new village was centered on a paved square, perhaps the marketplace, and contained a number of houses with walls of rubble, broken tiles, and spoils assembled without the use of mortar. Ancient marble blocks were used as foundations for internal supports of wood. The houses, built along a couple of narrow streets, had earth floors and extended over the area west and north of the former Church E, which was presumably still in use as a workshop. Objects found in the houses include coins of the seventeenth century, china of the eighteenth, Ottoman clay pipes, and slabs of glass, suggesting that there may have been glass working in the village.[24] These remains could well be appropriate to one of the quarters mentioned by Evliya. In size and technique they are certainly unpretentious but not much more primitive than those of the Byzantine period known from the Acropolis and the temple area.

Further information about Ottoman Sardis comes from the

travelers' narratives, which give some description of the village at PN and others on the site. The earliest western traveler to provide much information about the Turkish village is Thomas Smith, who visited Sardis in 1671.[25] He remarks on the "pitiful and beggarly villages, the houses few and mean," a description repeated with little variation by travelers of the following two centuries. He noted that since Sardis was on the main caravan route from Smyrna to Persia, it contained a caravansaray for travelers. In his day most of the inhabitants were shepherds; the Christian population had practically disappeared, being represented by only a few employed in menial jobs who had neither church nor priest, while the Turks had a mosque which had been converted from a church.[26]

As mentioned above, one of the major transformations which took place in Sardis under the Ottomans was the abandonment of the Acropolis and consequent reduction in the importance of the place. Another was the great growth of nomadism which began with the arrival of the Turks and prevailed to such an extent in the eighteenth and early nineteenth centuries that the land around Sardis fell out of cultivation and the village came to have few, if any, permanent inhabitants.

Turcomans are mentioned in the region of Saruhan as early as the late fourteenth century, when Ottoman sultans ordered groups of them transferred to Europe.[27] The first of these passages refers to a transfer of populations ordered by Murat I in 1385, at a time when Saruhan was still independent. It is not clear whether this event reflects cooperation between Saruhan and the Ottomans or is included, perhaps anachronistically, to illustrate the power which Murat had over the other emirates of Anatolia.

The Turcoman tribes were naturally more interested in grazing lands for their flocks and herds—both sheep and cattle are mentioned—than in settled agriculture. Because their lives depended on regular migrations between winter pastures in the plain and summer pastures in the mountains, there was considerable conflict between their interests and those of the settled population, whose fields they would attempt to appropriate for grazing lands and whose property and animals they frequently plundered.

The earliest Turcomans to arrive, who made up the bulk of Turkish immigration into the region, found much of the land depopulated and frequently established themselves in villages, and became peasants. Significantly, most of the village names attested from the Saruhanid period are derived from tribal names.[28] Many, naturally, did not choose to change their way of life, and the Ottoman government, which made extensive use of the nomads in the army, attempted to impose order on them and force them to settle in one place, especially during the sixteenth century and later. In the seventeenth century, the Ottoman government exacerbated the nomad problem in Western Anatolia by attempting to break up and sedentarize the great tribal confederations of eastern Turkey. Many of the nomads thereupon drifted to the west to become involved in frequent difficulties with the settled population.[29] In the region of Sardis the nomads were finally settled only in the last century, completing a process which had lasted some 500 years. Local toponymy reveals the overwhelming predominance of the Turcoman influx into the area. The great majority of place names are derived from tribes, or tribal or clan leaders; very few represent survivals from the classical or Byzantine periods.[30] Unfortunately, few toponyms of the region appear in dated documents so far published; it is therefore not possible to work out a chronology of nomad settlement or consider in any detail the various states of the development.

The extensive immigration of nomads and their reluctance to settle in one place naturally gave rise to a major alteration in the settlement pattern of the area. This is already apparent in the seventeenth century account of Sardis by Kâtip Çelebi, for whom Sardis was only a place with ruins near a hot spring on the road leading to the pastures of Mount Tmolus, half a day away. The town had yielded in importance to the pasture (source 39). The nomads who used the road through Sardis presumably alternated between winter quarters in the Hermus plain and summer pastures in Mount Tmolus, where they could find many fairly large and fertile valleys. Only one tribe is mentioned with specific pastures: the tribe of Kacar, which spent the summer in the Tmolus range and had its winter pastures around Sirke in the upper Hermus Valley, about ninety kilometers east of Sardis.[31] In the immediate vicinity of Sardis the tribe of Karacakoyunlu is mentioned in a document of 1605, without indication of its range of habitation, and a register of 1866-1875 shows that the tribes of Alıcı, Karayahşı, and Karasığıralıcısı were settled there.[32] Travelers from the late seventeenth through the early nineteenth centuries make fre-

quent mention of the Turcomans and, in the latter period, com-
ment significantly on the desolate aspect of the countryside,
no doubt the consequence of the reversion of much of the land to
nomadism.[33]

In the long period of nomadism, conflict between the tribes, the
settled population, and the governmental authorities was endemic. A few instances noted in the documents illustrate the
troubles of the time, which were exacerbated, especially in the
seventeenth century, by revolts and brigandage. In 1654 a tribe of
Turcomans from Manisa moved to Bin Tepe (the site of the Necropolis of the Lydian kings) and caused great disturbance by rob-
bing the locals of their animals. In 1692 an official traveling to his
duties in the east was ambushed and killed by Turcomans near
Mermere and the taxes he had collected were stolen. Eight years
later the Kacar tribe arrived at Kemer in the province of Adala,
plundered neighboring villages, and killed a governor with a hundred of his attendants, stealing their horses, camels, and other
possessions. In 1758 the tribe of Caber, which was supposedly
settled near Ephesus, moved to the *kaza* of Sardis and for eight
years oppressed the local villagers by attacking them and stealing
their animals at night.[34] The archaeological record seems to have
provided an illustration of these troubles: a hoard of gold coins
from Bin Tepe, of which the one example recovered was dated
1580, may represent the plunder concealed by some Turcoman
bandits.[35] Under these conditions trade and city life naturally suffered a severe decline.

The mention of a Chane (han, i.e., caravansaray) by Thomas
Smith is also significant. By the middle of the seventeenth century
Smyrna had become the center for caravan trade between the
coast, the interior, and Persia.[36] Since Sardis lay on the main road
between Smyrna and the east, it should have benefited from this
development, especially with the construction of a new paved
road along the Hermus Valley and through the town, probably
attributable to this time (fig. 32).[37] The caravansaray was perhaps
also a construction of the period.[38] However, these developments
failed to bring prosperity to the town: the caravansaray was described as "ruinous and inconvenient"[39] by Chishull in 1699, and
later travelers give the impression of anything but a flourishing
town. The growth of nomadism and the insecurity of the times no
doubt discouraged commercial venture at Sardis, which by that
time was probably replaced as the regional center by Salihli.

The remark of Smith that there were hardly any Christians left at Sardis in his day is only surprising in that any would have retained their religion without priest or church for some three centuries. Van Egmont, who visited in the early eighteenth century, reported that there was not a Christian among the inhabitants. Both writers mention a mosque with antique columns in its portico, a building which had apparently been converted from a Christian church; Evliya Çelebi also indicates that there was a mosque at Sardis (source 38), and Chandler in 1764 wrote that it was ruinous. No trace of the building has been found, but if it had indeed been a church, the most plausible candidate would be the former Church E at PN, though nothing in the remains suggests that it was ever a mosque. The accounts of Spon and Chandler, however, make it clear that the village they describe was at PN.[40]

The numerous travelers of the eighteenth and nineteenth centuries add little to the information so far presented. They are unanimous in describing the Turkish village as small and poor, and frequently write of the presence of the Turcoman nomads and the desolation of the countryside. Boissier (1828) and Beaujour (1829) even noted that Sardis was virtually deserted, but their statements may perhaps be attributed to their neglect of the villages on the site or to a temporary absence of the Turcomans who inhabited them.[41]

By the early nineteenth century, some stability had been reestablished and recovery was taking place. In 1826, Arundell remarked on the frequency of the caravan trade—caravans were passing Sardis almost hourly—and noted that the town had two Christian inhabitants. Similarly, the Rev. Pliny Fisk, a protestant missionary from Massachusetts who visited Sardis on November 12 and 13, 1820, reported the presence of three or four Greeks who lived in a mill where they were employed grinding grain. The reverend and his companions held their Sabbath service in the upper part of the mill. The place was otherwise sparsely inhabited by Turks, for whom the pious missionary had few kind words. They lived in a "few mud huts," one of which he described: "It was about ten feet square, the walls of earth, the roof of bushes and poles covered with soil and grass growing on it. There was neither chair, table, bed nor floor in the habitation." Since earlier travelers indicate specifically that there were no longer any Christians at Sardis, the presence of these may be taken to reflect the colonization of western Anatolia by Greeks from the islands, Thrace, and the Greek mainland. These Greeks first began to settle in large numbers at the end of the eighteenth century, then poured into the country during the nineteenth. Their first major centers were Ayvalık on the Aeolian coast and Smyrna, but they soon spread inland wherever trade or industry presented opportunities for their talents. With the construction of the railway network centered on Smyrna in the second half of the nineteenth century, the Greeks established settlements throughout the fertile valleys of the Aegean region, so that they formed a substantial proportion of the population of western Asia Minor by the end of the century.[42]

The only detailed description of the Turkish village of Sardis comes from the pen of Charles MacFarlane, an acute observer whose books on Turkey are the source of much valuable and curious information.[43] MacFarlane wrote a detailed narrative of his visit to the site in 1828, including in it a description of the native village and houses, "a half temporary hamlet, composed of a half dozen houses built of clay and loose stones, and a few black tents."[44] This village was on the north side of the Acropolis, perhaps built among the ruins of Building A, where a village stood in the early twentieth century. After a tour of the site, he accepted the hospitality of one of the local Turcomans, "member of the small migratory tribe then encamped at Sart." The house where he lodged reflected the transitory character of its occupants. It consisted of a "rude little cabin, pitched by the side of which was a conical tent." The cabin, of one room with a fire in the middle, contained no furniture except the pilaf kettle, two wicker stools, a straw mat, and some sheepskins.[45] For dinner the travelers were given pilaf mixed with yogurt, roast lamb, and coffee. MacFarlane remarked at length on the kindness and civility of his hosts as well as the simplicity of their life. Such a description accords well with the meager physical remains of the village at PN and illustrates the nature of the Turkish settlement. Habitation was not intended to be permanent; the tents were as prominent a feature as the houses, which themselves were of the greatest simplicity, appropriate to a nomadic existence. Whether these particular houses were newly built for the occasion or restored each time a tribe settled in the site is not mentioned.

A similar, if more cursory description appears in the narrative of Richard Burgess, who passed through Sardis in 1834. He remarked the presence of three Christians, the miller, his wife and son, as the lone representatives of that church. Their nearest neighbors were some Turcomans who had erected their tents and a few mud huts on the Pactolus and about the site of the Stadium. Otherwise, the country was practically deserted: as he traveled from Sardis to the Gygean lake, Burgess "passed a number of black booths of Turcomans scattered about the marshes, which only so far redeemed the depopulation of this wide district." If the caravan route brought some prosperity to the village, the wide tract of the Hermus Valley to the north was still virtually uninhabited because of the nomads and lack of irrigation.[46]

Travelers of the nineteenth century showed an ever diminishing interest in the Turkish village as the scientific study of classical antiquity progressed. To some extent visitors to the seven churches of the Apocalypse formed an exception, for they tended to be fond of describing and commenting on the decline of sites which had been great when Christian, using as a text the obscure words of Saint John. One such visitor was Abbé Le Camus, who arrived in Sardis on May 1, 1896. He described the two miserable houses with roofs of branches which made up the village of Sart and noted that their fifteen or twenty inhabitants were dressed in rags, worn out with fever, and their children consumed by worms (fig. 39). The cafe on the main road from Casaba to Alaşehir was deserted, since the railway had destroyed the caravan trade on which the settlement had formerly subsisted.[47]

The last indication of conditions in Turkish Sardis is provided by the first scientific excavator of the site, Howard Crosby Butler. In his discussion Butler made passing mention of the village settlements of Sart, one of them built inside Building A, another at PN, and two more north and south of the Artemis Temple. The last was a primitive-looking village of mud houses, with, in addition, thatched houses, houses of wattles and matting, and a goat-hair tent.[48] The long effort of the Ottoman government to convert the nomads into farmers and thus to diminish their depredations and increase agricultural production had been continuing for two centuries by 1910. In the region of Sardis, it seems to have been a slow and difficult process which was hardly completed by the beginning of the present century.

This narrative of Sardis, which has traced its fortunes through a long period of change and decline, may come to an end with the beginning of systematic excavation before the first World War.

The flourishing metropolis of Late Antiquity had yielded to the fortified town of the Byzantine Age, which, in its turn, had finally been reduced to a squalid village. The excavations, by uncovering the glorious monuments of that village's past, have brought it renewed fame and introduced a new period of the city's history. At the same time, the half century of peace following the establishment of the Turkish republic has brought a renewed prosperity to the region and its most flourishing days since the end of the Roman Empire. But for this period, the main focus of interest lies no longer in the present but in the past, not in the growth of the modern villages but in the chronicle of the excavations and the description and analysis of the discoveries. These cannot be discussed here, but will be presented in detail in other volumes of this series, for which the present narrative may serve as a partial introduction.

IV. The Sources

The pages which follow contain a selection from the sources on which the history of Sardis has been based. I have not attempted to include every mention in late antique and Byzantine writers, but to restrict the collection to those which provide some historical or topographical information. I have thus excluded all sources which deal with bishops who did not visit the city. Those and other casual mentions will be found in the footnotes to the text.

The sources are compiled in the order in which they are mentioned in the text; that is, they are in roughly chronological order. Their number is too few to make a classification according to topic worthwhile. The chronological limits, as agreed with J. G. Pedley, are Diocletian through the Ottoman period, with sources on early Christianity included here except those already printed by Pedley; see his *Ancient Literary Sources on Sardis* (Sardis Monograph 2, Cambridge, Mass. 1972) vii, and sources 222-224.

The texts are presented with a translation—my own, except for those reproduced from *Sardis* VII—and whatever further annotation may seem appropriate. In several inscriptions, I have ignored abbreviations and simple restorations. For those already published, I have used the texts in *Sardis* VII. Unpublished inscriptions are reproduced from the files of the Sardis Expedition; they appear here simply as a convenience to the reader with the kind permission of Professor Louis Robert, who will publish them properly.

The Weapons Factory

1. *Notitia dignitatum,* ed. O Seeck (Berlin 1876) 32.   ca.400

Sub dispositione viri illustris magistri officiorum fabricae infrascriptae: . . . Asiae una: Scutaria et armorum, Sardis Lydiae.

Under the administration of the illustrious master of the offices, the following factories: . . . one in Asia: Shield-works and weapons factory, Sardis in Lydia.

2. Unpublished Sardis inscription IN 64.3, found in MTW.
4th-6th c.

λεκτὶς διαφέρων [Π]ανίονος φαβρικησίου καὶ δουκηναρίου

Tombstone belonging to (P)anion, worker in the *fabrica* and *ducenarius*

I have restored the initial letter of the name as P- *exempli gratia*. For inscriptions in similar lettering, see *Sardis* VII, 167, 170.

Sardis as a Military Base

3. Zosimus IV.8.   366

ὃ δὲ μετὰ τὴν νίκην ταῖς Σάρδεσιν ἐπιδημήσας κἀκεῖθεν ἐπὶ Φρυγίαν ἐλάσας.

After his victory, (Valens) stayed at Sardis and from there marched towards Phrygia.

4. Eunapius frag. 45 (*FHG* IV. 33).   368

῞Οτι συνηρτῆσθαι τοῦ πολέμου δοκοῦντος Μουσώνιος ἵππον ἐπιβὰς ἐξήει τῶν Σάρδεων. Καὶ ὁ Θεόδωρος τὸν συγγραφέα μεταπεμψάμενος ἐδάκρυσε τὴν ἔξοδον, καὶ ἀνδρὶ τἆλλα γε ἀτεράμονι καὶ ἀτέγκτῳ δάκρυα κατεχεῖτο τῶν παρειῶν ἀκρατέστερον. ῞Οτι τὸ ἐπὶ Μουσώνιον ἐπίγραμμα τὸ παρὰ Θεοδώρου τοιοῦτόν ἐστιν·
   ῎Ενθα μὲν Αἴας κεῖται ἀρήϊος, ἔνθα δ' ᾿Αχιλλεὺς,
   ἔνθα δὲ Πάτροκλος θεόφιν μήστωρ ἀτάλαντος·
   ἔνθα δ' ἐπὶ τρισσοῖσι πανείκελος ἡρώεσσι
   ψυχὴν καὶ βιότοιο τέλος Μουσώνιος ἥρως.

When the war had begun, Musonius got on a horse and departed from Sardis. Theodore sent for the writer (i.e. Eunapius) and wept at the departure. Tears poured abundantly down the cheeks of a man otherwise hard and unfeeling. This is the epigram of Theodore on Musonius:

Martial Ajax lies here, and Achilles there;
and there Patroclus, counsellor equal to the gods;
and there the hero Musonius, most like those three
heroes in his spirit and in the end of his life.

It is difficult to regret the loss of the works of Theodore, the Sardian poet.

5. Zosimus V.9.   396

Βάργος ἐκ τῆς ἐν Συρίᾳ Λαοδικείας ὁρμώμενος, ἀλλᾶντας ὠνίους ἐπ' ἀγορᾷ προτιθείς, ἐπί τισιν ἁλοὺς ἀτοπήμασιν ἀπὸ τῆς Λαοδικείας εἰς τὰς Σάρδεις ἦλθε φυγάς, εἶτα κἀκεῖσε φανεὶς οἷος ἦν, ἐπὶ πονηρίᾳ διεβεβόητο. τοῦτον ὁ Τιμάσιος ταῖς Σάρδεσιν ἐπιδημήσας, στωμύλον ἰδὼν δεινόν τε κολακείᾳ ῥᾳδίως ὑπαγαγέσθαι τοὺς προστυγχάνοντας, ᾠκειώσατό τε καὶ παραχρῆμα στρατιωτικοῦ τέλους ἔταξεν ἄρχειν·

Bargus, a native of Laodicea in Syria who sold sausages in the agora, was caught in some improprieties, and fled from Laodicea to Sardis. There, he showed his true character, and became renowned for his wickedness. When Timasius stayed in Sardis, he saw that he was talkative and clever at easily winning everyone over by flattery. He made him his friend and immediately put him in charge of a body of soldiers.

Looting of Sardis by Constantine   ca. 330

6. Pseudo-Codinus, *Origines Constantinopolis*, in *Scriptores originum Constantinopolitanarum*, ed. Th. Preger (Leipzig 1907) 189.

Ὁμοίως καὶ ἀπὸ Ἀθήνας καὶ Κυζίκου καὶ Καισαρείας καὶ Τράλλης καὶ Σάρδης καὶ Μωκησοῦ καὶ ἀπὸ Σεβαστείας καὶ Σατάλων καὶ Χαλδείας καὶ Ἀντιοχείας τῆς μεγάλης καὶ Κύπρου καὶ ἀπὸ Κρήτης καὶ Ῥόδου καὶ Χίου καὶ Ἀτταλείας καὶ Σμύρνης καὶ Σελευκείας καὶ ἀπὸ Τυάνων καὶ Ἰκονίου καὶ ἀπὸ Βιθυνῶν Νικαίας καὶ ἀπὸ Σικελίας καὶ ἀπὸ πασῶν τῶν πόλεων ἀνατολῆς καὶ δύσεως ἥκασι διάφοραι στῆλαι παρὰ τοῦ μεγάλου Κωνσταντίνου.

Similarly, many monuments were brought by Constantine the Great from Athens, Cyzicus, Caesarea, Tralles, Sardis . . . and all the cities of the east and west.

Sardis Spared from Gothic Attack   399

7. Zosimus V.18

ἐφείπετο δὲ αὐτῷ καὶ ὁ Τριβίγιλδος, διὰ τῆς ἄνω Λυδίας ἄγων τοὺς
ὑπ' αὐτὸν τεταγμένους, ὥστε μηδὲ θεάσασθαι τὰς Σάρδεις, ἢ τῆς
Λυδίας ἐστὶ μητρόπολις. ἐπεὶ δὲ εἰς Θυάτειρα συνέμιξαν ἀλλήλοις,
μετέμελε τῷ Τριβιγίλδῳ τὰς Σάρδεις ἀπορθήτους ἀφέντι ῥᾴδιον ὂν
τὴν πόλιν ἑλεῖν πάσης ἔρημον οὖσαν ἐπικουρίας. ἀναστρέφειν οὖν
ἔγνω σὺν τῷ Γαΐνῃ καὶ τὴν πόλιν κατὰ κράτος ἑλεῖν· κἂν εἰς ἔργον
αὐτοῖς ἡ γνώμη προῆλθεν, εἰ μὴ γενόμενος ὄμβρος ἐξαίσιος, καὶ τήν
τε γῆν ἐπικλύσας καὶ τοὺς ποταμοὺς καταστήσας ἀπόρους, ταύτην
αὐτῶν ἐνέκοψε τὴν ὁρμήν.

Tribigild followed him, leading his troops through upper Lydia, so that he did not see Sardis, which is the metropolis of Lydia. When they joined forces in Thyateira, Tribigild was sorry that he had left Sardis untaken, since it would have been easy to take the city, which was destitute of any defense. He and Gainas therefore decided to turn back and take the city by force. Their decision would have been realized if a violent rainstorm had not flooded the land and made the rivers impassable and cut off their attack.

Sardis in Late Antique Literature

8. Nonnus, *Dionysiaca* 13.464-467.   5th c.

Λυδῶν δ' ἁβρὸς ὅμιλος ἐπέρρεεν, οἵ τ' ἔχον ἄμφω
Κίμψον ἐϋψήφιδα καὶ ὀφρυόεσσαν Ἰτώνην,
οἵ τε Τορήβιον εὐρύ, καὶ οἱ πλούτοιο τιθῆνας
Σάρδιας εὐώδινας, ὁμήλικας ἠριγενείης

The luxurious crowd of Lydians poured in; those who lived in pebbly Cimpsus and craggy Itone; those in wide Torrhebus and the inhabitants of fertile Sardis, nurse of wealth, agemate of the dawn.

Nonnus, *Dionysiaca* 41.85-88

οὐ τότε Ταρσὸς ἔην τερψίμβροτος, οὐ τότε Θήβη,
οὐ τότε Σάρδιες ἦσαν, ὅπη Πακτωλίδος ὄχθης
χρυσὸν ἐρευγομένης ἀμαρύσσεται ὄλβιος ἰλύς,
Σάρδιες, Ἠελίοιο συνήλικες·

Tarsus the delight of men did not yet exist, nor did Thebe; nor
did Sardis yet exist, where glistens the blessed mud of the bank
of the Pactolus which disgorges gold; Sardis, the agemate of
the Sun.

Nonnus, *Dionysiaca* 41.354-358

πρεσβυτέρη πολίων πρεσβήια ταῦτα φυλάσσω·
εἶτ᾽ οὖν Ἀρκαδίη προτέρη πέλεν ἢ πόλις Ἥρης,
Σάρδιες εἰ γεγάασι παλαίτεραι, εἰ δὲ καὶ αὐτὴ
Ταρσὸς ἀειδομένη πρωτόπτολις, εἰ δέ τις ἄλλη,
οὐκ ἐδάην·

I am guarding these privileges for the oldest of cities; whether
Arcadia was the first, or the city of Hera, or whether Sardis is
older, or Tarsus praised as the first city, I have not learned.

See Louis Robert, *Villes d'Asie Mineure*[2] (Paris 1962) 298f, 313-317.

9. Macedonius Consul, *Anthologia Graeca* IX.645.   ca. 550

Τμώλῳ ὑπ᾽ ἀνθεμόεντι ῥοὴν πάρα Μαίονος Ἕρμου
    Σάρδιες ἡ Λυδῶν ἔξοχός εἰμι πόλις.
μάρτυς ἐγὼ πρώτη γενόμην Διός, οὐ γὰρ ἐλέγχειν
    λάθριον υἷα Ῥέης ἤθελον ἡμετέρης.
αὐτὴ καὶ Βρομίῳ γενόμην τροφός· ἐν δὲ κεραυνῷ
    ἔδρακον εὐρυτέρῳ φωτὶ φαεινόμενον·
πρώταις δ᾽ ἡμετέρῃσιν ἐν ὀργάσιν οἰνὰς ὀπώρη
    οὔθατος ἐκ βοτρύων ξανθὸν ἄμελξε γάνος.
πάντα με κοσμήσαντο, πολὺς δέ με πολλάκις αἰὼν
    ἄστεσιν ὀλβίστοις εὗρε μεγαιρομένην.

Under flowering Tmolus, beside the stream of Maeonian
Hermus, I am Sardis, the eminent city of the Lydians. I was the
first witness of Zeus, and I did not wish to disgrace the secret
son of our Rhea. I became the nurturer of Bromius (Bacchus); I
saw him shining with far-reaching light in the thunderbolt. It
was first in our meadows that the season squeezed out the

golden brilliance of the wine from the richness of the grapes. Everything adorned me; many an age often found me envied by the most blessed cities.

Industry and Commerce

10. Sardis VII, 169. 4th-6th c.

μημόριον διαφέρον Εὐχρωμείου τοῦ καὶ Λεοντείου μανγαναρείου ὑδραλέτα.

Tomb belonging to Euchromius also called Leontius, water-mill engineer.

11. Sardis VII, 166. 4th (?) c.

τὸ ἡρῶον [κ- τὰ ἐν] αὐτῶ ἐνσόρια πάντα Αὐρηλί[α]ς 'Ησυχίου Μηνοφίλου Σαρδιανῆς κ- τοῦ ἀνδρὸς αὐτῆς Αὐρ. Ζωτικοῦ Σαρδιανοῦ, γερουσιαστοῦ, ἀρτοπώλου πολειτικοῦ.

The sepulchre and all the coffins therein (are the property) of Aurelia Hesychion, daughter of Menophilus, citizen of Sardis, and of her husband Aurelius Zoticus citizen of Sardis, member of the *gerousia*, municipal bread-seller.

12. Sardis VII, 167. 4th (?) c.

λε[κ]τὶς διαφέρων Εἰουλιανῷ βρακαρίῳ

Tomb of Julianus, maker of trousers

I have restored the initial word by analogy with source 2.

13. Sardis VII, 168. 4th c.

καμ(άρα) ὑπηρεσίας εἱματιοπωλῶν.

Vault of the clothes-dealers' assistants.

14. Sardis VII, 18. April 27, 459

[ἐξομοσί]α [τῶν τε οἰκοδόμων καὶ τεχνιτων τῶν τ]ῆ[ς λ]αμ-(προτάτης) Σαρδ(ιανῶν) μητρο[πόλεως. ὑ]πατίας Φλ(αβίου) Πατρικίου τοῦ λαμ(πρ9τάτου) καὶ τοῦ δηλοθησομένου, πρὸ πέν[τ]ε καλανδῶ(ν) Μαΐων ἐν τῆ λαμ(προτάτη) καὶ δὶς νεοκόρω <ν> Σαρδ-(ιανῶν) μητροπ(όλει) ἰνδ(ικτιῶνος) ιβ' εὐτυχεστάτης καὶ μηνὸς

Δεσίο[υ] τετάρτη, ὁμολογοῦμεν Αὐριλιανῷ τῷ θαυμασιωτάτῳ καὶ
καθοσιωμ(ένῳ) μαγιστριανῷ καὶ ἐκδ(ίκῳ) τῆς αὐτῆς περιφανοῦς
[μ]ητροπ(όλεως) τὰ ὑποτεταγμένα· κατηγορίας διαφόρους [δε]-
ξαμένη ἡ σὴ θαυμασιότης κατὰ διαφόρων τινῶ[ν τὴ]ν ἡμετέρ[α]ν
μετιόντων τέχνην ὡς ἐνχειριζο[μέν]ων ἔργα οἰκοδομικὰ κα[ὶ] ἀτελῆ
ταῦτα καταλιμπα[νόντ]ω[ν] καὶ ἐμποδιζόντων τοῖς ἐργοδότες,
ἀναστῖλε [τὴν τοι]αύτην κατὰ τῶ[ν] ἐργοδοτῶν γιγνομέν[ην
ἀδικίαν] περὶ πολλοῦ πο[ι]ουμένη <ν> ἐπεζήτησ[εν πρὸς ἡμ]ᾶς
τὴ[ν] ὁμολογίαν τε καὶ ἐξομοσίαν [τὴν ἐπὶ τῷ ἑξῆ]ς· ὁ[μ]ολογοῦ-
[μεν] καὶ ἐξομ[ν]ύμεθα τὴν [ἁγίαν καὶ ζω]οπ[ο]ιὸν Τ[ριάδα] καὶ
τὴν σω[τ]ηρίαν κα[ὶ] [νίκην τοῦ δεσπό]του τ[ῆς οἰκου]μένης
Φλ(αβίου) [Λ]έοντο[ς τοῦ αἰωνίου Αὐγού]στου [Αὐτ]οκράτο-
[ρ]ος πάντα τὰ ἔ[ργα ὅσων ἡμῖν ἔκδοσις γ]ίνετ[ε] παρὰ οἱουδήποτε
τῶν [ἐργοδοτῶν ἀναπλη]ρο[ῦ]ν, ἑτοίμου ὄντος τοῦ ἐργοδότου [ἡμῖν
διδόναι τοὺς] συ[ν]αρέσαντας [μ]ισθούς· εἰ δὲ οἱα[δήποτε παραίτη-
σις] πα[ρα]γένηται τ[ῷ ἐ]ργολαβήσαντι [ἐπὶ προφάσει αὐτοῦ ε]ἴτ[ε]
ἰδιωτεικ[ῇ] εἴτε δημοσίᾳ, [ὑπὲρ αὐτοῦ ἐξ ἡμῶν ὑπεισιέν]αι ἕτερον
τεχνίτην τό [τε κτιζόμενον ἔργον παντ]ε[λ]ῶς ἀν[απ]ληροῦν, δηλονότι
[ἡμῶν ὄντος τοῦ τοῦτο πα]ρα[ιτ]ουμέν[ου], ἤτοι τοῦ ἐναρξ[αμένου
τούτου τεχ]νίτου ἤ[τ]οι τοῦ ἀ[ν]τ' αὐτοῦ ὑπεισιόντο[ς,] [μηδὲ
ἐπισχούσης τὸ ἔ]ργον μηδεμίας ἡμ[ῶ]ν προφάσεω[ς· εἰ δὲ ὁ
ἐργολαβήσας] ἅπαξ οἰῳδήποτε τ[ρό]πῳ τὸν ἐρ[γοδότην κωλύη
κ]τι[ζ]ομένου καθὼς ἔφημ[εν τοῦ] ἔργου, ἡμ[ῶν ὄντος εἴτε τοῦ ἐ]ξ
ἀρχῆς ἀρξαμένου εἴτ[ε τοῦ ὑπὲ]ρ οἱου[δήποτε τεχν]ίτου ὑπεισιόντος,
το[ι]αύτ[ης κωλύσεως] [διδόναι ἡμᾶ]ς μισθοὺς κατὰ τὸ γενόμ-
[ε]νο[ν μετα]ξὺ [αὐτοῦ τε τοῦ] ἐργοδότου καὶ αὐτοῦ τοῦ τεχνίτου
σύμφω[νον· τοῦ δὲ ἐργο]δότου ἀνεξικακοῦντος, ε[ἴ] π[οτ'] ἐ[φ'
ἑ]πτὰ ἡμέραι[ς] [κωλύθη τοῦ ἔρ]γου, τῷ τεχνίτῃ <ν> τῷ ἐργολα-
βήσαντει τὸ [ἔργον ὑπῖναι· εἰ] δὲ συμβῇ καὶ ἀρρωστίᾳ περιπεσ[ῖ]ν
τὸν τε[χνίτην, εἴκοσι] ἡμέρας περιμένιν τὸν ἐργοδότ[ην], με(τ)ὰ δὲ
[τὴν ἀνεξικα]κίαν τῶν εἴκοσι ἡμερῶν, εἰ μὲν ὑ[γι]άνη [ἀμελῇ δὲ τοῦ
ἐργάζεσ]θαι ἐπὶ τὸ τ[η]ν[ι]καῦτα, ὑπεισιένα[ι ἕ]τερον [ὡς τοῦ
παραιτησαμέ]νου ποιούμ[εθα] τὸν λόγον· καὶ π[αραι]τουμένου [τοῦ
ἐργολαβήσαντος, εἰ μ]ηδὲν κατὰ τὰ προγεγραμμέ[ν]α εὑρεθίη [μήτε
πράττων μήτε ἐργαζ]όμενός τις ἐξ ἡμῶν, συν[τ]ιθέμεθα [καὶ
ὁμολογοῦμεν ἐκτί]σιν λόγῳ προστίμου εἰς ἔργα τῆς πόλ[ε]ως, [καὶ
παραυτίκα εἰσπ]ραξόμενον χρυσᾶ νομίσματα ὀκτὼ [τὸν ἔκδικον
ἐγκαλέσι]ν τῷ τῆς [ἀδ]ικίας ἐγκλήματι κατὰ τὰς [θείας διατάξεις
οὐ]δὲν ἧττον καὶ μετὰ τὴν τοῦ προστίμο[υ] [εἴσπραξιν· βεβαί]ας
καὶ ἀρραγοῦς καὶ ἀσαλεύτου μενο[ύσης τῆς παρούσης ὁ]μολογίας
εἰς τὸ διηνεκές, καὶ ἀναπ[οτρέπτως τελουμένης] πάντοθεν
ἀκόλουθον πᾶσιν τοῖς προ[διορισθεῖσιν καὶ ὁμ]ολογηθεῖσιν παρ'
[ἡ]μῶν· καὶ ὑπεθέμεθα [εἰς τὴν ἔκτισιν τοῦ πρ]οστίμο[υ], ἐνεχύρου

λόγω τῷ γενικῷ [καὶ ἰδικῷ, πάντα ἡμῶ]ν τὰ ὑπάρχοντα καὶ [ὑ]πάρ-
ξοντα [ἐν παντὶ εἴδει καὶ γέ]νι. καὶ πρὸς τὰ προγεγ[ρα]μμένα
[πάντα ἐπερωτηθέντες] παρὰ τῆς σῆς θαυμασιότητος ὁμ[ολογήσαμεν
τῇδε τῇ ὁ]μολογίᾳ καὶ ἐξομοσίᾳ, ἡμέρα [καὶ ὑπατία τῇ προγε]-
γραμμένη.

Declaration under oath by the Builders and Artisans of the most distinguished metropolis of the Sardians (= 'cautio iuratoria' given to the 'defensor' of Sardis by the local corporation of Building Artisans).

In the consulship of the most distinguished Flavius Patricius and of the consul who shall have been proclaimed, on the fifth before the calends of May (= April 27, A.D. 459), in the most distinguished metropolis of the Sardians twice honoured with an emperor's temple, in the twelfth most happy indiction and on the fourth of the month Daisios, we agree with the most excellent Aurelianus, devoted commissioner and *defensor* of the said renowned metropolis, as hereinafter set forth:

Whereas your excellency has received divers accusations against divers persons practising our craft, to the effect that they take in hand pieces of building work, leave these unfinished and obstruct the employers, and deeming it highly important to abolish an injustice so detrimental to the employers, has requested from us this agreement and declaration under oath in the following terms:

We do agree and make oath by the holy and life-giving Trinity and by the safe preservation and victory of the lord of the inhabited world, Flavius Leo, everlasting Augustus and Emperor,

(1) That we will complete all pieces of work given out to us by any one of the employers, provided the employer is prepared to pay us the wages mutually agreed upon;

(2) Should the man undertaking the work have any plea on which he declines it for some reason of his own either private or public, another artisan from among us shall take his place and shall entirely complete the work under construction, on the distinct understanding that the man declining it, whether he be the artisan who began it or the man who shall have taken his place, is one of ourselves and that no reason of our own stands in the way of the work;

(3) Should the man undertaking the work once hinder the employer in any way while it is, as we said, under construction, if he who either began it from the beginning or shall have taken the place of any artisan is one of ourselves, we shall for such hindrance pay indemnities according to the contract between the individual employer and the individual artisan;

(4) Should the employer show indulgence, if he be for seven days hindered from working the work shall be left to the artisan undertaking it;

(5) Should the artisan fall ill, the employer shall wait twenty days, and if after such indulgence for twenty days the man should get well, but show no disposition to work at that time, another shall take his place on the terms stipulated by us as to the man who declines:

(6) If, when the man undertaking the work declines it, some one of us be found neither doing anything nor performing work in accordance with the provisions herein written, we promise and agree that we will make payment by way of fine to be used for the city's public works, and that the *defensor* shall forthwith exact eight pieces of gold, and notwithstanding and even after exaction of the fine, shall prosecute under the divine edicts on the charge of wrong-doing; the present agreement remaining firm, unbroken and undisturbed in perpetuity, and being irrevocably carried out in strict conformity with all things above determined and promised by us;

(7) And for the full discharging of the fine we pledge, under a lien both general and individual, all our property present and future of every kind and sort.

And when as to all things above written the question was put to us by your excellency, we gave our assent to this agreement and declaration under oath on the day and in the consulship above written.

Building Inscriptions

15. (Unpublished).   4th-6th c.

ἐπὶ Σεου(ή)ρ(ου) Σιμπλικίου τοῦ λαμπ(ροτάτου) κόμ(ητος)
πρώτ᾽(ου) βαθμ᾽(οῦ) διέπ(οντος) τὴν ἔπαρχ(ον) ἐξουσίαν καὶ τοῦτο
τὸ ἔργον τῆς ἀ[λει]πτηρίας ἀνενεώθη

The work of the *aleipteria* also was restored under Severus Simplicius, *clarissimus* count of the first rank, holding the office of governor.

For the term *aleipteria*, see C. Foss, "Aleipterion," *GRBS* 18 (1975).

16. (Unpublished).   4th-6th c.

Θαῦμα μ' ἔχει πόθεν ἔργον . . . γαῖα
δώματος ὑψορόφου χρυσαυγέος ἀπλέτ[ου . . .]
. . . τὸ γῆρας . . .
. . . νονιος πάτρης γενέτη[s . . .]
῾Ως ἴδεν ὡς κόσμ[ησε . . . αὐ]τίκα τεῦξεν
κόσμον ἀεὶ ζώοντα τὸν οὐ φθόνος οἶδεν . . .
ὤπασε δ' εὐρὺ θέμιλον ἀναπτύξας . . .
αἰὲν ὀπιπευ[. . .]
'Ανανεώθη χρυσοροφ[. . .]τῆς πόλεως ἰνδ. η' μηνὸς 'Ιουλίῳ σκούτ-
λωσιν [. . .] στρώσεις δὲ τοῦ ἐδ[άφους . . .] δίχα τοῦ μουσίου καὶ τῶν
ἄλλων

Wonder seizes me, whence the work . . . earth
Of the immense, high-roofed, gold-gleaming chamber
. . . old age . . .
. . . nonius, son of the country . . .
As he saw how he had decorated . . . he immediately created
An ever-living decoration which envy never . . .
He granted a wide foundation, unfolding . . .
Always gaze . . .
The golden-roofed . . . was restored . . . of the city, in the eighth indiction, in the month of July; thus the revetment . . . laying the floor . . . apart from the mosaic and the other . . .

I have not attempted any restoration of this fragmentary poem, which will be published properly by Professor Robert. For poems of similar style and content, see Louis Robert, *Epigrammes du Bas-empire* (= *Hellenica* IV, Paris 1948).

17. (Unpublished).   4th-6th c.

οἱ κρήνης ποτ' ὕπερθε μέσην κατ' ἄγυιαν ὁδοῖο
πᾶσι παρερχομένοισιν ὁρώμενοι εἰσὶ δράκοντες
οὗτοι χαλκείῃσιν ἑλισσόμενοι φολίδεσσιν
οὓς Βασιλίσκος ἔθηκε δικασπόλος ἔνθα κομίσσας
χρυσῷ ἐρευθομένους ὑπὸ δε‹ι›ράδα μέχρι καρήνων
νέρθεν ἄνω πέμποντας ἐπὶ στόμα χεύματα πηγῆς

These are the snakes which were once seen by everyone passing by, above the fountain in the middle of the public road. Basiliscus, who held the office of judge there, set them up, wound round with brazen scales, reddened with gold from their necks to their heads, sending up the streams of the fountain from below to their mouth.

Cf. Robert, *Epigrammes*, for similar poems.

18. (Unpublished).　　4th-6th c.

ἐκτίσθη ὁ ἔμβολος ἀπὸ τοῦ ʿΥπεπηνοῦ ἐνβόλου ἄχρι τοῦ τετραπύλου
ἐκκοπίσης τῆς πίλης καὶ παντὸς τοῦ τόπου

The colonnaded street was built from the street of Hypaepa as far as the Tetrapylon after the gate had been cut out and the whole area (cleared).

19. (Unpublished).　　4th-6th c.

ἐκχωσθέντος χωρὶς πόρων πολιτικῶν

Cleared out without public expense.

Found with the above, and presumably referring to related operations.

20. *Sardis* VII, 83.　　4th-6th c.

Οὗτος ὁ τῆς ᾿Ασίης ὑψαυχένα θῶκον ὑπάρχων
　　πυργώσας καθαροῖς δόγμασιν ᾿Αχόλιος,
ὧι βουλὴ μεγάλων ἀγαθῶν χάριν εἰκόνα βαιὴν
　　στήσαμεν, εὐνομίης μάρτυρα πιστοτάτην,
ἠδ᾿ ὅτι λαϊνέων δαπέδων κρηπῖδα τορήσας
　　τεῦξεν ᾿Ελευθερίης ἐνναέταις τέμενος.

This is that Acholius who fortified the lofty seat of vicars of Asia with his faultless ordinances, to whom for his great good deeds we the Council set up a small statue, a most faithful witness of his good administration, and because by laying a foundation of stone floors he created for the inhabitants a precinct of freedom.

For a discussion of this poem, see Robert, *Epigrammes*, 45ff.

Pagans and Christians

21. *Sardis* VII, 19.   After 539

γνῶ(σις) τῶν διατυπωθ(έντων) ἤτοι κ- ἐξωρισθέντων ἀνοσίων κ-
μυσερῶν 'Ελλήνων παρὰ 'Υπερεχίου τοῦ ἐνδοξωτάτου ῥεφερε-
(νδαρίου) κ- θί(ου) δικαστοῦ· [. . .]ιπος εἰς τὸν τῶν ἀρόστων
ξενδ[ν]α [ἐξωρίσθη] ἐπὶ ἔτη ι'.

Statement of the decisions rendered and furthermore of the
unholy and abominable pagans interned by the most honour-
able Hyperechius, referendary and imperial judge: . . . pus was
(interned) for ten years in the hospital for the sick.

The text of the last line is uncertain; for a different reading and interpretation, and for a detailed commentary, see Gregoire, *Recueil*, 324.

22. Eunapius, *Vitae Sophistarum* 503.   ca. 375

Τοῦ δὲ τῶν χριστιανῶν ἐκνικῶντος ἔργου καὶ κατέχοντος ἅπαντα,
διὰ μακροῦ τις ἀπὸ τῆς 'Ρώμης εἰσεφοίτησεν ἄρχων τῆς 'Ασίας
('Ιοῦστος ὠνομάζετο), πρεσβύτης μὲν ἤδη κατὰ τὴν ἡλικίαν, γενναῖος
καὶ ἄλλως τὸ ἦθος, καὶ τῆς ἀρχαίας καὶ πατρίου πολιτείας οὐκ
ἀπηλλαγμένος, ἀλλὰ τὸν εὐδαίμονα καὶ μακάριον ἐκεῖνον ἐζηλωκὼς
τρόπον, πρός τε ἱεροῖς ἦν ἀεί, καὶ μαντείας ἐξεκρέματο πάσης, μέγα
φρονῶν ὅτι τούτων ἐπεθύμησέν τε καὶ κατώρθωσεν. οὗτος εἰς τὴν
'Ασίαν διαβὰς ἐκ τῆς Κωνσταντινουπόλεως, καὶ τὸν ἡγεμόνα τοῦ
ἔθνους καταλαβὼν ('Ιλάριος ἐκεῖνος ἐκαλεῖτο) συγκορυβαντιῶντα
πρὸς τὴν ἐπιθυμίαν, βωμούς τε ἀνέστησεν αὐτοσχεδίους ἐν Σάρδεσιν
(οὐ γὰρ ἦσαν αὐτόθι), καὶ τοῖς ἴχνεσι τῶν ἱερῶν, εἴπου τι ἴχνος
εὑρέθη, χεῖρα ἐπέβαλεν, ἀνορθῶσαι βουλόμενος.

When the work of the Christians was conquering and taking
possession of everything, there arrived from Rome after a long
time a certain ruler of Asia named Justus, a man old in years,
noble and different in character, who had not departed from
the ancient and ancestral customs, for he was a zealous fol-
lower of that happy and blessed worship. He was always at
the temples, depending on every kind of divination, and took
great pride in his zeal for these things and his restoration of
them. When he crossed into Asia from Constantinople, he
found that the governor of the country (whose name was
Hilarius) shared in his inspiration. He built improvised altars

at Sardis (for there were none there) and wherever a trace was to be found, he set his hand to the remains of the temples with the intention of rebuilding them.

PLRE, s.v. Hilarius 10, dates this event to the time when Chrysanthius was an old man, probably in the reign of Theodosius. There is no real evidence, but such activity could hardly have taken place after 391, when Theodosius prohibited sacrifices and closed the temples. As early as 381, however, the same emperor had imposed heavy penalties on sacrifice for the purpose of divination (Jones, *Later Roman Empire*, 167f.). It would, therefore, be most reasonable to assume that Justus and Hilarius visited Sardis during the more tolerant reign of Valens.

23. *Synaxarium ecclesiae Constantinopolitanae* May 26, col. 711f.   ca. 257

Τῇ αὐτῇ ἡμέρᾳ ἄθλησις ἑτέρου ἁγίου ἱερομάρτυρος Θεράποντος. Ὃς ἦν ἱερεὺς κατὰ τὴν μητρόπολιν Σάρδεις· καὶ διὰ τὴν ἀρίστην αὐτοῦ πολιτείαν κρατηθεὶς παρὰ τοῦ ἄρχοντος Οὐαλεριανοῦ τοὺς χριστιανοὺς διδάσκων, δεσμεῖται καὶ ποινὰς ὑφίσταται. Μετὰ ταῦτα ἄγεται δέσμιος εἰς Συναὸν καὶ Ἄγκυραν καὶ ἐπὶ τοῦ Ἀστελῆ καλουμένου ποταμοῦ ὕπτιος ἐπ' ἐδάφους ἁπλωθεὶς καταξαίνεται ῥάβδοις τὰς σάρκας· καὶ πιανθεῖσα ἡ γῆ τῷ αἵματι αὐτοῦ φυτὸν βαλάνου ἀνέδωκε μέγιστον λίαν· ὃ μέχρι τῆς σήμερον δείκνυται ἀείφυλλον ὄν, πᾶσαν νόσον καὶ πᾶσαν μαλακίαν ἰώμενον· ἔπειτα ἄγεται ἐκεῖθεν ἐπὶ τὸ θέμα τῶν Θρακησίων παρὰ τὸν ποταμὸν Ἕρμον, ἐν ᾧ ἡ ἐπισκοπὴ ἡ λεγομένη Σάταλα, ὑπὸ τὴν μητρόπολιν Σάρδεις τελοῦσα. καὶ πολλαῖς ὑποβληθεὶς αἰκίαις ἔσχατον τὸν τοῦ μαρτυρίου στέφανον ἐκομίσατο.

On the same day, the suffering of another holy martyr, Therapon, a priest in the metropolis of Sardis. Seized by the ruler Valerian who taught (?) the Christians, he was bound and underwent punishment. Afterwards he was led bound to Synaus and Ancyra and to the river called Asteles. Stretched out on the floor, his flesh was torn with rods. The earth, enriched by his blood, brought forth a great oak tree which is shown, always blooming, up to the present day; it cures every disease and weakness. From there, he was led beside the river Hermus in the Thracesian theme, in which is the bishopric of Satala, subordinate to the metropolis of Sardis. After submitting to many blows, he gained the final crown of martyrdom.

For the location of the martyrdom, see Robert, *Villes*² 93-103, 280-313.

24. Ibid., July 10, col. 812.   3rd c. (?)

> *Τῇ αὐτῇ ἡμέρᾳ ἄθλησις τοῦ ἁγίου μάρτυρος 'Απολλωνίου. Οὗτος ἦν ἐκ τῆς πόλεως Σάρδεων τῆς ἐν Λυδίᾳ· καὶ προσαχθεὶς Περινίῳ τῷ ἄρχοντι ἐν τῷ 'Ικονίῳ ἐνδημοῦντι, ὡμολόγησεν ἑαυτὸν εἶναι χριστιανόν. 'Αναγκασθεὶς δὲ εἰς τὴν τύχην τοῦ βασιλέως ὀμόσαι, ἔφη μὴ εἶναι θεμιτὸν εἰς βασιλέα ὀμνύειν θνητόν, καὶ μάλιστα τὸν ποιητὴν καὶ δημιουργὸν τοῦ σύμπαντος μὴ ἐπιγινώσκοντα. 'Επὶ τούτοις ἐν ξύλῳ σταυροῦ ἀναρτηθεὶς τῷ Θεῷ τὸ πνεῦμα παρατίθεται.*

On the same day, the suffering of the holy martyr Apollonius, a native of the city of Sardis in Lydia. When he was led before the governor Perinius who was staying in Iconium, he confessed that he was a Christian. When he was forced to swear by the good fortune of the Emperor, he said that it was not lawful to swear by a mortal king, especially by one who did not recognize the Maker and Creator of all. Thereupon he was crucified and committed his soul to God.

25. Socrates VII. 29.   ca. 430

> *"Οσα δὲ περὶ 'Ασίαν, Λυδίαν τε καὶ Καρίαν κακὰ τοῖς Τεσσαρεσκαιδεκατίταις ἐποίησε, καὶ ὁπόσοι δι' αὐτὸν πολλοὶ περὶ Μίλητον καὶ Σάρδεις ἐν τῇ γενομένῃ στάσει ἀπέθανον, παραλιπεῖν μοι δοκῶ.*

How much evil he caused for the Quartodecimans in Asia, Lydia, and Caria, and how many perished in the riots which he caused in Miletus and Sardis I think I should pass over.

Arab Capture of Sardis   716

26. *Chronicon anonymum ad a.d. 819 pertinens*, ed. I.-B. Chabot in *CSCO, Scriptores Syri* III.xiv, p. 10

(Original text in Syriac)

In the year 1027 (Seleucid era) Suleyman assembled troops and workmen and they went by sea and encamped in Asia; and they took two cities, Sardis and Pergamum, and other fortresses; they killed many men and led many into captivity; and the Syrians who were there they carried away and let go in peace.

The same text appears in another anonymous Syriac chronicle of the year 846: "A Syriac Chronicle of the Year 846," ed. E. W. Brooks, *ZDMG* 51 (1897) 583 (= *CSCO, SS,* III.iv, *Chron. Min.* II.4). It is reproduced in Arabic by the 15th-century Egyptian chronicler, Abu'l-Mahasin ibn Taghribardi in *Al-Nujūm az-Zāhira fi Mulūk Misr wa Qāhira* (Cairo 1929) I, 235.

Euthymius at Sardis   ca. 790

27. "The Unpublished Life of Euthymius of Sardis," ed. A. Papadakis in *Traditio* 26 (1970) 73.

Διὰ τὸ ἄγνωστον τοῦ λαοῦ καὶ ἀτίθασον διδακτικὸς ὢν ὁ ἅγιος, καὶ λόγον ζωῆς ἐν τῷ κόσμῳ ἐπέχων, ᾤχετο μὲν οὖν αὐτίκα πρὸς τὸ ποίμνιον, καὶ δὴ παρὰ τοῦ ἀρχιποιμένος δοθέντα αὐτῷ λογικὰ πρόβατα, ἡμίθνητα καὶ ἡμίζωα ἐφευρηκὼς διὰ τὸ τῆς πίστεως αὐτῶν ἀδρανές.

Since the saint was apt at teaching the ignorance and wildness of the people and offering the word of life to the world, he went straightaway to his flock. There, he found the sheep capable of speech which had been given to him by the High Shepherd half dead and half alive because of the feebleness of their faith.

The passage continues at considerable length with a vapid description of the restoration of orthodoxy which Euthymius accomplished in his diocese.

The Cities of Asia   ca. 935

28. Constantine Porphyrogenitus, *De Thematibus,* ed. A. Pertusi (Vatican 1952) 68.

Εἰσὶ δὲ πόλεις περὶ τὴν Ἀσίαν εἴκοσι· πρώτη μὲν Ἔφεσος, δευτέρα δὲ Σμύρνα, τρίτη Σάρδεις, τετάρτη Μίλητος, πέμπτη Πριήνη, ἕκτη Κολοφών, ἑβδόμη Θυάτειρα, ὀγδόη τὸ Πέργαμον, ἐνάτη Μαγνησία, δεκάτη Τράλλη, ἑνδεκάτη Ἱεράπολις, δωδεκάτη Κολοσσαὶ αἱ νῦν λεγόμεναι Χῶναι, οὗ ἔστι ναὸς διαβόητος τοῦ ἀρχαγγέλου Μιχαήλ, τρισκαιδεκάτη Λαοδίκεια, τεσσαρεσκαιδεκάτη Νύσσα, πεντεκαιδεκάτη Στρατονίκεια, ἑξκαιδεκάτη Ἀλάβανδα, ἑπτακαιδεκάτη Ἀλίνδα, ὀκτωκαιδεκάτη Μύρινα, ἐννεακαιδεκάτη Τέως, εἰκοστὴ Λέβεδος, [εἰκοστὴ πρώτη Φιλαδέλφεια] καὶ ἄλλαι τινές. Καὶ ταῦτα μὲν περὶ τοῦτον.

There are twenty cities in Asia: 1. Ephesus 2. Smyrna 3. Sardis 4. Miletus 5. Priene 6. Colophon 7. Thyateira 8. Pergamum 9. Magnesia 10. Tralles 11. Hierapolis 12. Colossae now called Chonae, where the famous church of the Archangel Michael is located 13. Laodicea 14. Nyssa 15. Stratonicea 16. Alabanda 17. Alinda 18. Myrina 19. Teos 20. Lebedus (21. Philadelphia) and some others.

The last city has been rejected by the editor as an obvious interpolation. I have discussed this list in "Byzantine Cities", 7-12, 398, and concluded that it was the usual wretched compilation from late antique sources slightly modified to suit the boundaries of the Thracesian theme in the writer's own time.

Reconquest of Sardis from the Turks   1098

29. Anna Comnena XI.5

'Ο δὲ δοὺξ οὐ κατὰ πόδας τούτους ἐδίωκεν, ἀλλὰ τὴν συντομωτέραν ὁδεύσας τάς τε Σάρδεις καὶ τὴν Φιλαδέλφειαν ἐξ ἐπιδρομῆς κατέσχε τὴν τούτων φρουρὰν Μιχαὴλ τῷ Κεκαυμένῳ πιστεύσας.

The duke (John Ducas) did not follow in the steps of the Turks but took a shorter road and suddenly seized Sardis and Philadelphia; he entrusted the guardianship of these to Michael Cecaumenus.

Emperor and Sultan at Sardis   1257

30. Acropolites, ed. Heisenberg (Leipzig 1903) 143

'Ο μὲν οὖν βασιλεὺς διαπεραιωθεὶς τὸν 'Ελλήσποντον, ὡς εἶχε τάχους περὶ τοὺς τῆς Λυδίας τόπους κεχώρηκε καὶ περὶ τὰς Σάρδεις τὰς σκηνὰς ἔπηξεν. ὁ δὲ περσάρχης σουλτάν, ὁ φυζακινῆς ἐλάφου κραδίην ἔχων, εἶπεν ἂν ποιητής, τὴν χώραν τούτου καταλιπών, ἐπείπερ καὶ τὸ τούτου στράτευμα καταλέλυται, φυγὰς πρὸς τὸν βασιλέα χωρεῖ. ὁ δὲ ἐδέξατο τοῦτον καὶ δωρήμασιν αὐτόν τε καὶ τοὺς ἀμφ' αὐτὸν φιλοτίμως ἐδεξιώσατο.

The Emperor (Theodore II) crossed the Hellespont and proceeded as quickly as possible to Lydia, and pitched his tents around Sardis. The Sultan, the leader of the Persians, who had the heart of a shy deer as the poet would say, left his own country, since his army had been destroyed, and came as a fugitive to the emperor, who received him and proudly honored him and those around him with gifts.

Early Turkish Raids on Sardis   ca. 1275

31. Ducas, ed. Grecu (Bucharest 1958) 205f.

Ἐν ταῖς ἡμέραις δὲ τοῦ βασιλέως Μιχαὴλ τοῦ Παλαιολόγου, τοῦ πρώτως βασιλεύσαντος ἐν Παλαιολόγοις, ἦλθόν τινες Ἰταλοὶ αἰτοῦντες τὸ ὄρος δοθῆναι αὐτοῖς καὶ λαμβάνειν κατ' ἔτος τὸ συμφωνηθέν. Τότε καὶ οἱ Τοῦρκοι ἐνεδρεύοντες ἦσαν λῃστρικῶς τὰ πέριξ μέρη Λυδίας τε καὶ Ἀσίας καὶ κατέτρεχον ἕως Σάρδεων καὶ αὐτῆς Μαγνησίας.

In the time of the emperor Michael Palaeologus, the first of the Palaeologi, some Italians came asking him to give them the mountain of Phocaea and receive in return an agreed annual payment. At that time, the Turks, like bandits, were overrunning and devastating the surrounding territory of Lydia and Asia and penetrated as far as Sardis and Magnesia itself.

Citadel of Sardis Divided   1304

32. Pachymeres II. 402-405

Ἦν μὲν οὖν τὰ καθ' ἡμᾶς καὶ λίαν δεινά, τῶν μὲν ἐκτὸς πόλεως οὐδὲν ὑποστάντων τὴν τῶν Περσῶν ἀνυπόστατον ῥύμην, καὶ διὰ τοῦτο τῶν μὲν φονευομένων τῶν δ' ἀπανισταμένων, τῶν μὲν εἰς πόλεις καὶ φρούρια τῶν δ' εἰς νήσους, ἄλλων δέ καὶ εἰς τὰ κατ' ἀντιπεραίαν ἀσφαλῆ, ὅπου ἂν καὶ σωθεῖεν, βλεπόντων καὶ ὁρμώντων, τῶν δ' ἐντὸς καὶ λίαν ἐνδεῶς ἐχόντων τῶν ἀναγκαίων διὰ τὴν τῶν ἐξωτερικῶν ἐξαπώλειαν. βασιλεὺς μὲν οὖν διὰ ταῦτα ὡς οἷόν τ' ἦν ἀντιπαλαμώμενος πρὸς τὰς τῶν δεινῶν ἐπιρροίας, Ἀλανῶν μὲν ἐκείνων καὶ τῶν ἰδίων ἀπεγνωκώς, ἐπὶ σαθροῖς δὲ σαλεύων τοῖς ξενικοῖς, πέμπει καὶ πρὸς Καζάνην τὸν τῶν ἀνατολικῶν Τοχάρων, ὡς αὐτοὶ φαῖεν ἄν, Κάνιν, καὶ γαμικὰς ἐπιμιξίας προτείνει, καὶ ἐπαμύνειν προσαξιοῖ τοῖς τῶν Ῥωμαίων ἐσχάτως ἔχουσι πράγμασιν. ὁ δὲ καὶ τὴν ἀξίωσιν δέχεται, καὶ τὸ κῆδος (ἐπὶ γὰρ φυσικῇ θυγατρί, ἧς αὐτὸς βασιλεὺς πατὴρ ἐνομίζετο, συνεφώνει) προσαπεδέχετο, καὶ ὑποσχέσεις ἀσφαλῶς ἐδίδου μετελεύσεσθαι τοὺς ἀλάστορας. τοῦτο φημισθέν, ὡς εἰκός, τοῖς μὲν λοιποῖς ἄλλως ᾠκονομεῖτο ἡ περὶ τὰς συστολὰς σπουδή, κἂν ἠφροντίστουν τὸ τέως· ἑνὶ δὲ τούτων τῷ Ἀλάϊδι τὰ κατὰ τὴν Λυδίαν καταδραμόντι, ὥστε καὶ λείαν Μυσῶν, οὐ Λυδῶν φανῆναι τἀκεῖ,

κατασεισθέντι τῇ φήμῃ τοὺς λογισμοὺς ἔδοξε προνοεῖν ἑαυτῷ τε καὶ
τοῖς ἰδίοις τῶν ἐκ φυλακῆς συμφερόντων. ἀμέλει τοι καὶ τοῖς κατὰ
τὸ τῶν Σάρδεων φρούριον ὀχυρὸν ἄλλως ὂν ὡς παλαιᾶς ἀκρόπολιν
πόλεως, καθ' ἓν ἄβατον μέρος καὶ τὸ λοιπὸν ἀπόκρημνον, διὰ τὴν παρ'
ἐκείνων ἐγκεκλεισμένην ἐπίθεσιν πέμπων ἐπὶ ῥηταῖς ὁμολογίαις
συνέπραττεν, ἐφ' ᾧ τοῦ φρουρίου διαμεμερισμένου μακρῷ τινὶ τείχει
καὶ ἀσφαλεῖ ἥμισυ μὲν ἐκείνους ἥμισυ δ' αὐτοὺς ἔχειν, κἀντεῦθεν
δεσμοῖς ὁμονοίας συνδεῖσθαι, καὶ ἀνέδην ἐξιόντας ἐκείνους μὲν
τοῖς ἰδίοις ἔργοις προσανέχειν ἐξ ὧν τραφήσονται, αὐτοὺς δὲ τὰ
οἰκεῖα πάντως ποιεῖν, αὐτῶν μέν, ὡς εἰκός, ἀπέχοντας, ἄλλοις δ'
ἐπιτιθεμένους ἐξ ὧν κερδανοῦσι τὸν οἰκεῖον τρόπον καὶ ληστρικόν.
ἐκεῖνοι μὲν οὖν τοιαῦτ' ἠξίουν, καὶ λιπαρῶς ἀντείχοντο τοῦ
φρουρίου· τοῖς δὲ τὸ μὲν ἀνθίστασθαι μάταιον ἐνομίζετο, τὸ δ'
εὐπειθεῖν, εἰ καὶ μὴ σφίσιν αὐτοῖς ἀσφαλὲς διὰ τὴν τῶν ἐχθρῶν
γειτνίασιν (οὐδὲ γὰρ ἦν ἀρνειοῖς καὶ λύκοις κοινὰ ταμέσθαι τὰ ὅρκια),
ὅμως διὰ τὴν ἐφεστῶσαν ἀνάγκην καὶ τοῦ ὑδρεύεσθαί τε καὶ κατα-
σπείρειν ἕνεκα ἀνεκτὸν ἐδόκει, καὶ συγκατέβαινον. καὶ δὴ πολλούς
τινας τῶν Περσῶν ὑποδέχονται (σωροὺς δὲ χρημάτων αὐτῶν, ὡς
εἰκός, σὺν αὐτοῖς εἶδέ τις ἄν), παρὰ τοσοῦτον οὐ συνοικοῦντες τοῖς
εἰσαχθεῖσι παρ' ὅσον τὸ μεταξὺ τεῖχος σφᾶς ἀπ' ἀλλήλων διεῖργε.
κατά τινα δὲ πυλίδα καὶ συμμετεῖχον ἀλλήλοις ἔνιοι, ὡς ἐλέγετο.
ταῦτα γοῦν ἦσαν ἐπὶ χρόνον, καὶ ἀνακωχὴν τῶν κακῶν κατὰ τὸ
φρούριον εἶχον. ἐπεὶ δὲ τὰ μὲν τῆς φήμης τῶν Τοχάρων κατ' ὀλίγον
ἠσθένουν καὶ ἤδη θάρρος εἶχον ἐκεῖνοι καὶ τῶν φόβων ἑαυτοὺς
ἀνελάμβανον, οἱ τέως ἱκέται ἑαυτῶν γίνονται καὶ τῶν προτέρων
ἀναμιμνήσκονται καὶ ἐπιχειρεῖν τοῖς γειτονοῦσι βουλεύονται. ἦν δὲ
ἄρα τὸ σόφισμα καθ' αὑτῶν· ἐξ ἴσου γὰρ καὶ Ῥωμαῖοι ἀντεπιβου-
λεύειν ἐκείνοις ἔχοντες πρὸς τοῦτο καὶ διυπνίζοντο παρ' ἐκείνων, τὸ
φθῆναι πρᾶξαι παρὰ τὸ παθεῖν κερδαλεώτερον ἡγησάμενοι. καὶ δὴ
προλαβόντες τὴν ἐπιβουλὴν πέμπουσι πρὸς τὸν τηνικάδε τῶν Ῥωμα-
ϊκῶν ταγμάτων ἄρχοντα πριμικήριον ἐξ ἀξιώματος τῆς αὐλῆς. καὶ
νυκτὸς ἐκεῖνος λαὸν ἱκανὸν ἐξετοιμασάμενος προσβάλλει τῷ φρουρίῳ,
καὶ ἐμφανὴς ἦν τοῖς μὲν προσδοκώμενος τοῖς δ' ἀπροσδόκητος. ὅθεν
καὶ οἱ μὲν ἀσμένως δέχονται τοῦτον, τοῖς δ' ἐφίσταται κοιμωμένοις
δεινὸς ὄνειρος, καὶ ἐντεῦθεν διατεθείκει σφᾶς τὰ παγχάλεπα.

Our situation was indeed terrible. Those outside the city could
not at all resist the irresistible onrush of the Persians, on
account of which some were being killed and others emi-
grated; some into the cities, fortresses and islands, others
looked to and made for the safe places on the mainland opposite, wherever they might be safe. Those within the city were
in extreme need of the necessities of life because of the destruc-

tion of those outside. The emperor, therefore, managing as well as he could against the onflow of disaster and despairing of those Alans and his own men, since he was unable to rely on undependable mercenaries, sent to Kazanes, the Khan, as they themselves would say, of the eastern Tochari (Mongols) and proposed a marriage alliance, and asked him to help the affairs of the Romans which were in the worst possible way. The Khan received the request and accepted the marriage alliance—it was a question of an illegitimate daughter, whose father was thought to be the emperor—and he gave firm promises to pursue the destroyers.

After this was announced, the eagerness to restrain their attacks was managed differently by the others, even if they disregarded it for the time being. But one of them, Alais, who had ravaged Lydia so that it seemed to be the plunder of the Mysians not of the Lydians, was shaken by the news and thought it best in his calculations to take care of himself and his men and to think about a safe place for the treasures which he had gathered. He sent, therefore, to those on the citadel of Sardis, which was especially strong since it was the acropolis of an ancient city—one part was inaccessible and the rest precipitous—and because of their protected situation proposed an agreement on these terms: that each of them would hold half of the citadel, which would be divided by a long and firm wall; that from then on they would be bound by the bonds of concord; that the defenders would continue freely to go out to their own work by which they would be maintained; and that the Turks would busy themselves with their own business entirely, keeping off from the defenders and attacking others from whom they would make profit according to their own piratical way of life.

The defenders, then, considered these things and persistently clung to the citadel. But they thought that it was pointless to resist, and to obey, even if it might not be safe for them because of the proximity of the enemy—for lambs and wolves could not make a covenant together—nevertheless seemed tolerable because of the impending necessity and in order to get water for themselves and sow their fields; and so they agreed. Thus they received a great many Persians—indeed, one might have seen heaps of their money with them—but they did not dwell together with those who were brought in, though they were so near, since the wall between them separated them from each other. Things continued this way for a while, and they had a cessation of troubles in the fortress.

But when after a while, the rumor about the Tocharians became weaker, the Turks took courage again and recovered from their fear. Those who had previously been suppliants got control of themselves, remembered their past actions, and planned to attack their neighbors. But their scheme turned out against them, for the Romans equally were making counterplots against them for the same end and were awakened by them, thinking that it was more profitable to act first than to suffer. And so, anticipating their plot, they sent to the commander of the Roman forces at that time, who had the court rank of primicerius. That man prepared a sufficient force and assaulted the citadel at night; he was clearly expected by the defenders and unexpected by the Turks. Thus, the former received him gladly, while to the others he appeared as a terrible dream while they slept and treated them most savagely.

The difficulties presented by the complex turgidity of Pachymeres are reflected in the inelegance of the translation. Like most other Byzantine writers, Pachymeres used antiquated terms to cloak the realities of his own day: the Persians of this passage, for example, are actually Turks, as the Tochari are the Mongols; cf. source 30.

Poems of Nicephorus Chrysoberges   ca. 1215

33. S.G. Mercati, *Collectanea Byzantina*, 590f.

Βροτοί, βλέποντες τὸ ξίφος τεταμένον,
ὅσοι βέβηλοι καὶ ῥάθυμοι τὸν τρόπον,
ἢ συστάλητε πρὸς μετάνοιαν τάχει,
ἢ μηδὲ προσψαύσητε τῇ θείᾳ πύλῃ.

Ἐγὼ γὰρ ὁ πρὶν τῆς παλαιᾶς προστάτης
ταύτης ἐτάχθην τῆς νέας Ἐδὲμ φύλαξ
ἀρχιστράτηγος ταγμάτων οὐρανίων.

Ἐγὼ χάριτος καὶ διαθήκης νέας
εὐαγγελιστὴς καὶ μετανοίας πύλας
πιστοῖς ἀνοίγω καὶ χαρὰν προμηνύω
τοῖς ὧδε προστρέχουσι πίστει καὶ φόβῳ.

Ποίμνης ἐτάχθην Σάρδεων ἐγὼ φύλαξ
καὶ πρὸς πύλας ἕστηκα τῆς ἐκκλησίας,
κἀντεῦθεν πάντας ἐγγεγραμμένους φέρω
ὅσοιπέρ εἰσιν ἐν βίβλῳ σεσωσ[μένων].

Mortals, such as are unholy and careless, as you look at the drawn sword, either draw towards repentance quickly or never touch the holy gate. For I, earlier protector of the old Eden, have now been made guardian of this new one, I, the commander of the heavenly hosts.

I, the evangelist of grace and the New Testament, open the gates of Paradise to the faithful and foretell joy to those who come forward here in faith and fear.

I have been appointed guardian of the flock of Sardis and stand next to the gate of the church; here I bear the names of all those who are inscribed in the book of salvation.

The poems were intended to accompany pictures of the respective saints—the Archangel Michael, John the Evangelist, and the Archangel Gabriel—on the walls of the church, near the entrance. See the explanations of Mercati 579-583, based largely on the fifteenth century Byzantine painters' manual, the *Hermeneia zographikes technes*, ed. A. Papadopulos-Kerameus, (St. Petersburg 1909), *q.v.* 219 for a similar representation of Gabriel.

Archdiocese of Sardis Suppressed   1369

34. Fr. Miklosich and Io. Müller, *Acta et diplomata Graeca medii aevi* (Vienna 1860) I, cclv, pp. 509-510.

† Πρᾶξις συνοδικὴ ἐπὶ τῷ Φιλαδελφείας †.

† Ὁ δὲ πάντα μεταποιῶν χρόνος καὶ ἀμείβων καὶ εἰς τὸ μὴ ὂν χωρεῖν παρασκευάζων τὰ καλῶς ἔχοντα μέχρι τοῦδε τὰ ἑαυτοῦ ποιῶν καὶ τῆς ἰδίας φυσικῆς ἀκολουθίας ἐχόμενος καὶ τὴν τῶν Σάρδεων μεγάλην μετρόπολιν, ἐφ' οὕτω δόξης προήκουσαν καὶ τοσαύτην περιφάνειαν σχοῦσαν ἀπό τε χρόνου καὶ τῆς τῶν ἐν αὐτῇ καλλίστης εὐταξίας τε καὶ παιδεύσεως, ὡς καὶ ταῖς μεγίσταις καὶ πρώταις συναριθμηθῆναι τῶν μητροπόλεων, καὶ τὸ πρωτεῖον πλὴν ὀλίγων τινῶν κατὰ πασῶν ἐπιφέρεσθαι καὶ τὸ κράτος, κἂν ταῖς ἁπάντων ἐγκειμένην γλώσσαις, ὡς ἥδισμά τι τερπνὸν καὶ καλλώπισμα τῶν ὅσαι τῆς Ἀσίας προκάθηνται πόλεων, εἰς τοσοῦτο νῦν ἀμορφίας προήνεγκε ταύτην καὶ οὕτω τὸ κατ' αὐτὴν, θεοῦ δηλαδὴ συγχωροῦντος, διέθετο, ὡς μηδὲ σχῆμα γοῦν πόλεως ἀποσώζειν καὶ μικρόν τινα χαρακτῆρα ἀντὶ παραδείσου τρυφῆς, ἀφανισμοῦ καὶ ἀπωλείας πεδίον γεγενημένην.

καὶ ταῦτα μὲν τῷ χρόνῳ ποιεῖν καὶ τὰ πολλῷ τούτων ἔτι χείρω τοῖς πᾶσι προσαπειλεῖν ἔθος, ὕλην εὑρίσκοντι τὴν καθ' ἡμῶν ἀγανάκτησιν τοῦ θεοῦ διὰ τὸ τῶν ἁμαρτιῶν ἡμῶν πλῆθος, μάλα δικαίως ἡμῖν ἐπιγιγνομένην. τοῖς δέ γε τῆς ἀσφαλείας αὐτῶν καὶ τῆς εἰς τὸ κρεῖττον ἐπανορθώσεως ἀνάγκην ἔχουσι κήδεσθαι τῶν ἀπολωλότων τὰ καταλειφθέντα μέρη συνάγειν προσήκει καὶ τούτοις φυλακὴν εἰς τὸ ἑξῆς χορηγεῖν, ὡς ἂν τῆς χρονικῆς ἐπιβουλῆς ἀνώτερα τὰ τῆς ῥηθείσης ἐκκλησίας περιλειφθέντα ἐκ πολλῶν μικρὰ λείψανα πνευματικῆς ἐπισκέψεως ἀξιῶσαι τῶν προσηκόντων ἂν εἴη, τὸν καλὸν ἐκεῖνον μιμουμένους ποιμένα, ὃς τὰ πολλὰ τῶν προβάτων καταλιπών, καλῶς ἔχοντα, ἐπὶ τὴν τοῦ ἀπολωλότος ἑνὸς ζήτησιν καθῆκεν. ἔνθεν τοι καὶ τὴν ἁγιωτάτην Φιλαδελφείας μητρόπολιν, πολλὰ φιλουμένην θεῷ καὶ διὰ τοῦτο καὶ μέχρι τέλους ἀνάλωτον τηρουμένην καὶ μηδενί ποτ' ἂν τῶν ἐθνῶν αὐχένα κλῖναι προστεταγμένην, ποιμένα τε πλουτοῦσαν τὸν Ἀαρὼν τὸν τοῦ θεοῦ ἐκλεκτὸν καὶ ταῖς αὐτοῦ σὺν τοῖς λόγοις τε καὶ διδάγμασιν εὐχαῖς κατεστηριγμένην, μητέρα τούτων δὴ τῶν καταλειφθέντων καὶ μητρόπολιν καλὸν ἔδοξεν ἡμῖν καταστῆσαι, οὐ δόξαν μᾶλλον αὐτῇ παρεχομένην, ὅσον αὐτοῖς τὴν ἀπ' αὐτῆς σωτηρίαν καὶ τὴν ἀσφάλειαν. συνδιασκεψαμένη τοίνυν τὰ περὶ τούτου ἡ μετριότης ἡμῶν τῇ περὶ αὐτὴν ὁμηγύρει τῶν ἱερωτάτων ἀρχιερέων καὶ ὑπερτίμων, τῷ Ἐφέσου, τῷ Κυζίκου, τῷ Νικαίας, τῷ Χαλκηδόνος, τῷ Βρύσεως, τῷ Περιθεωρίου καὶ τῷ Μιλήτου, πέπραχε τὴν μὲν ἐνορίαν πᾶσαν τῶν Σάρδεων, ὅση τίς ἐστιν, εἶναι ὑπὸ τὴν ἁγιωτάτην ταύτην μητρόπολιν, ταύτην δ' ὡσαύτως τὴν τῶν Σάρδεων κεκτημένην τόπον καὶ θρόνον, τοῦτο εἰς τὸν ἑξῆς ἅπαντα χρόνον εἶναι, ὅπερ αἱ Σάρδεις ἦσαν, καλῶς ἔχουσαι καὶ μήπω τῇ τῶν ἐθνῶν φθορᾷ, θεοῦ παραχωρήσαντος, ἐκδοθεῖσαι. ἐξέσται τοίνυν τὸ ἀπὸ τοῦδε τῷ ἱερωτάτῳ μητροπολίτῃ Φιλαδελφείας, ὑπερτίμῳ καὶ ἐξάρχῳ πάσης Λυδίας, ἐν ἁγίῳ πνεύματι ἀγαπητῷ ἀδελφῷ καὶ συλλειτουργῷ τῆς ἡμῶν μετριότητος, γνησίῳ ὄντι ἀρχιερεῖ καὶ τῆς περιλειφθείσης ἐνορίας τῶν Σάρδεων, μετέχειν πάντων τῶν ἀνηκόντων τῷ τοιούτῳ θρόνῳ, ἤγουν τοῦ τε τόπου καὶ τῆς ἐν ταῖς ἱεραῖς συνάξεσι στάσεως καὶ καθέδρας, τοῦ τε διακόνους καὶ πρεσβυτέρους χειροτονεῖν, ἐπισκόπους ἐν ταῖς ὑπ' αὐτὰς ἐκκλησίας ἐγκαθιστᾶν καὶ ἁπλῶς εἰπεῖν πάντα ποιεῖν καὶ πράττειν, ὅσα πᾶσι τοῖς γνησίοις ἀρχιερεῦσιν ἐν ταῖς ὑπ' αὐτοὺς ἐκκλησίαις ἀνήκει ποιεῖν, τῶν καταλειφθέντων μερῶν ἐκείνης ὑποκειμένων τῇ ἁγιωτάτῃ μητροπόλει Φιλαδελφείας, ὀφειλούσῃ καὶ τὸν τόπον ἔχειν καὶ τὴν τιμὴν καὶ τὸν θρόνον ἐκείνης, ὡς εἴρηται, ὀφειλόντων πάντων τῶν ἐν αὐταῖς εὑρισκομένων χριστιανῶν ὑποκεῖσθαι αὐτῷ δὴ τῷ ἱερωτάτῳ μητροπολίτῃ Φιλαδελφείας καὶ πειθαρχεῖν, ὡς γνησίῳ ἀρχιερεῖ καὶ διαλλακτῇ καὶ μεσίτῃ αὐτῶν τὰ πρὸς τὸν θεόν, μηδενὸς ὄντος τοῦ πλεονεκτικῷ τινι τρόπῳ παρεισαχθέντος καὶ ἐν τῇ ἐνορίᾳ τούτων ἱερατικόν τι βουληθησομένου ποτὲ διαπράξασθαι. εἰς

γὰρ τὴν περὶ τούτου ἀσφάλειαν ἀπολέλυται καὶ ἡ παροῦσα συνοδικὴ
πρᾶξις τῆς ἡμῶν μετριότητος †.

August 6877 (= 1369), 7th indiction. *Synodic act, to the
bishop of Philadelphia.*

Time, which alters and changes all things, and causes those
which have been well off until now to proceed into oblivion,
and makes them its own, and holds to its own natural succession, has brought even the great metropolis of Sardis, which
had advanced so far in reputation and had such fame both for
its antiquity and for the outstanding good order and discipline
of its people that it was reckoned among the greatest and first
of the metropolises and had first rank and power of all except
a few, which was even on the tongues of all men so that it was
some sweet joy and ornament of those cities which presided
over Asia, into such unsightliness and has so arranged its condition, with the manifest consent of God, that it does not even
preserve the appearance and some small character of a city but
has become a field of obliteration and destruction in place of a
garden of luxury. For it is the custom of Time to act this way
and to threaten everyone with things far worse even than
these, finding as its matter the irritation of God against us
because of the multitude of our sins; this indeed comes upon us
justly.

It is fitting that those who are obliged to be concerned with
their security and the restoration of affairs to the better to
collect those parts which remain from what is lost and to provide them with protection for the future, so that it would seem
right to judge worthy of spiritual attention that which remains
of the aforesaid church—small remains out of many—and has
survived the conspiracy of Time, imitating the Good Shepherd, who left the many sheep who were well and made a
search for the one which was lost.

It has therefore seemed right to us to appoint the holy
metropolis of Philadelphia, much beloved by God and therefore preserved untaken till now, never forced to bend its neck
to any of the nations, wealthy in its pastor, that Aaron chosen
by God, and confirmed by his words, teachings and prayers,
mother and metropolis of those remains, not so much to pro-

vide glory for itself as for them deliverance and safety from it. Our Moderation, therefore, having examined this together with the synod assembled around us of the most holy and reverend archbishops of Ephesus, Cyzicus, Nicaea, Chalcedon, Brysis, Peritheorion, and Miletus, has made the whole territory of Sardis, such as it is, subordinate to that most holy metropolis, which will possess the rank and seat of Sardis for all future time, in the same way as Sardis was in a good state and not yet given over, God allowing, to the destruction of the enemy.

The most holy metropolitan of Philadelphia, therefore, reverend exarch of all Lydia, beloved brother in the Holy Spirit and colleague of our Moderation, the true high priest of the surviving territory of Sardis, will be allowed in the future to share in all that belongs to that throne, that is to say, its rank, position and seat in the holy synods, the ordination of deacons and priests, the appointment of bishops in the churches under it; to speak simply, to do all that is proper for all high priests to do in the churches under them.

The remaining parts will be subject to the most holy metropolis of Philadelphia, which shall hold the rank, honor and seat of Sardis, as has been said, and all Christians who are found there will be obliged to be subject to and to obey that most holy metropolitan of Philadelphia as a true high priest and their reconciler and mediator before God. Let no one in the future, introduced by any ambitious means, seek to accomplish any priestly act in their territory. For the security of this matter the present synodic act of our Moderation has been issued.

The same events are referred to in almost identical language in another document on p. 46 of the same collection. The "Aaron chosen by God" is a reference to the famous bishop of Philadelphia, Macarius Chrysocephalas, who presided over his see for forty-six years, from 1336-1382, at a time when all others in Anatolia had fallen to the Turks. The reference in the penultimate sentence is to the poverty of the church in those times, when priests and bishops frequently would trespass on territories which were not subject to them in order to collect fees: see Vryonis, *Decline of Hellenism,* 327-332.

Sardis Under the Turks

35. Ducas 39.   1390

Λαβὼν δὲ τὰς δυνάμεις πάσας, ὀπισθορμῶν ἐν τῇ Λυδίᾳ παραγίνεται, τὴν πορείαν ἀπὸ τοῦ Τμώλου, τοῦ μεγίστου ὄρους τῆς Λυδίας, εἰς Σάρδεις, μητρόπολιν τῆς Λυδίας, κατελθών.

Taking all his forces, Bayezid hastened back and arrived in Lydia, making his way down from Mount Tmolus, the greatest mountain of Lydia, into Sardis, the metropolis of Lydia.

The language of Ducas is archaistic; in his time, of course, Sardis was no longer metropolis of Lydia.

36. Ducas 103.   1402

πάντα πλοῦτον σωρεύσας ἦλθεν εἰς Μαγνησίαν τὴν ἐν Σιπύλῳ κειμένην. Κἀκεῖ συναθροίσας πάντα τὰ τῆς Λυδίας χρύσεά τε καὶ ἀργυρᾶ κειμήλια καὶ πάντα τὸν ἐν ταῖς Σάρδεσι καὶ Φιλαδελφείᾳ καὶ Ἀττάλῳ σωρεύσας πλοῦτον, ἦλθεν εἰς Σμύρναν.

Tamerlane came to Magnesia which lies under Mount Sipylus and there he gathered all the gold and silver treasures of Lydia. Piling up all the wealth of Sardis, Philadelphia, and Attalus, he came to Smyrna.

See Appendix II.

37. Ducas 117.   ca. 1405

καὶ πρὸς ἑαυτὸν ἑλκύσας τὰς πάσας πόλεις τὰς πρὸς Μαίανδρον καὶ τὰς πρὸς ἄρκτον, Φιλαδέλφειαν, Σάρδεις, Νύμφαιον, μέχρι τον Ἕρμωνος ποταμοῦ, καὶ οἰκίσας τοὺς πιστοτάτους αὐτῷ καὶ τὴῦ πᾶσαν ἡγεμονίαν εἰς χεῖρας τῶν αὐτοῦ συγγενῶν καὶ φίλων ἐνθείς.

. . . and Junayd drew to himself all the cities on the Maeander and those on the north: Philadelphia, Sardis, and Nymphaeum, as far as the Hermon River. He established his trusted friends in them and put his whole dominion into the hands of his relatives and friends.

The Hermus River is occasionally called Hermon in Byzantine sources; change of gender or declension is not an uncommon phenomenon.

38. Evliya Çelebi, *Seyahatname* (Istanbul 1935) IX.55.

ca. 1680

Evsafi kal'ai Sart yani hasini sarb
Velâdeti hazreti Resulden evvel sene 882 tarihinde İskenderi
Kübra hafvinden Kıdefa nam melike binti Yanive kıralenin
binasıdır Badehu Aydin Bay Oğulları elinden sene tarihinde
Yıldırım Han fethidir Ayın (Aydın) hakinde [lacuna] hüküm-
dür (hükûmettir) Ve yüz elli akçe kazadır Ve mahiye kırk para
kuradır Ve kal'ası yine Bozdağa muttasıl olan Cebeli Sartin
dameninde bir mürtefi mahalde şekli murabba' bir şeddadî
bina bir küçük kal'adır Amma gayet sarb binadır Kavidir İç el
olmak ile dizdarı ve neferatı olmadığından maada kal'anın içi
olkadar mamur âbâdân değildir Lâkin aşağı varuşu sehl
mamurdur üç mahalle ve yedi yüz toprak örtülü hanelerdir Ve
[lacuna] mibrabdır [lacuna] Camii [lacuna] mada zaviyeleri ve
esvakı muhtasarı ve hanları ve hamamı vardır Ve bağ bağçesi
çokdur Ve müşebbek besatinlerinde âbdar kavunu ve karpuzu
meşhurdur Ve sahralarında penbesi dünyayı zeyn etmişdir Ve
haftada bir azim bazar olub nice bin tüccar ehli bihar cem olub
beyi ve şira iderler Andan yine canibi garba bir ulu sahra icre
nehri Gedüse cereyan ider kim ta Alaşehir ile Sart ve şehri
mabeyninden beru gelir Hakir bu nehri atlar ile ubur idüb ve
Çomaklı yaylasında sehl teneffüs idüb Çomaklı Sultanı ziyaret
idüb âbı hayatlar nuş idüb mamur kuraları ubur ederek 9
saatde

Description of the Castle of Sardis, the Inaccessible Fortress

This is a construction of a queen named Kidefa, daughter of
Queen Yanive, in the year 882 before the birth of the
illustrious Prophet, after the appearance (?) of Alexander the
Great. Afterwards, it was conquered by Yıldırım Han (Bayezid) from the sons of Aydın Bay in the year . . . It is a unit of
government in the land of Aydın. It is a *kaza* of 150 *akches*. It
has 40 villages. Its castle is a small castle, a square dominating
building, in an elevated position at the foot of the mountain of
Sardis adjoining Boz Dagh. But it is an extremely inaccessible
building. It is strong. Besides having no castle warden or garrison within, its interior is not especially flourishing and prosperous. But its lower approach is easy and inhabited; there are

three quarters and 700 houses with earth roofs. There are . . .
mihrabs and . . . mosques, with dervish-lodges, unpretentious
markets, hans, and a bath. It has many gardens and vineyards. The cantaloupes and watermelons which grow in its
neat gardens are famous. The cotton of its plains has adorned
the world. There is a great bazaar every week where a few
thousand merchants—people of the seas—gather and buy and
sell. To the west in a great plain flows the river Gediz, which
comes as far as Alaşehir and Sardis and the cities between
them. The author crossed this river on horseback and took an
easy breath in the yayla of Çomaklı. After visiting Çomaklı
Sultan and drinking the water of life, he crossed through prosperous villages and came in nine hours to Gördes.

The text of this passage is corrupt and incomplete; parts of the translation
are therefore quite tentative. The new edition of Zuhuri Danişman, *Evliya
Çelebi Seyahatnamesi* (Istanbul 1971), XIII.65, presents an abridged translation of the passage into modern Turkish. For "700 houses," Danişman writes
"750," probably representing the reading of a different manuscript. The sum
"150 *akches*" refers to the salary of the *kadi*. It was the maximum which a
local administrator would receive, and was the standard sum in the whole
region; only the governor of an important city would have a higher salary;
that of Alaşehir, for example, was paid 300 *akches*, and the governor of
Manisa 500. An *akche* was a small and thin silver coin. See R. Repp. "Ottoman Learned Hierarchy," in *Scholars, Saints and Sufis*, ed. N. Keddie
(Berkeley 1972) 18 n.4.

39. Kâtip Celebi (Haci Kalfa), *Cihannumā* (Constantinople 1145H
= 1732).   ca. 1650

كرمابهٔ صــارت مغنيسا ايله بوز طاغ اراسنرهٔ يول اوزرينرهٔ صــارت
قصبهدن برمنزل شرق و جنوبه دوشر.

(transcription) Germabe-i Sart Mağnisa ile Boz Dağ arasında
yol üzerinde Sart kasabadan bir menzil şark ve cenuba düşer.

The hot spring of Sart is on the road between Manisa and Boz
Dagh; it is one stage southeast of Sart.

صرت بوز طاغ ييلاقنه كيدن يول اوزرهٔ مغنيسادن شرق جنوبه
دوشر بوز طاغك غرب و ثماليدر مغنيسادن بعدى بر مرحلهدر

بوندن بوز طاغ ییلاق برجّق مرحله‌در اوائله بر عظیم شهردر
حالا اثارسوری باقیدر و اقارصوی وآر بوز طاغ ییلاقنه متصل
اولان بعض جبالك ذیلنده‌در بوز طاغ آیدین بلندن آشیلوب برکی
اوزرینه اینلور.

(transcription) Sart Boz Dağ yaylağına giden yol üzere Mağnisadan şark cenuba düşer Boz Dağı n garb ve simalidir. Mağnisadan bu'du bir merhaledir bundan Boz Dağ yaylağı bir bucuk merhaledir. Evailde birazim şehirdir halen eser-i suru bakidir. Ve akar suyu var. Boz Dağyaylağina muttasıl olan ba'z cebalın zeylindedir. Boz Dağ Aydın belinden aşılıp Birgi üzerine inilir.

Sart is on the road which goes to the summer pastures of Boz Dagh (Mount Tmolus); it is southeast of Manisa and northwest of Boz Dagh. Its distance from Manisa is one day's journey, and from there to Boz Dagh is one and a half day's journey. In ancient times, it was a great city, but now only traces of its walls remain. It has flowing water. Joined to Boz Dagh, it is at the foot of part of the mountain range. Crossing Boz Dagh by the pass of Aydın, you descend to Birgi.

Appendices

Bibliography

Notes

Appendix I

The Metropolitan Bishops of Sardis

The list which follows is based upon that of Archbishop Germanos, *Melete*, 40-63, with the corrections of V. Laurent in *EchO* 29 (1930) 186-192, and such additions and corrections as I have been able to make. For bishops discussed above, see the index; for others, a reference to Germanos (G.) or Laurent (L.) has been given, so that more detailed information, if desired, may be consulted. Numbers assigned to bishops of the same name are purely arbitrary, serving only to distinguish them one from another; there are too many lacunae in the list to determine how many bishops were called John or Peter, for example.

Clement	1st c.	
The "angel" of the Apocalypse	1st c.	
Melito	fl. 160-180	
Artemidorus	325	G.42
Leontius	359	G.43
Heortasius	360	G.44
(Candidus, Arian)	(363)	
Maeonius	431	G.45
Florentius	fl. 448-451	G.45f
Aetherius	457	G.46
Julianus	553	G.57
(Elisaeus, monophysite)	(571)	
Marinus	680	G.47
Euthymius	ca. 787-805	
John I	815	
Antonius I	early 9th c.	

John II	mid-9th c.	
Peter I	859-869	
Peter II	877	
Theophylact	879	G.52
Peter III	912	
Antonius II	ca.920	
Leo I	945	
Leo II	997	
John III	ca.1071-1082	L.189
John IV	1147	L.189
Theodore Galenus	1191-1196(?)	
Nicephorus Chrysoberges	1213	
Alexius	1216	G.55
Andronicus	ca.1250-1261	
Jacob Chalazas	1261-1282	
Andronicus (bis)	1282-1284	
Gerasimus of Corcyra	1285	L.191
Cyril	ca.1305-1315	
Gregory	ca.1315-1343	

Appendix II

Tamerlane and
The Conquest of Sardis

Scholars have so far not agreed about the fate of Sardis in the obscure period between its conquest by the Turks in the early fourteenth century, when it was still an important fortified town, and the arrival of European travelers in fair numbers in the seventeenth century, when the place had plainly declined to a village. The few sources for the intervening period have given rise to a variety of opinions. These range from the reasonable account of G. M. A. Hanfmann (*Encyclopedia Britannica* 1971), who ended the history of Sardis with its incorporation into the Ottoman domains in 1390, through the moderation of H. C. Butler who wrote (*Sardis* I, 4) that "there are no remains to suggest that (Sardis) has been anything more than a small village since the ravages of Timour Leng in the 15th century," to the pronunciamento of W. M. Ramsay (in Hasting's *Dictionary of the Bible*): "in 1402 Sardis was captured and destroyed by Tamerlane and it has never recovered from that crushing blow." J. H. Kramers (*Encyclopedia of Islam, s.v. Sart*), D. G. Hogarth (*Encyclopaedia Britannica* 1911), and A. Philippson (*Reisen*, II, 73) agreed with Ramsay with varying degrees of qualification, and it has been generally accepted that the attack of Tamerlane brought the history of Sardis to an end.

That point of view, however, is not supported by any real evidence. The material already presented shows that Sardis continued to exist, though certainly not as a great city, well into the fifteenth century, and only declined to a village after the final Ottoman conquest. It is at least possible to see whence the common error arose.

137

The conquests of Tamerlane in western Asia Minor are described in a brief and rhetorical passage of the Greek historian Ducas, who wrote around 1460 (source 36). This passage needs to be checked carefully against the oriental sources to see whether or not Tamerlane had anything to do with the destruction of Sardis. The most important of these sources are the *Zafername* of Sharaf ad-Din, written in 1425 on the basis of the unpublished official history of Tamerlane by Nizam ad-Din Shami, and the universal history of Mirkhwand (1423-1498). Supplemented by some later writers, these sources make it quite clear that Tamerlane and his main force never attacked Sardis.[1]

While he was staying at Kütahya, Tamerlane sent out several expeditionary forces to crush what remained of Ottoman resistance and to bring all of Asia Minor under his control. The attack on Sardis, though it is not specifically mentioned in any of the oriental sources, is certainly to be attributed to one of these expeditions. Immediately after the battle of Ankara, a division under Muhammed Sultan, the grandson of Tamerlane, rushed westwards to capture Suleyman Çelebi, the son of the sultan Bayezid. Muhammed reached Bursa in record time, but stopped to plunder and devastate the city, giving Suleyman an opportunity to escape to Europe. After he had sent the treasures of Bursa back to Tamerlane, Muhammed advanced to Mysia and the coast, then to Manisa, which he made his base. From Manisa, he sent out another force to conquer Bergama. Muhammed Sultan was present with all his men to aid his grandfather at the seige of Izmir, and withdrew with him as far as Develi Karahisar where he died in March 1403.

It is reasonable to presume, then, that Ducas either had unreliable sources or has deliberately conflated the narrative of several campaigns, perhaps attributing them all to Tamerlane for dramatic effect. The attack on Sardis and Philadelphia is to be assigned not to Tamerlane but to one of the expeditions which his grandson sent out from his base at Manisa. Since these expeditions destroyed some cities and held others for ransom, it is not possible

---

1. These sources have been analyzed in admirable detail by M. Alexandrescu-Dersca in her extremely useful work, *La campagne de Timur en Anatolie* (Bucharest 1942). Unfortunately, she does not mention the attack on Sardis. I have drawn freely on her work.

to say that Sardis was destroyed. Rather, the words of Ducas and the character of these campaigns make it most probable that Sardis was attacked and bought off its beseigers.[2]

The passage of Ducas is thus at least partly responsible for the notion that Tamerlane destroyed Sardis. The early travelers were also curious about the fate of the city, which they saw reduced to such poverty and misery. Jean-Baptiste Tavernier, who published his *Six Voyages* in 1670, reports a story that Sardis had held out against Tamerlane for six years and that the conqueror had in revenge destroyed it utterly. This is of course a traveler's tale with no basis in historical fact. It is curious, however, as an example of the growth of a local tradition which seems to have preserved some dim association of the great conqueror with the ruins. That is, if the tradition were purely local; it could as well have been told to the credulous traveler by some Greek dragoman from Izmir, who would have had traditions of his own to draw upon.

The archaeological and historical evidence presented in the text has already shown that the "conquest" or "destruction" of Sardis by Tamerlane was a myth. Examination of the sources can explain how such a myth might have arisen and consideration of the fiction reported by Tavernier can show how it developed and grew to flourish until quite recently.

2. Ducas' mention of a place called "Attalus" (in the passage quoted above) presents a special problem. He may be referring to the town of Attaleia in Lydia, which might seem appropriate to the context, or to the better known and far more important city of the same name in Pamphylia. I would incline to the second of these possibilities. Attaleia in Lydia was never a place of much import and appears in Byzantine sources only in the lists of bishops (the site is in the hills northwest of Thyateira; for its identification and description, as well as texts of inscriptions found there and all texts dealing with the place, see Keil and v. Premerstein, *Zweite Reise*, 60-66). Attaleia in Pamphylia, on the other hand, was a major center throughout the Byzantine period and is known to have been taken by one of the expeditions sent out by Timur (in addition to the narrative of Alexandrescu-Dersca, see the discussion in B. Flemming, *Landschaftsgeschichte von Pamphylien, Pisidien und Lykien im Spätmittelalter* [Wiesbaden 1964] 110-119). Considering the confused state of Ducas' narrative, this seems a reasonable, though not positive assumption.

Bibliography

Abbreviations throughout are those listed in the *American Journal of Archaeology* 74 (1970) 3-8, with the following additions:

AASS	*Acta Sanctorum*
ACO	*Acta Conciliorum Oecumenicorum*
BNJ	*Byzantinisch- Neugriechische Jahrbücher*
CSHB	*Corpus Scriptorum Historiae Byzantinae*
OCP	*Orientalia Christiana Periodica*
PLRE	*Prosopography of the Later Roman Empire*

Sources

Acropolites. Ed. A. Heisenberg. Leipzig 1903.

Acta Conciliorum Oecumenicorum. Ed. E. Schwartz. Berlin 1924-1940.

Al-Umari's Bericht über Anatolien. Ed. Fr. Taeschner. Leipzig 1929. Trans. E. Quatremere, *Notices et extraits* 13 (1838) 367 f.

Ammianus Marcellinus. Ed. J. C. Rolfe. Loeb Classical Library.

Anna Comnena. Ed. B. Leib. Paris 1945.

Ansbert. *Historia de Expeditione Friderici.* Ed. A. Chroust. *MGH, Scriptores rer. germ.* V. Berlin 1928.

Anthologia Graeca. Ed. H. Stadtmueller. Leipzig 1894.

Aşikpaşazade. *Die altosmanische Chronik des Aşikpaşazade.* Ed. F. Giese. Leipzig 1929.

Ausonius. Ed. Hugh White. Loeb Classical Library.

Basil of Caesarea. *Letters.* Ed. R. Deferrari. Loeb Classical Library.

Choniates, Nicetas. Ed. I. Bekker. *CSHB.*

Chronicon anonymum ad a.d. 819 pertinens. Ed. I.-B. Chabot. *CSCO, Scriptores Syri* III.xiv. Louvain 1937.

Claudian. Ed. M. Platnauer. Loeb Classical Library.

Codex Theodosianus. Ed. Th. Mommsen and P. Meyer. Berlin 1905. Trans. C. Pharr. Princeton 1952.

Constantine Porphyrogenitus. *De Thematibus.* Ed. A. Pertusi. Vatican 1952.

Diocletian. *Edictum de Pretiis.* Ed. S. Lauffer. Berlin 1971.

Dionysius of Tell-Mahre. *Chronique de Denys de Tell-Mahre.* Ed. and Trans. J.-B. Chabot. Paris 1895.

Ducas. Ed. V. Grecu. Bucharest 1958.

Eunapius. *Historiae fragmenta.* Ed. C. Muller in *FHG* IV.

———— *Vitae sophistarum.* Ed. I. Giangrande. Rome 1956.

Eusebius. *Historia ecclesiastica.* Ed. E. Schwartz and Th. Mommsen. Leipzig 1903-1908.

Euthymius. Aristeides Papadakis, "The Unpublished Life of Euthymius of Sardis." *Traditio* 26 (1970) 63-89.

Evliya Çelebi. *Seyahatname.* Istanbul 1935.

Evliya Çelebi Seyahatnamesi. Ed. Zuhuri Danişman. Istanbul 1971.

Grégoire, H. *Recueil des inscriptions grecques chrétiennes d'Asie Mineure.* Paris 1922.

Hierocles. Ed. E. Honigmann. Brussels 1939.

Himerius. Ed. A. Colonna. Rome 1951.

Historia Peregrinorum. Ed. A. Chroust. *MGH, Scriptores rer. germ.* V. Berlin 1928.

Iohannes Lydus. *De magistratibus.* Ed. R. Wuensch. Leipzig 1903.

Iohannes Malalas. *Chronographia.* Ed. L. Dindorf. *CSHB.*

Iohannis Sardiani commentarium in Aphthonii Progymnasmata. Ed. H. Rabe. Leipzig 1928.

John of Ephesus. *Ecclesiastical History.* Ed. and trans. E. W. Brooks. *CSCO, Scriptores Syri* III, 3. Louvain 1936.

———— *Lives of the Eastern Saints.* Ed. E. W. Brooks in *Patrologia Orientalis* 17, 18, 19. Paris 1923-1926.

Josephus. Ed. B. Niese. Berlin 1887-1894.

Justinian. *Novellae.* Ed.R. Schoell and W. Kroll. Berlin 1895.

Katip Çelebi (Haci Kalfa). *Cihannumā.* Constantinople 1145 H = 1732.

Lactantius. *De mortibus persecutorum.* Ed. J. Moreau. Paris 1954.

Mansi, J. D. *Sacrorum conciliorum nova et amplissima collectio.* Florence 1769 -

Marinus. *Vita Procli.* Ed. J. F. Boissonade. Leipzig 1814.

Miklosich, Fr. and Müller, Jos. *Acta et diplomata Graeca medii aevi.* Vienna 1860-1890.

Nicephori Chrysobergae ad Angelos orationes tres. Ed. M. Treu. Breslau 1892.

Nicephorus Blemmydes. *Curriculum vitae.* Ed. A. Heisenberg. Leipzig 1896.

Nicephorus Chrysoberges. "Poesie giambiche di Niceforo Chrysoberges, metropolita di Sardi," Ed. S. G. Mercati, *Collectanea Byzantina.* Bari 1970. I, 547-594.

———— *Die progymnasmata des Nikephoros Chrysoberges.* Ed. F. Widmann. *BNJ* 12 (1936) 12-41, 241-299.

Nicetas Paphlago. *Vita Ignatii.* Migne, *PG* 105.488-574.

Nicolaus Mesarites: Description of the Church of the Holy Apostles at Constantinople. Ed. G. Downey. *Trans. Amer. Phil. Soc.* 47 (1957).

Nonnus. *Dionysiaca.* Ed. W. H. D. Rouse. Loeb Classical Library.

Notitia dignitatum. Ed. O. Seeck. Leipzig 1876.

Oribasius. Ed. I. Raeder. *Corpus Medicorum Graecorum* VI. Berlin 1926-1933.

Pachymeres. Ed. I. Bekker. *CSHB.*

Peter of Atroa. *La vie merveilleuse de Saint Pierre d'Atroa.* Ed. V. Laurent. Brussels 1956.

——— *La Vita Retractata et les miracles posthumes de Saint Pierre d'Atroa.* Ed. V. Laurent 1958.

Philostorgius. *Historia ecclesiastica.* Migne, PG 65.455-638.

Priscus. *Fragmenta.* Ed. C. Müller in *FHG* IV.

Proclus. *Théologie platonicienne.* Ed. H. D. Saffrey and L. G. Westerink. Paris 1968.

Procopius. *De bellis.* Ed. J. Haury. Leipzig 1905.

Pseudo-Codinus. *Patria Constantinoupoleos* in *Scriptores Originum Constantinopolitanarum.* Ed. Th. Preger. Leipzig 1907.

Socrates. *Historia ecclesiastica.* Migne, *PG* 67.

Sozomen. *Historia ecclesiastica.* Ed. J. Bidez and G. Hansen. Berlin 1960.

Suidas. *Lexicon.* Ed. A. Adler. Leipzig 1928-1938.

Synaxarium ecclesiae Constantinopolitanae. Ed. H. Delehaye. Brussels 1902.

Synesius of Cyrene. *Epistulae.* Migne, PG 66.1321-1560.

Tafel, G., and Thomas, G. *Urkunden zur alteren Handels-und Staatsgeschichte der Republik Venedig.* Vienna 1856.

Theodore of Studium. *Opera.* Migne, PG 99.

——— *Epistulae* in M. Mai, *Nova patrum bibliotheca.* Rome 1871. VIII, 1-244.

Theodori Ducae Lascaris Epistulae. Ed. N. Festa. Florence 1898.

Theophanes. Ed. C. de Boor. Leipzig 1883.

Vita Euthymii Patriarchae CP. Ed. P. Karlin-Hayter. Brussels 1970.

Vita Stephani Iunioris. Migne, *PG* 100.1069-1186.

Zosimus. Ed. L. Mendelssohn. Leipzig 1887.

Modern Works

Ahrweiler, Helene. "L'histoire et la géographie de la région de Smyrne entre les deux occupations turques (1081-1317)." *Travaux et mémoires* 1 (1965) 1-204.

——— *Byzance et la Mer.* Paris 1967.

Akdağ, Mustafa. *Celali Isyanları.* Ankara 1963.

Akın, Himmet. *Aydın Oğulları Tarihi hakkında bir Araştırma.* Ankara 1968.

Alexandrescu-Dersca, M. *La campagne de Timur en Anatolie.* Bucharest 1942.

Arundell, Rev. F. V. J. *A Visit to the Seven Churches of Asia.* London 1828.

Barb, A. A. "The Magic Arts" in *The Conflict between Paganism and Christianity in the Fourth Century.* Ed. A. Momigliano. Oxford 1963.

Bates, George. *Byzantine Coins.* Sardis Monograph 1. Cambridge, Mass. 1971.

Beaujour, Felix. *Voyage militaire dans l'empire ottoman.* Paris 1829.

Beck, Hans Georg. *Kirche und Theologische Literatur im byzantinischen Reich.* Munich 1959.

Bell, H. W. See *Sardis XI.*

Berchem, D. van. *L'armée de Dioclétien et la réforme constantinienne.* Paris 1952.

Boissier, E. *Lydie, Lycie, Carie, 1842, 1883, 1887.* Ed. W. Barbey. Lausanne 1890.

Bond, Alvah. *Memoir of the Reverend Pliny Fisk.* Boston 1828.

Brehier, L. *Les institutions de l'empire byzantin.* Paris 1949.

Brett, G. "Byzantine Water Mill." *Antiquity* 13 (1939) 354-356.

Broughton, T. R. S. "Roman Asia" in T. Frank, ed., *An Economic Survey of Ancient Rome.* Baltimore 1938. IV, 499-916.

Brown, Peter. "Religious Dissent in the Later Roman Empire," *History* 46 (1961) 83-101. Reprinted in *Religion and Society in the Age of Saint Augustine.* London 1972. 237-259.

Browning, R. "The Correspondence of a Tenth-Century Byzantine Scholar." *Byzantion* 24 (1954) 397-452.

_____ "The Patriarchal School at Constantinople in the Twelfth Century." *Byzantion* 32 (1962) 167-202.

Buckler, W. H. "Lydian Records." *JHS* 37 (1917) 88-115.

_____ "Labour Disputes in the Province of Asia" in *Anatolian Studies Presented to Sir William Mitchell Ramsay.* Manchester 1923. 36-45.

_____ and Robinson, D. "Greek Inscriptions from Sardes IV." *AJA* 18 (1914) 35-74.

_____ See *Sardis VII.*

Burgess, Richard. *Greece and the Levant.* London 1835.

Bury, J. B. *A History of the Later Roman Empire from Arcadius to Irene.* London 1889.

_____ *History of the Later Roman Empire.* London 1923.

Butler, Howard Crosby. See *Sardis I* and *Sardis II.*

Cahen, Claude. "Notes pour l'histoire des turcomans d'Asie Mineure au XIIIe siècle." *Journal Asiatique* 239 (1951) 335-354.

_____ *Pre-Ottoman Turkey.* London 1968.

Calder, W. M. "Philadelphia and Montanism." *Bulletin of the John Rylands Library* 7 (1923) 309-354.

Cameron, A. *Claudian.* Oxford 1970.

Chandler, Richard. *Travels in Asia Minor.* London 1817.

Charanis, P. "A Note on the Byzantine Coin Finds in Sardis and their Historical Significance." *Epet.* 39/40 (1972-73) 175-180.

Chishull, Edmund. *Travels in Turkey.* London 1747.

Clark, D. L. *Rhetoric in Greco-Roman Education,* New York 1957.

Claude, D. *Die byzantinische Stadt im 6. Jahrhundert.* Munich 1969.

Constantelos, D.J. *Byzantine Philanthropy and Social Welfare.* New Brunswick 1968.

Cousin, G. "Voyage en Carie." *BCH* 24 (1900) 24-69.

Danişment, I. H. *Izahlı Osmanlı Tarihi Kronolojisi.* Istanbul 1950.

Darrouzes, J. *Epistoliers byzantins du Xe siècle.* Paris 1960.

―――― *Documents inédits d'ecclésiologie byzantine.* Paris 1966.

―――― *Georges et Dèmètrios Tornikès, Lettres et Discours.* Paris 1970.

―――― *Recherches sur les officia de l'église byzantine.* Paris 1970.

Deichmann, F. W. "Frühchristliche Kirchen in antiken Heiligtümern." *JdAI* 54 (1939) 105-136.

Delehaye, Hippolyte. "Les actes des martyrs de Pergame." *Anal. Boll.* 58 (1940) 192-176.

Diehl, Charles. "Rescrit des empereurs Justin et Justinien." *BCH* 17 (1893) 501-520.

―――― *Justinien et la civilisation byzantine au VIe siècle.* Paris 1901.

Dieterich, Karl. *Hellenism in Asia Minor.* New York 1918.

Dodds, E. R. *The Greeks and the Irrational.* Berkeley 1951.

Dölger, F. *Beiträge zur Geschichte der byzantinischen Finanzverwaltung.* Leipzig 1927.

Dvornik, F. *The Photian Schism.* Cambridge 1948.

Egmond, J. A. van, and Heyman, J. *Travels through Part of Europe, Asia Minor . . . etc.* London 1759.

Eichler, F. "Die österreichischen Ausgrabungen in Ephesos im Jahre 1964." *Anz. Wien* 102 (1965) 93-109.

Ensslin, W. *Zur Ostpolitik des Kaisers Diokletian.* SB München, Phil.-Hist. Klasse, 1942.

Fellows, Charles. *A Journal Written during an Excursion in Asia Minor.* London 1839.

Fıratlı, Nezih, "An Early Byzantine Hypogeum Discovered at Iznik." *Melanges Mansel* (Ankara 1974) 919-932.

Flemming, B. *Landschaftsgeschichte von Pamphylien, Pisidien und Lykien im Spätmittelalter.* Wiesbaden 1964.

Forbes, R. J. "Power" in *A History of Technology.* Ed. C. Singer *et al.* Oxford 1956. II, 589-622.

―――― *Studies in Ancient Technology* II². Leyden 1965.

Foss, Clive. "Historical Note on the Church at Sige" in H. Buchwald, *The Church of the Archangels in Sige.* Vienna 1969.

―――― "Byzantine Cities of Western Asia Minor." Diss. Harvard 1972.

―――― "Aleipterion." *GRBS* 18 (1975).

―――― "The Destruction of Sardis in 616 and the Value of Evidence." *JÖB* 24 (1975).

―――― "The Persians in Asia Minor and the End of Antiquity." *EHR* 90 (1975).

―――― and G.M.A. Hanfmann. "Regional Setting and Urban Development" in G.M.A. Hanfmann and J.C. Waldbaum, *A Survey of Sardis and the Major Monuments Outside the City Walls.* Sardis Report 1. Cambridge, Mass. 1975.

Frantz, Alison. "From Paganism to Christianity in the Temples of Athens." *DOPapers* 19 (1965) 185-205.

Fuchs, Fr. *Die höheren Schulen von Konstantinopel im Mittelalter.* Leipzig 1926.

Galanté, Abraham. *Histoire des juifs d'Anatolie.* Istanbul 1939.

Geanakoplos, Deno. *Emperor Michael Palaeologus and the West.* Cambridge, Mass. 1959.

Germanos, Bishop of Sardis. *Historikē Meletē peri tēs Ekklesias tōn Sardeōn.*

Constantinople 1928.

Gibb, H.A.R. and Bowen, H. *Islamic Society and the West.* London 1950.

Gibbon, Edward. *The Decline and Fall of the Roman Empire.* (Numerous editions.)

Gökbel, A., and Sölen, H. *Aydın İli Tarihi.* Aydin 1936.

Gökbilgin, M. Tayyib. *Rumelide Yürükler, Tatarlar ve Evlâd-i Fâtihân.* Istanbul 1957.

Gökçen, Ibrahim. *Saruhanda Yürük ve Türkmenler.* Istanbul 1946.

Gouillard, J. "Une oeuvre inédite du patriarche Méthode: la vie d'Euthyme de Sardes." *BZ* 53 (1960) 36-46.

Grégoire, H. "Epigraphie chrétienne II." *Byzantion* 1 (1924) 703-710.

_____ "Du nouveau sur la hierarchie de la sècte montaniste." *Byzantion* 2 (1925) 329-335.

Hanfmann, G. M. A. "A Preliminary Note on the Glass Found at Sardis in 1958." *Journal of Glass Studies* 1 (1959) 51-54.

_____ "On Late Roman and Early Byzantine Portraits from Sardis." *Hommages à Marcel Renard* III. Collection Latomus 103. Brussels 1969. 288-295.

_____ *Letters from Sardis.* Cambridge, Mass. 1972.

_____ and Waldbaum, Jane C. *A Survey of Sardis and the Major Monuments Outside the City Walls.* Sardis Report 1. Cambridge, Mass. 1975.

Hansen, Donald. "L'antica Sardi cristiana." *Bibbia e Oriente* 4 (1962) 189ff.

Hasluck, F. W. "The Rise of Modern Smyrna." *BSA* 23 (1918-19) 139-147.

_____ *Christianity and Islam under the Sultans.* Oxford 1929.

Hefele, K. *Histoire des conciles.* Tr. H. Leclercq. Paris 1907.

Heisenberg, A. "Kaiser Johannes Batatzes der Barmherzige." *BZ* 14 (1905) 160-233.

Hendy, Michael. *Coinage and Money in the Byzantine Empire 1081-1261.* Washington 1969.

Hergenröther, J. *Photios.* Regensburg 1867-1869.

Honigmann, E. *Evèques et évêchés monophysites d'Asie antérieure au VIe siècle.* *CSCO Subsidia* 2. Louvain 1951.

Hörandner, W. "Leon Metropolit von Sardes und die Briefsammlung in Neap. III A 6." *Byz. Forschungen* 2 (1967) 227-237.

Humann, C. *Magnesia am Mäander.* Berlin 1904.

Inalcık, H. "The Emergence of the Ottomans" in *The Cambridge History of Islam.* Cambridge 1970.

Johnson, Sherman. "Christianity in Sardis" in *Early Christian Origins.* Ed. A. Wikgren. Chicago 1961. 81-90.

Jones, A. H. M. *The Greek City.* Oxford 1940.

_____ "Were Ancient Heresies National or Social Movements in Disguise?" *Journal of Theological Studies* 10 (1959) 280-297. Reprinted as a separate pamphlet, Philadelphia 1966.

_____ *The Later Roman Empire.* Oxford 1964.

_____ Martindale, J.R., and Morris, J. *The Prosopography of the Later Roman Empire (PLRE).* Cambridge 1971.

Kaegi, W.E. "The Byzantine Armies and Iconoclasm." *Byzantinoslavica* 27 (1966) 48-70.

Karayannopoulos, J. *Die Entstehung der byzantinischen Themenordnung.* Munich 1959.

Kaufmann, C.M. *Handbuch der altchristlichen Epigraphik.* Freiburg 1917.

Keil, Josef. "Die Familie des Prätorianer Präfekten Anthemius." *Anz. Wien* 79 (1942) 195-203.

_____ *Führer durch Ephesos.* Vienna 1964.

_____ and Premerstein, Anton von. *Bericht uber eine (. . . zweite, dritte) Reise in Lydien, Denkschriften der Wiener Akademie* 53 (1908); 54 (1911); 57 (1914).

Kraabel, Alf. "Judaism in Western Asia Minor under the Roman Empire." Diss. Harvard Divinity School 1968.

_____ "Melito the Bishop and the Synagogue at Sardis." *Studies Presented to George M.A. Hanfmann.* Mainz 1971. 77-85.

Krumbacher, K. *Geschichte der byzantinischen Literatur.* Munich 1897.

Kustas, G.L. "The Function and Evolution of Byzantine Rhetoric." *Viator* 1 (1970) 55-73.

Laiou, A. *Constantinople and the Latins.* Cambridge, Mass. 1972.

Lampakis, G. *I. efta asteres tis apokalipseos.* Athens 1906.

Lampe, G. W. H. *A Patristic Greek Lexicon.* Oxford 1961.

Laurent, V. "A propos de l'oriens Christianus." *EchO* 29 (1930) 176-192.

_____ *La collection Orghidan.* Paris 1952.

Le Camus, Abbé E. *Voyage aux sept églises de l'apocalypse.* Paris 1896.

Lemerle, P. *L'Emirat d'Aydin, Byzance et l'Occident.* Paris 1957.

_____ "Thomas le Slave." *Travaux et mémoires* 1 (1965) 255-297.

_____ *Le premier humanisme byzantin.* Paris 1971.

Lewy, Hans. *Chaldaean Oracles and Theurgy.* Cairo 1956.

Liebeschuetz, J. *Antioch.* Oxford 1972.

Lloyd, A. C. "The Later Neoplatonists" in *Cambridge History of Later Greek and Early Medieval Philosophy.* Cambridge 1967. 272-325.

Lopez, R. *Genova Marinara nel Duecento: Benedetto Zaccaria.* Messina 1933.

L'Orange, H.P. *Art Forms and Civic Life in the Later Roman Empire.* Princeton 1965.

Lucas, Paul. *Voyage du Sieur Paul Lucas . . .* Paris 1712.

MacFarlane, Charles. *Constantinople in 1828.* London 1829.

MacMullen, Ramsay. "Inscriptions on Armor and the Supply of Arms in the Roman Empire." *AJA* 64 (1960) 23-40.

_____ *Soldier and Civilian in the Later Roman Empire.* Cambridge, Mass. 1963.

_____ "Social Mobility and the Theodosian Code." *JRS* 54 (1964) 49-53.

Magie, D. *Roman Rule in Asia Minor to the End of the Third Century After Christ.* Princeton 1950.

Mango, Cyril. *The Homilies of Photius.* Cambridge, Mass. 1958.

Marrou, Henri. *A History of Education in Antiquity.* London 1956.

Martin, E.J. *A History of the Iconoclastic Controversy.* London 1930.

McCall, Marsh. *Ancient Rhetorical Theories of Simile and Comparison.* Cambridge, Mass. 1969.

Melikoff, I. *La geste de Melik Daniṣmend.* Paris 1960.

Mitten, David. "Two Bronze Objects in the MacDaniel Collection." *HSCP* 69 (1965) 163-167.

Moritz, L.A. *Grain-Mills and Flour in Classical Antiquity.* Oxford 1958.

Müller-Wiener, Wolfgang. "Mittelalterliche Befestigungen im südlichen Ionien." *Ist. Mitt.* 11 (1961) 5-122.

Nautin, P. "La conversion du temple de Philae en église chrétienne." *Cahiers archeol.* 17 (1967) 1-43.

Niebuhr, Carl. *Reisebeschreibung.* Hamburg 1837.

Norden, W. *Das Papsttum und Byzanz.* Berlin 1903.

Pargoire, J. "Saint Euthyme et Jean de Sardes." *EchO* 5 (1901) 157-161.

_____ *L'église byzantine de 527 à 847.* Paris 1905.

Parsons, A.W. "A Roman Water-Mill in the Athenian Agora." *Hesperia* 5 (1936) 70-90.

Pedley, John. *Ancient Literary Sources on Sardis.* Sardis Monograph 2. Cambridge, Mass. 1972.

Planhol, X. de. *De la plaine pamphylienne aux lacs pisidiens.* Paris 1958.

_____ "Geography, Politics and Nomadism in Anatolia." *International Social Science Journal* 11 (1959) 525-531.

_____ "L'évolution du nomadisme en Anatolie et en Iran." *Viehwirtschaft und Hirtenkultur.* Ed. Laszlo Földes. Budapest 1969. 69-93.

Polemis, D. *The Doukai.* London 1968.

Ramsay, W. M. *The Historical Geography of Asia Minor.* London 1890.

Refik, Ahmet. *Anadoluda Türk Aşiretleri.* Istanbul 1930.

Ricaut, Paul. *The Present State of the Greek and Armenian Churches.* London 1679.

Robert, Louis. *Epigrammes du Bas-Empire.* Hellenica IV. Paris 1948.

_____ *Villes d'Asie Mineure*[2]. Paris 1962.

_____ *Nouvelles inscriptions de Sardes.* Paris 1964.

Rostovtzeff, M. *The Social and Economic History of the Roman Empire.* Oxford 1957.

Saldern, Axel von. "Glass from Sardis." *AJA* 66 (1962) 5-12.

Sardis I: The Excavations. Part I: 1910-1914 by Howard Crosby Butler. Leyden 1922.

Sardis II: Architecture. Part I: The Temple of Artemis by Howard Crosby Butler. Leyden 1925.

Sardis VII: Greek and Latin Inscriptions by W. H. Buckler and D. M. Robinson. Leyden 1932.

Sardis XI: Coins by H. W. Bell. Leyden 1916.

Sardis Report 1. See Hanfmann and Waldbaum.

Schreiner, P. "Zur Geschichte Philadelphias im 14. Jahrhundert." *OCP* 35 (1969) 375-417.

Seager, Andrew. "The Building History of the Sardis Synagogue." *AJA* 76 (1972) 425-435.

Ševčenko, Ihor. "The Capital and the Provinces." *DOPapers* 28 (1974).

Shear, T.L. "Seventh Preliminary Report on the Excavations at Sardis." *AJA* 26 (1922) 389-409.

Smith, M. L. *Ionian Vision: Greece in Asia Minor 1919-1923.* New York 1973.

Smith, Thomas. *Remarks upon the Manners, Religion, and Government of the Turks, together with a Survey of the Seven Churches of Asia . . .* London 1678.

Spon, Jacob. *Voyage en Italie et du Levant*. Amsterdam 1679.

Starr, Joshua. *The Jews in the Byzantine Empire*. Athens 1939.

Stein, Ernest. *Histoire du Bas-Empire*. Paris 1949.

Sternbach, L. "Analecta byzantina." *Ceské Museum Filologické* 6 (1900) 305ff.

Stratos, A.N. *Byzantium in the Seventh Century*. Amsterdam 1968.

Sümer, F. *Oğuzlar*. Ankara 1967.

Taeschner, Fr. "Die Verkehrslage und das Wegenetz Anatoliens in Wandel der Zeiten." *Petermanns Mitteilungen* 72 (1926) 202-206.

Talbot, Alice-Mary. *The Correspondence of the Patriarch Athanasius I with the Emperor Andronicus II*. Dumbarton Oaks publications (forthcoming).

Teall, John. "Barbarians in Justinian's Armies." *Speculum* 40 (1965) 294-322.

Thompson, Homer. "Athenian Twilight." *JRS* 49 (1959) 60-90.

Uluçay, M. Çağatay. *Saruhanda Eşkiyalık ve Halk Hareketleri*. Istanbul 1944.

_____ *Saruhanoğulları ve Eserlerine dair Vesikalar*. 2 vols. Istanbul 1940-1946.

_____ and Gökçen, I. *Manisa Tarihi*. Istanbul 1939.

Uzunçarşılı, I. Hakki. *Anadolu Beylikleri*. Ankara 1969.

Uzunçarşılıoğlu, I. H. *Kütahya Şehri*. Istanbul 1932.

Vermeule, C. *Roman Imperial Art in Greece and Asia Minor*. Cambridge, Mass. 1968.

Vryonis, Speros. *The Decline of Medieval Hellenism in Asia Minor and the Process of Islamization from the Eleventh through the Fifteenth Century*. Berkeley 1971.

Walzing, J. P. *Etude historique sur les corporations professionnelles chez les romains*. Louvain 1896.

Wheler, George. *A Journey into Greece*. London 1682.

Wittek, P. *Das Fürstentum Menteşe*. Istanbul 1934.

_____ *The Rise of the Ottoman Empire*. London 1938.

Yeğül, Fikret. "Early Byzantine Capitals from Sardis: A Study in the Ionic Impost Type." *DOPapers* 28 (1974).

Zacos, G. and Veglery, A. *Byzantine Lead Seals*. Basel 1972.

Notes

I. Late Antique Sardis

1. See Foss and Hanfmann, "Regional Setting," for the growth of the city in Antiquity.

2. Fortifications in Asia Minor: D. Magie, *Roman Rule in Asia Minor to the End of the Third Century After Christ* (Princeton 1950) 1566-1568, 1572.

3. City Wall: *Sardis I*, 29-31; *BASOR* 206 (1972) 31-33. The wall is published with detailed description by G. Hanfmann and D. Van Zanten in *Sardis Report 1*, where the meagre evidence for dating is discussed and the alternative possibility of c.400 considered. The silence of the archaeological record is not to be attributed to coincidence. Among the large number of dedications to emperors found at Sardis, none dates to the period between Severus Alexander and Diocletian, a phenomenon noted by C. Vermeule, *Roman Imperial Art in Greece and Asia Minor* (Cambridge, Mass. 1968) 332, and to be explained by the troubles and economic crises of the time.

4. These lists are the *Laterculus Veronensis* and the list of bishops present at the Nicene Council, both dating from the reign of Constantine, and the *Synecdemus* of Hierocles from the time of Justinian. For Sardis and the Lydian cities in Hierocles, see the edition of E. Honigmann (Brussels 1939) 25f.

5. See the *notitae* (lists of bishops of the Eastern Church) tabulated in W. M. Ramsay, *The Historical Geography of Asia Minor* (London 1890) 120, and Germanos, *Historikē Meletē peri tēs Ekklesias tōn Sardeōn* (Constantinople 1928) 75-86.

6. For Hilarius and Panhellenius, see A. H. M. Jones, J. R. Martindale, and J. Morris, *The Prosopography of the Later Roman Empire (PLRE)* (Cambridge 1971) *s. vv.*; for Severus Simplicius, "-nonius," and Basiliscus see sources 15, 16, 17; for anonymous governor see *Sardis VII*, 20.

149

7. The subject of corruption in Late Antiquity is surveyed in A. H. M. Jones, *The Later Roman Empire* (Oxford 1964) 391-401.

8. Synesius, *Epistula* 127.

9. Claudian, *In Eutropium* I.203; A. Cameron, *Claudian* (Oxford 1970) 120.

10. For the history of the municipal councils in the period, see Jones, *Later Roman Empire*, 724-760, and D. Claude, *Die byzantinische Stadt im 6. Jahrhundert* (Munich 1969) 107-161.

11. *Boulē* and *gerousia* inscriptions: *BASOR* 206 (1972) 25; nature and function of *gerousia:* Magie, *Roman Rule*, 855-860; *gerousia* of Sardis: *Sardis* VII, 8, 30, 32, 48.

12. On the *defensor*, see A.H.M. Jones, *The Greek City* (Oxford 1940) 208f; Jones, *Later Roman Empire*, index, *s.v. defensor civitatis;* and Claude, *Byz. Stadt*, 114-117.

13. For the highway system of Lydia in Late Antiquity and the Byzantine and Ottoman periods, see Foss and Hanfmann, "Regional Setting." The work of Diocletian and Constantine is attested by the following milestones: Sardis-Smyrna road: *CIL* III.7197/7199 (=14201[6]), 7198, 14404[b], 474; Keil and Premerstein, III, 7. Sardis-Thyateira-Pergamum: Keil and Premerstein, I, 52, 63; II, 20; *CIL* III.7196; *Sardis* VII, 84. Sardis-Daldis: Keil and Premerstein, I. 67. Sardis-Bagis and Silandus: ibid., I, 84; *CIG* 3449. For later milestones, see below, n. 18.

14. See R. MacMullen, "Inscriptions on Armor and the Supply of Arms in the Roman Empire," *AJA* 64 (1960) 29-31 for an excellent discussion of the whole question.

15. This point is made by Iohannes Malalas 13 (ed. Bonn 307) and discussed by W. Ensslin, *Zur Ostpolitik des Kaisers Diokletian*, SB München, Phil.-Hist. Klasse, 1942, 65.

16. Lactantius, *De mortibus persecutorum* 7 (Nicomedia); Iohannes Malalas 307 (Antioch, Edessa, Damascus).

17. *Comitatenses:* D. van Berchem, *L'armée de Dioclétien et la réforme constantinienne* (Paris 1952) 103-116. Troops stationed in the cities: Zosimus II.34.

18. The highway repairs are indicated by milestones: Smyrna-Sardis road: *CIL* III.471 (Valentinian and Valens), 7200 (=14201[7]) (Gratian, Valentinian, Theodosius, Arcadius), 14201[8] (idem). Thyateira-Sardis: two unpublished stones from Kanboğaz near the Gygean Lake: (1) Arcadius and Honorius, reused by Theodosius II and Valentinian III (2) Theodosius, Arcadius, and Honorius, reused by Theodosius II and Valentinian III (C. Foss, MS report 1972). Daldis-Sardis: Keil and Premerstein, I, 67 of the Tetrarchy and Constantine, with a later reuse attested by the apparently meaningless IOYMENTI, which is to be corrected to ⁻I OYAΛENTI, i.e., Valens and his colleagues. The importance to the army of the highway through Lydia in this period is reflected by an anecdonte in Zosimus IV. 30. Theodosius ordered barbarian troops stationed on the Danube frontier to be transferred to Egypt and Egyptians to replace them on the frontier. As the two bodies proceeded to their respective destinations, they met at Philadelphia in Lydia and got into a brawl. This shows that the highway through Sardis was a major axis in the imperial network. Tombstones of soldiers: *Sardis* VII, 170, tomb of a *ducenarius* of the fourth century; ibid., 173, a *decanus* oᶠ the

fourth-sixth centuries. Neither of these titles is unambiguously military. A *ducenarius* might be either soldier or civilian; the *fabricensis* of source 2, for example, had the rank of *ducenarius*. *Decanus* could denote a minor official of the governmental bureaucracy or the army, or an undertaker: see the discussion in *Sardis* VII, 173. An unpublished inscription from HOB (IN 59.19) in lettering of the fourth or fifth century is less ambiguous: it was the tombstone of a centurion.

19. Zosimus IV.4-8; Ammianus Marcellinus XXVI.5.8-10.6. The topographical details are not very clear in either of these narratives.

20. Zosimus V.13,18. His account (from which the narrative presented here is adapted) sounds highly rhetorical but is considerably less so than that of Claudian, *In Eutropium* II, which agrees with it in general outline.

21. I have not attempted here to collect references to Sardis in late antique and Byzantine literature. In the Byzantine period, mentions of Sardis, the Pactolus, and Croesus are common enough, but mostly as banal as their English equivalent, "rich as Croesus."

22. Justinian, *Novel* 166, succinctly analyzed in Bury, *Later Roman Empire*[2], 445 n.2. For the whole question of deserted lands, see the discussion of Jones, *Later Roman Empire*, 812-823.

23. Iohannes Lydus, *De magistratibus* III. 58-61, 70.

24. See the discussion of C. Diehl, *Justinien et la civilisation byzantine au VIe siècle* (Paris 1901) 269-313 and cf. n. 28 below.

25. See below, notes 73, 74.

26. Procopius, *Bell. Pers.* II.22-23; see also J.B. Bury, *History of the Later Roman Empire* (London 1923) II. 62-66, and Ernest Stein, *Histoire du Bas-empire* (Paris 1949) II, 756-761, with full references to the sources. For the effects of the plague on manpower, see John Teall, "Barbarians in Justinian's Armies," *Speculum* 40 (1965) 305-307, 319-322.

27. Justinian, *Novel* 145; see also Stein, *Bas-empire*, II, 749-751.

28. Text and commentary: Charles Diehl, "Rescrit des empereurs Justin et Justinien," *BCH* 17 (1893) 501-520, with corrections in H. Grégoire, *Recueil des inscriptions grecques chretiennes d'Asie Mineure* (Paris 1922) 314. For the site and its remains, some of them Byzantine, see G. Cousin, "Voyage en Carie," *BCH* 24 (1900) 67f. There is no reason to suppose, as does H. Leclerq in *DACL*, *s.v. Ephèse* col. 138, that the oratory of Saint John was the great basilica dedicated to him in Ephesus. The church in the inscription is called *oratorium* and *eukterion*; such terms would not be appropriate to the large church in Ephesus: see G.W.H. Lampe, *A Patristic Greek Lexicon* (Oxford 1961) *s.v. euktērion*.

29. See, for example, M. Řostovtzeff, *The Social and Economic History of the Roman Empire* (Oxford, 1957) 406, 478, with the general discussion 433-501; cf. Magie, *Roman Rule*, 688-722.

30. Summarized from Diehl, "Rescrit," 512-520. The subject requires a more detailed treatment than would be appropriate here. In a consideration of the reign of Justinian, the remarks of P. Lemerle, *Le premier humanisme byzantin* (Paris, 1971) 68-73, should also be taken into account. He comments on the disastrous decline of learning and culture, and concludes: "le 'siècle de Justinien' est un temps mort, consommé dans les entreprises où la vanité à disputé à la naiveté . . ."

31. For the resources of the region of Sardis, see Foss and Hanfmann, "Regional Setting."

32. On the *fabricae* and *fabricenses* in general, see Jones, *Later Roman Empire*, 834-836.

33. For particular factories, see R. MacMullen, "Inscriptions," 29 and R. MacMullen, *Soldier and Civilian in the Later Roman Empire* (Cambridge, Mass. 1963) 24-26, 30f.

34. The *fabricae* are discussed in detail by J. P. Walzing in *Etude historique sur les corporations professionnelles chez les romains* (Louvain 1896) II, 239-243; see also O. Seeck in *RE, s.v. fabricenses*.

35. *Codex Theodosianus, Nov. Th.* 6 (trans. C. Pharr).

36. For the products of the shops, see *BASOR* 170 (1963) 49-51; 191 (1968) 17-22; and 199 (1970) 74.

37. Sources 12, 13, discussed in detail below.

38. *BASOR* 191 (1968) 18.

39. *BASOR* 154 (1959) 27.

40. A. von Saldern, "Glass from Sardis," *AJA* 66 (1962) 5-12; see also G. Hanfmann, "A Preliminary Note on the Glass Found at Sardis in 1958," *Journal of Glass Studies* 1 (1959) 51-54.

41. Two gems are illustrated in *BASOR* 170 (1963) 44 (Shops) and 50 (Synagogue).

42. *Sardis* VII, 18, discussed below.

43. For illustrations of the mosaics of PN, see *BASOR* 166 (1961) 20 and 170 (1963) 23f, 26f; of the Synagogue, *BASOR* 174 (1964) 33; 182 (1966) 49; 187 (1967) 22f; 203 (1971) 18. Note particularly the series of restored drawings of the Synagogue mosaics in *BASOR* 187 (1967) 26, 28, 30f, 33, 35, 37. On the sculpture of late antique Sardis, see G. Hanfmann, "On Late Roman and Early Byzantine Portraits from Sardis," *Hommages à Marcel Renard* III, Collection Latomus 103 (Brussels 1969) 288-295.

44. The shift of markets from the agora to colonnaded streets is discussed by D. Claude, *Byz. Stadt*, 60-68; it is particularly evident at Ephesus, where the main street of the late antique city, the Embolos, was colonnaded and lined with shops and the southern Agora was given up and built over with houses in Late Antiquity: Josef Keil, *Führer durch Ephesos* (Vienna 1964) 121-124 (Embolos), F. Eichler, "Die österreichischen Ausgrabungen in Ephesos im Jahre 1964," *Anz. Wien* 102 (1965) 96 f (Agora).

45. The stone was found northeast of the temple, but the location of the mill has not been determined. It may have occupied the same spot as the modern mill of which the remains are still visible below Building D, the Justinianic church. For that mill, see the map in *Sardis* I, 30.

46. For a general survey of water mills in Late Antiquity, see R. J. Forbes, *Studies in Ancient Technology* II[2] (Leiden 1965) 80-106, summarized in "Power" in *A History of Technology*, ed. C. Singer *et al.* (Oxford 1956) II, 589-622. Mills of Arles and Rome: ibid., 598-600; price edict: Diocletian, *Edictum de pretiis*, ed. S. Lauffer (Berlin 1971) 15.54 (a watermill cost 2000 denarii, a horse-mill 1500 and a donkey-mill 1250); mill in Constantinople mosaic: G. Brett, "Byzantine

Water Mill", *Antiquity* 13 (1939) 354-356 with plate VII; mill of Athens: A.W.Parsons, "A Roman Water-mill in the Athenian Agora," *Hesperia* 5 (1936) 70-90 and H. Thompson, "Athenian Twilight," *JRS* 49 (1959) 69f. Marble mill in Gaul: Ausonius, *Mosella* 362-364. See also L. A. Moritz, *Grain-Mills and Flour in Classical Antiquity* (Oxford 1958) 131-139.

47. Forbes, "Power," 601. The subject of technology does not seem to be discussed in Jones, *Later Roman Empire*. This section has been read by my colleague, Professor Eric Robinson, and has benefitted greatly from his perceptive and helpful comments.

48. On bakers and the bread supply, see Jones, *Later Roman Empire*, 629, 699f, 735.

49. For distribution of bread in provincial cities, see Waltzing, *Corporations* II, 219 n.4, and J. Liebeschuetz, *Antioch* (Oxford 1972) 126-132.

50. See the article "bracae" in Daremberg-Saglio, Diocletian, *Edictum de Pretiis* 7.42 and *Codex Theodosianus* XIV. 10.2 and 3.

51. For discussions and interpretations of this document, see T. R. S. Broughton, "Roman Asia," in T. Frank, *An Economic Survey of Ancient Rome* (Baltimore 1938) IV, 848f, and, in much more detail, W. H. Buckler, "Labour Disputes in the Province of Asia," in *Anatolian Studies Presented to Sir William Mitchell Ramsay* (Manchester 1923) 36-45.

52. The nature of late antique government is well surveyed in Jones, *Later Roman Empire*, 366-410 ("The Administration"); see also 470-522 ("Justice") and 523-562 ("Senators and *Honorati*"). The difference between appearances given by the laws and actual practice is brought out by R. MacMullen in "Social Mobility and the Theodosian Code," *JRS* 54 (1964) 49-53. For expressions of the formalism of the age, see the excellent and provocative work of H. P. L'Orange, *Art Forms and Civic Life in the Later Roman Empire* (Princeton 1965). The author, however, seems to take too much imperial propaganda at its face value and to believe that the administrative system (and its reflection in art and architecture) was more rigid and simple than it actually was.

53. The restorations of the Gymnasium and the details of work on other buildings will be treated below in the section on the expansion of the city in Late Antiquity. A fragmentary inscription, IN 70.7, reused in the Synagogue, may refer to construction by another governor. It names a certain Maeonius and mentions a *krēpeida kraterēn*.

54. Jones, *Greek City*, 253 and Claude, *Byz. Stadt*, 76.

55. On *xenones* see D. J. Constantelos, *Byzantine Philanthropy and Social Welfare* (New Brunswick 1968) 185-221.

56. For the nature and extent of education in Late Antiquity, with particular reference to the municipal schools, see H. Marrou, *a History of Education in Antiquity* (London 1956) 305-313.

57. The practices and doctrine of the theurgists are discussed by E. R. Dodds, "Theurgy," in *The Greeks and the Irrational* (Berkeley 1951) 283-311 (reprinted from *JRS* 37, 1947) and reconstructed in considerable detail from surviving fragments by Hans Lewy, *Chaldaean Oracles and Theurgy* (Cairo 1956); for the origin and meaning of the terms "theurgy" and "theurgist," see Lewy, 461-466.

For the philosophical background see A. C. Lloyd, "The Later Neoplatonists" in *Cambridge History of Later Greek and Early Medieval Philosophy* (Cambridge 1967) 272-325. The work of Eunapius is full of narratives of miracles; see especially 458f (Iamblichus), 467-471 (Sosipatra), 475 (statue of Hecate).

58. For the prevalence of magic in Late Antiquity, see A. A. Barb, "The Magic Arts," in *The Conflict between Paganism and Christianity in the Fourth Century*, ed. A. Momigliano (Oxford 1963) 100-125.

59. Eunapius 500; see also Jones, *PLRE*, *s.v.* Some of his works, in both Greek and Latin, survived in the time of Eunapius.

60. Training in the philosophers and oratory was part of a normal education. See Proclus, *Théologie platonicienne*, ed. H. D. Saffrey and L. G. Westerink (Paris 1968) ix-xxvi ("Vie de Proclus") and xxxv-xlviii ("L'école d'Athènes au IVe siècle").

61. I presume that the phrase of Eunapius 500, "he was so lifted up and aroused by the plumage of his soul" refers to such initiation. For the sacrament of theurgical elevation, see Lewy, *Chaldaean Oracles*, 177-226.

62. For the career of Chrysanthius, see Eunapius 500-505, 476-478, and passim.

63. See Eunapius frag. 15 in *FHG* IV, 21 and Suidas, *s.v. Musonius*.

64. Eunapius frag. 45 in *FHG* IV, 33f, and Jones, *PLRE*, *s.v.*

65. Eunapius 498f, 505; H. Schröder, "Oribasius" in *RE, Supp.* VII, 797-812.

66. Encouragement of Eunapius and memoir: Eunapius frag. 8 in *FHG* IV, 15; the medical books are published with the other works of Oribasius in the *Corpus Medicorum Graecorum*.

67. Eunapius 499.

68. For the career, writings, and philosophy of Eunapius, see the article of W. Schmid in *RE*. Both Schmid and Jones, *PLRE*, *s.v.*, write that Eunapius was of a poor family. This notion is based on nothing more than Eunapius' own statement (485) that when he arrived in Athens he possessed nothing but the learning of the ancients. This need hardly be taken literally. Eunapius' parents, whom he nowhere names, could afford to send him from Sardis to Athens for five years' study; on his voyage there he was accompanied by numerous relatives, an unlikely circumstance for a poor man. More revealing of his economic status is his connection by marriage with Chrysanthius, a man of a senatorial family. If the proposed identification of the rhetorician Eunapius as the father or grandfather of the writer is correct, there can be little doubt that he came from a prominent family.

69. Eunapius 504f.

70. Eunapius 505. It is not known whether Tuscianus and Patricius of Lydia had anything to do with the school of Sardis. The former taught in Athens in the mid fourth century, the latter was executed in the persecution of magicians carried out by Valens in 371. For Tuscianus see *RE, s.v.* (Güngerich); for Patricius see Zosimus IV. 15. Polybius, who wrote technical treatises on rhetoric, was a native of Sardis, but his date is uncertain; he may have lived in the third century. See, most recently, Marsh McCall, *Ancient Rhetorical Theories of Simile and Comparison* (Cambridge, Mass. 1969) 137, 255. Polybius is possibly

to be identified with the dedicant of an inscription set up in Sardis to accompany a bust of Cicero: *Sardis* VII, 49.

71. For the persecutions of Justinian and the end of classical learning, see Lemerle, *Humanisme*, 68-73.

72. Eunapius 501.

73. In the period after Eunapius, the fate of paganism in Lydia is not altogether clear. Himerius (ed. A. Colonna, Rome 1951) XLVI.6 and XLVII.6 mentions the worship of Dionysus in Lydia as if it were current in his own day, the late fourth century. Nonnus, writing in the fifth century, shows considerable familiarity with the Dionysiac rituals and traditions of the Sardis region, but does not imply that the pagan worship continued in his own time. On the other hand, Proclus the Neoplatonist philosopher was exiled from Athens around 450 and spent a year in Lydia; while there, he studied the ancient rites which were preserved. Paganism, perhaps including ritual which had died out in Greece, was evidently still practiced in Lydia in the mid-fifth century: see Marinus, *Vita Procli*, ed. J. F. Boissonade (Leipzig 1814) cap. 15. Archaeological evidence may provide some confirmation. An inscription of about 400 from Hypaepa, a town near Sardis noted for the worship of the Persian Artemis, mentions an *archimagus*, a Zoroastrian high priest. Josef Keil in "Die Familie des Prätorianer Präfekten Anthemius," *Anz. Wien* 79 (1942) 201-203 elaborated a theory that the magi were tolerated in Hypaepa in the fifth century as the Christians were in Persia according to the treaty which Anthemius concluded with Yezdigerd I in 408. Such an explanation, however, may be otiose. Louis Robert in *Hellenica* IV (1948) 19f pointed out that the late inscription of Anthemius does not form a unity with the text which mentions the *archimagus* and is inscribed on a different side of the stone. He raised the possibility that the stone had been reused and that the *archimagus* may have lived much earlier. There were, however, Zoroastrians in Cappadocia in the late fourth century: see Basil of Caesarea, *Ep.* 258, written in 377; cf Priscus frag. 31 in *FHG* IV. 105, referring to events of ca. 464. Their doctrine had been widespread in Asia Minor for centuries and could have survived the triumph of Christianity for a time.

74. John of Ephesus, *Ecclesiastical History* III.36. The numbers of pagans and churches varies somewhat in the different accounts: see E. Honigmann, *Evêques et évêchés monophysites d'Asie antérieure au VIe siècle. CSCO Subsidia* 2 (Louvain 1951) 208 n.6.

75. Obadiah 20; Josephus, *Ant.* 12.147-153, 14.235, 14.260. For the early history of the Jews at Sardis, see Kraabel, "Judaism," 198-203, and Louis Robert, *Nouvelles inscriptions de Sardes* (Paris 1964) 37-58.

76. For the Synagogue, see below. For the inscriptions, see Robert, *Nouvelles inscriptions*, 37-58 and *BASOR* 187 (1967) 27-32.

77. Note the remarks of G. M. A. Hanfmann in *BASOR* 187 (1967) 50.

78. For the school, see Kraabel, "Judaism," 222-226.

79. Goldsmiths: Robert, *Nouvelles inscriptions*, 55. Glassmakers: *BASOR* 191 (1968) 28. Councillors: Robert, *Nouvelles inscriptions*, 55f, *BASOR* 187 (1967) 32. *Comes: BASOR* 206 (1972) 20.

80. A. Seager, "The Building History of the Sardis Synagogue," *AJA* 76

(1972) 432-435. The Jewish community of Sardis is not mentioned in the Byzantine period. It may have declined with the general depopulation of the area in the seventh and eighth centuries, or succumbed to one of the frequent persecutions which Byzantine emperors from Heraclius (602-641) to Romanus Lecapenus (920-944) carried out. For those, see Joshua Starr, *The Jews in the Byzantine Empire* (Athens 1939) 1-10. In the same work, 83-242, a collection of sources mentioning Jewish communities is presented; none appears from Lydia—the nearest seem to have been at Ephesus and Chonae. The sources for the whole period are, of course, fragmentary and deficient. For the Jews of the region in the Ottoman period, see below, Chap. III, n. 42.

81. Clement of Sardis: *Synaxarium* 621; of Sardica: ibid. 36, 787; helper of Paul: Philippians iv.3. See the discussion in *AASS Apr.* III, 4.

82. Revelation iii.1-6; Pedley, *Ancient Literary Sources on Sardis*, Sardis Monograph 2 (Cambridge, Mass. 1972) nos. 223, 224. On this passage and the early church at Sardis in general, see Sherman Johnson, "Christianity in Sardis," *Early Christian Origins*, ed. A. Wikgren (Chicago 1961) 81-90.

83. On Melito, see Eusebius, *Hist. Eccl.* IV.13, IV.26, V.24; Johnson "Christianity," 83-87; and especially, A. T. Kraabel, "Melito the Bishop and the Synagogue at Sardis," *Hanfmann Studies*, 77-85. Melito is sometimes referred to as a saint and is accepted as such by J. M. Sauget in *Bibliotheca Sanctorum, s.v. Melitone.* The evidence, however, is almost nonexistent. Melito does not appear in the *Synaxarium* (the calendar of the Greek Church), or the index of Byzantine saints, the *Bibliotheca Hagiographica Graeca.* Nor does he figure in the Martyrologium Romanum. According to the important discussion in *AASS Apr.,* I, 10-11, some calendars are reported to include Melito; others, however, have in his place a certain *beatus* Melito, bishop and confessor of Sardinia. The sanctity of this individual is doubtful, but, if he ever existed, he may serve to account for the reported presence of his more famous namesake in some unpublished calendars. In any case, there is no evidence of a cult of Melito of Sardis in east or west. It is not improbable that his espousal of the Quartodeciman cause was sufficient grounds to deny him sainthood, and, perhaps, to account for the loss of his works. The question of the sanctity of Melito is not entirely academic. It is not certainly known to whom any of the churches of Sardis was dedicated. If Melito was not a saint, his name can at least be eliminated from speculation. The romantic and colorful suggestion of G. Lampakis in *I Efta Asteres tis Apokalipseos* (Athens, 1909) 350 that the body of Melito lay in a crypt underneath the holy altar of the cathedral of Sardis (the present Church D) remains a possibility. The statement that Melito lay buried at Sardis is quoted by Eusebius (*Hist. Eccl.* v.24) from a letter of Polycrates of Ephesus written c. 195 before the Quartodecimans were generally recognized as heretics. It does not provide evidence that Melito was considered a saint; in fact, most of the holy men mentioned in the letter as celebrating Easter like Melito are not venerated by the Orthodox Church.

84. *Sardis* VII 164.

85. For a list of known bishops of Sardis, see Appendix I, and for the rank of Sardis in the church, see Germanos, *Melete*, 23-25.

86. Sozomen IV.24; Johnson, "Christianity," 89.

87. Philostorgius, *Hist. eccl.* VIII.2, 4.

88. Chrysostom: Socrates VI.19. For the Quartodecimans, see the clear sketch in Cyril Mango, *The Homilies of Photius* (Cambridge, Mass. 1958) 279-282, commenting on a text which shows that the heresy was still alive in the ninth century.

89. *ACO* I.i.7.100-105.

90. Originally published and misunderstood by W. H. Buckler, "Lydian Records," *JHS* 37 (1917) 95-99. The correct interpretation was given by H. Grégoire, "Du nouveau sur la hiérarchie de la secte montaniste," *Byz.* 2 (1925) 329-335. The article of W. M. Calder, "Philadelphia and Montanism," *Bulletin of the John Rylands Library* 7 (1923) 309-354, is of negligible value for Philadelphia in spite of its title, since the identification of Philadelphia as a cradle of Montanism is based on one of W. M. Ramsay's more infelicitous conjectures. On Calder's article, see the remarks of H. Grégoire "Epigraphie chrétienne II," *Byz.* 1 (1924) 703-710.

91. For the letter of Florentius, see *ACO* II.i.100 and K. Hefele, *Histoire des conciles* (Paris 1907) 518 ff. For the activities of Florentius, see Germanos, *Melete*, 45f. That work, on 39-63, contains a discussion of all the then known bishops of Sardis from the first century through the fourteenth, and may be consulted for information about each of them.

92. Mansi VII. 571-573. The history and doctrine of the monophysites may be found described in any standard work on the period; the discussion of Ed. Gibbon, *The Decline and Fall of the Roman Empire*, cap. xlvii, is better than most. Some historians have supposed that the controversies of the age had their roots in social and economic problems, that the heretics were oppressed peasantry, incipient nationalists, or something of the sort. Such notions have been successfully disposed of by A. H. M. Jones in "Were Ancient Heresies National or Social Movements in Disguise?" *Journal of Theological Studies* 10 (1959) 280-297; cf. Peter Brown, "Religious Dissent in the Later Roman Empire," *History* 46 (1961) 83-101.

93. John of Ephesus, *Lives of the Eastern Saints* 333; on the monophysite church and its growth in the sixth century, see the detailed study of E. Honigmann, *Evêques*.

94. John of Ephesus, *Ecclesiastical History* III. i. 15, Honigmann, *Evêques*, 230f. For the activities of Jacob Baradaeus in Asia Minor, see ibid., 168-177, and for John of Ephesus 207-215, 220f, and above.

95. For these, see *Sardis* VII, 188-190. The last of these mentions an unnamed bishop. His name was restored as Theophylactus by H. Gregoire (325) on the basis of an earlier reading which seems untenable if the drawing reproduced in *Sardis* VII is at all accurate. "Theophylactus" therefore is not to be added to the list of bishops of Sardis as proposed by V. Laurent in *EO* 29 (1930) 190. Numerous Christian tombstones and other fragments have been uncovered by the present expedition. They will be published by Louis Robert in a forthcoming volume of this series.

96. The section which follows is descriptive; references for individual buildings will be given in the next section which deals with the changes in Sardis in Late Antiquity.

97. It is possible that the building went through an intermediate stage as a civic basilica; see the discussion in A. Seager, "Building History," 430-433.

98. The *praetorium* is mentioned in H. Delehaye "Les actes des martyrs de Pergame," *Anal. Boll.* 58 (1940) 163.

99. *Sardis* I, 33. L. Vann will discuss the identification of this building in a forthcoming study. It may have been a basilica or part of a gymnasium.

100. *Sardis* I, 31 and L. Vann, forthcoming.

101. *Sardis* I. 31. A building southeast of the Theater, formerly called the Odeon, now the Hillside Chambers, appears to be a commercial structure. These and other unexcavated buildings will be published by L. Vann.

102. For the geological history of the temple area, see the report of W. Warfield in *Sardis* I, 175-180.

103. The sculpture is not yet published; for the graffiti, see below.

104. On this church, see *Sardis* I. 33 and D. Hansen, "L'antica Sardi cristiana," *Bibbia e Oriente* 4 (1962) 171. The dating to the time of Justinian was first suggested by A. H. S. Megaw and will be supported by L. Vann in his forthcoming publication of the building.

105. For the history of this building in Late Antiquity, see *BASOR* 157 (1960) 38-43.

106. Tomb of Sabina: *Sardis* I, 170, 174, *Sardis* V, 3-17 (sarcophagus). Christian tomb: *Sardis* I, 174, 181-183 with plates IV and V. For the "Peacock Tomb," see below. The stylistic resemblance between the paintings of the two tombs is so close that Professor Hanfmann, in a personal communication, has suggested that they may be by the same hand. A tomb with similar frescoes from Nicaea has been published by N. Fıratlı; "An Early Byzantine Hypogeum Discovered at Iznik," *Melanges Mansel* II (Ankara 1974) 919-932; see 929-932 for discussion of the frescoes in relation to others of the same type, including those of Sardis.

107. For the building history of the Gymnasium in Late Antiquity, see the preliminary reports in *BASOR* 162 (1961) 40-43; 182 (1966) 30f; 187 (1967) 50-58; 191 (1968) 33; 206 (1972) 24-31.

108. The capitals are the subject of a thorough study by Fikret Yeğül, "Early Byzantine Capitals from Sardis: A Study in the Ionic Impost Type," *DOPapers* 28 (1974).

109. The restored drawing reproduced in fig. 10 includes much which has been lost through the gradual deterioration of the plaster. The following inscriptions have been read:

a) . . . εὐχή   ". . . vow"
b) βοήθι τὸ Φη . . .   "help Phe . . ."
c) κύρι βοήθι   "Lord help . . ."
d) κύρι βοήθι τὸ δοῦλον σου Κοσταντῖνον   "Lord help thy servant Constantine"
e) χ̅ε̅   "Christ . . ."
f) βοή]θι τοῦ δούλου σου   "Help thy servant . . ."
g) κ̅ε̅ βοήθι τοῦ δούλου σου Θε[. . .]   "Lord help thy servant Th . . ."

I am indebted to Professor John Kroll for these readings.

110. For the Synagogue, see Seager, "Building History," 425-435, and the preliminary reports in *BASOR* 170 (1963) 38-38; 174 (1964) 30-38; 177 (1965) 17-19; 182 (1966) 34-45; 187 (1967) 10-50; 191 (1968) 26-32; 199 (1970) 45-51; 203 (1971) 12-18; 206 (1972) 20-23. See also Kraabel, "Judaism," 227-240.

111. For the Marble Street see *BASOR* 166 (1962) 40-45, and for the importance of colonnaded streets in Late Antiquity, see n. 44 above.

112. For the Byzantine Shops, see *BASOR* 154 (1959) 16-18; 157 (1960) 32-35; 166 (1962) 40-45; 170 (1963) 49-51; 174 (1964) 45-47; 177 (1965) 19-20; 186 (1967) 28-31; 191 (1968) 16-22; 199 (1970) 44. Coins: G. Bates, *Byzantine Coins*, Sardis Monograph 1 (Cambridge, Mass. 1971) 149f; Glass: n. 40 above.

113. For the House of Bronzes, see *BASOR* 154 (1959) 22-27; 157 (1960) 22-28; 182 (1966) 8, 15f. For the embers shovel, see D. G. Mitten, "Two Bronze Objects in the MacDaniel Collection," *HSCP* 69 (1965) 163-167. Late repairs are dated by coin finds, tabulated in Bates, *Byzantine Coins*, 150.

114. For buildings in this area see *BASOR* 162 (1961) 17; 170 (1963) 13; 174 (1964) 6-8.

115. Colonnaded street: *BASOR* 177 (1965) 14-17.

116. Tetrapylon: *BASOR* 199 (1970) 28f; 203 (1971) 11.

117. *BASOR* 162 (1961) 26f.

118. For the church, see the preliminary report in *BASOR* (forthcoming), and G. M. A. Hanfmann, MS report Sept. 1973. Law of 386: *Codex Theodosianus* IX.17.7. A similar instance of a church built in a graveyard is presented by the church at the Temple of Artemis.

119. G.M.A. Hanfmann, MS report Sept. 1973; *BASOR* 170 (1963) 18-20.

120. For the sector PN, see the preliminary reports in *BASOR* 162 (1961) 24-29; 166 (1962) 15-19; 170 (1963) 18-23; 174 (1964) 20-24; 182 (1966) 25.

121. Tombs at PN: *BASOR* 174 (1964) 22-24; 191 (1968) 10f. *Sardis* I, 155, 167. Peacock tomb: *BASOR* 166 (1962) 30-33; 199 (1970) 55-58. Other tombs: *BASOR* 157 (1960) 13-16; 162 (1961) 17f; 166 (1962) 52.

122. PN: *BASOR* 174 (1964) 24. HOB: *BASOR* 157 (1960) 26.

123. Villa at PC: *BASOR* 166 (1962) 33. Mosaics illustrated: G. M. A. Hanfmann, *Letters from Sardis* (Cambridge, Mass. 1972) 78 fig. 50. Villa near temple: T. L. Shear, "Seventh Preliminary Report on the Excavations at Sardis," *AJA* 26 (1922) 389-409.

124. Graves around temple: *Sardis* I, 126f; *BASOR* 199 (1970) 54. Tombstones: *Sardis* VII, 165-167, 169, 170, 173.

125. The coins are tabulated in *Sardis* XI, xii f.

126. Church M: *Sardis* I, 70, 112-115; *BASOR* 166 (1962) 49-54.

127. Enclosure (called Building U) and other buildings in temple precinct: *BASOR* 199 (1970) 29-35. The sector is published in detail in Sardis Report 1.

128. Law of Theodosius II: *Codex Theodosianus* XVI.10.25. This law, which did not provide for the conversion of temples into churches, as is sometimes maintained, is discussed by A. Frantz, "From Paganism to Christianity in the Temples of Athens," *DOP* 19 (1965) 187f. For demons surviving in the material of temple buildings, see F. W. Deichmann, "Frühchristliche Kirchen in antiken Heiligtümern," *JdAI* 54 (1939) 107, and for the whole question of conversion of

temples into churches, passim. For crosses carved on buildings, see Deichmann, "Frühchristliche Kirchen," 109-111; Gregoire, *Recueil*, 165, 166, 320; C. M. Kaufmann, *Handbuch der altchristlichen Epigraphik* (Freiburg 1917) 140, 414, and especially for crosses in a temple converted into a church, P. Nautin, "La conversion du temple de Philae en église chrétienne," *Cahiers archaeol.* 17 (1967) 14ff, 21-24. The Sardis inscriptions are discussed with full references in W. Buckler and D. Robinson, "Greek Inscriptions from Sardis IV," *AJA* 18 (1914) 44.

129. Enlargement of church: *BASOR* 166 (1962) 50, 54; S. W. Jacobs, MS report 1961. The church will be published by Professor Jacobs in a forthcoming volume of the Sardis Reports.

130. Destruction of temple: *Sardis* I, 49, 67, 68, and K. Frazer in Sardis Report 1 (coin of Constantine with marble chips).

131. See my discussion in "Byzantine Cities," 178, 199-202.

132. *Codex Theodosianus* XV.1, *De operibus publicis*.

II. Byzantine Sardis

1. For the evidence of burning and destruction, see *BASOR* 154 (1959) 16; 174 (1964) 29; 187 (1967) 57 (Gymnasium); 170 (1963) 48; 187 (1967) 14 (Synagogue); 157 (1960) 24 (HOB).

2. For the numismatic evidence see Bates, *Byzantine Coins*, 1 f, and his tabulation of the coin finds by sector, 149f. Hoard of coins from the temple: *Sardis* XI, viii. The validity of this evidence has unreasonably been called into question by P. Charanis in "A Note on the Byzantine Coin Finds in Sardis and their Historical Significance," *Epet.* 39-40 (1972-1973) 175-180. Professor Charanis has objected that the feeble literary sources make no mention of the capture of Sardis, and expresses considerable confusion about the use of archaeological and numismatic evidence. I have discussed the evidence and the methodology to be employed in "The Destruction of Sardis in 616 and the Value of Evidence," *JÖB* 24 (1975).

3. I have discussed these campaigns and the destruction which they wrought in "The Persians in Asia Minor and the End of Antiquity," *EHR* 90 (1975). where the evidence from Sardis is presented in a broader context. For a narrative of the war based on the literary sources, see A.N. Stratos, *Byzantium in the Seventh Century* (Amsterdam 1968) 105f, 115, 117, 360f.

4. Road rebuilding: *BASOR* 166 (1962) 45; 186 (1967) 28f. The coins are published with findspots in Bates, *Byzantine Coins*, 113-119.

5. Wall described and illustrated: *Sardis* I, 21-25. Construction: *BASOR* 162 (1961) 33.

6. Gate of Persecutions and fortifications connected with it: W. Müller-Wiener, "Mittelalterliche Befestigungen im südlichen Jonien," *Ist. Mitt.* 11 (1961) 91-95, 108f. The dating of these walls is not certain, and there may be reason to attribute their construction to the Dark Ages: see my discussion in "Byzantine Cities," 206f. Walls of Magnesia: C. Humann, *Magnesia am Mäander* (Berlin 1904) 2, 19, 33; Müller-Wiener (above) 88.

7. In this context, it should be remembered that the builders of the wall removed all earlier remains. An unpublished tombstone (IN. 60.3) in crude late antique lettering found on the Acropolis may indicate some habitation there before the fortifications were built.

8. Remains: *BASOR* 162 (1961) 33f; 166 (1962) 37-39; 170 (1963) 32. They are described in more detail in the MS reports of D. Hansen (1960), C. Greenewalt (1961) and W. Kohler (1962). Plan: *BASOR* 166 (1962) 38. Coins: Bates, *Byzantine Coins*, 651 (Maurice), 1089, 1092, 1099 (Constans II), 1103 (Justinian II). This is admittedly a very small sample, but the lack of earlier coins on the Acropolis is significant.

9. Sardis II, 13, *BASOR* 162 (1961) 33. This is possibly the same earthquake as that which destroyed the Gymnasium: *BASOR* 162 (1961) 43.

10. Coins: *Sardis* XI, 82-95; Bates, *Byzantine Coins*, 95-121. The basilica at PN was not destroyed in 616, but may have been temporarily abandoned; see below.

11. These buildings will be published by L. Vann.

12. The Greek sources, e.g. Theophanes 390, do not mention the attack on Sardis, but only that Maslama wintered in Asia.

13. *BASOR* 162 (1961) 34; 166 (1962) 37-39; 170 (1963) 32f., to be supplemented by the MS reports (above, chap. II, n. 8).

14. Battle: Theophanes 417.

15. *Chronique de Denys de Tell-Mahre*, ed. and trans. J.-B. Chabot (Paris 1895) 36, and 30-39 for the course of the plague in general with especial reference to the author's native Mesopotamia. For this plague, see Theophanes 422f, and J. B. Bury, *A History of the Later Roman Empire from Arcadius to Irene* (London 1889) II, 453-457.

16. Theophanes 473.

17. For the theme system, see J. Karayannopoulos, *Die Entstehung der byzantinischen Themenordnung* (Munich 1959), with full references.

18. For the functions of the *dioiketes*, see F. Dölger, *Beiträge zur Geschichte der byzantinischen Finanzverwaltung* (Leipzig 1927) 70f. Seals: Zacos and Veglery, *Byzantine Lead Seals*, nos. 1918 (George of Sardis), 2183 (Michael of Lydia, ninth century), and 2426 (Theodore of Lydia, eighth century).

19. The persecutions of Lachanodracon are described at length by Theophanes 445. They are put into the context of the military and religious conflicts of the time by W. E. Kaegi, "The Byzantine Armies and Iconoclasm," *Byzantinoslavica* 27 (1966) 48-70. Kaegi demonstrates that iconoclasm cannot be reduced to a simple opposition between orthodox westerners and iconoclast easterners, at least as far as the army is concerned. E. J. Martin, *A History of the Iconoclastic Controversy* (London 1930) provides a general survey; see pp. 38-71 for the persecutions of Constantine V.

20. *Synaxarium eccl. cp.* 62; the text states that the two saints were martyred under Leo III, who is not otherwise known to have carried out such violent persecutions. Attribution to him, the founder of the movement and therefore the symbol of impiety, is the kind of commonplace produced by ignorance; the life shows little real knowledge of the saints. Considering the historical circumstances, it is far more likely that they were executed under Constantine V.

21. For the career of Euthymius, see J. Gouillard, "Une oeuvre inédite du patriarche Méthode: la vie d'Euthyme de Sardes," *BZ* 53 (1960) 36-46, which analyzes the contents of an unpublished *vita*. A less detailed life is published in full by Aristeides Papadakis; "The Unpublished Life of Euthymius of Sardis," *Traditio* 26 (1970) 63-89. As far as Euthymius is concerned, the work of J. Pargoire, "Saint Euthyme et Jean de Sardes," *EO* 5 (1901) 157-161, is outdated, but it provides a useful sketch of the career of his successor, John. For the treatise, see J. Darrouzès, *Documents inédits d'ecclésiologie byzantine* (Paris 1966) 8-20, 108-115. For a seal of Euthymius, see Zacos and Veglery, *Byzantine Lead Seals*, no. 1332.

22. See Pargoire, "Saint Euthyme," and the letters of Theodore of Studium in *PG* 99.1368f and in A. Mai, *Nova patrum bibliotheca* (Rome 1871) VIII, 74ff.

23. Zacos and Veglery, *Byzantine Lead Seals*, no. 1327.

24. *Pierre d'Atroa* cap. 24, 39.

25. Ibid. caps. 19, 26, 28.

26. Ibid. cap. 41; for the possible identity of the attackers, see V. Laurent, *La Vita Retractata et les miracles posthumes de Saint Pierre d'Atroa* (Brussels 1958) 41f.

27. For Thomas the Slav, see P. Lemerle, "Thomas le Slave" *Travaux et mémoires 1* (1965) 255-297, a critical study of the sources and problems to be used in preference to earlier works there cited.

28. The former is edited by H. Rabe: *Iohannis Sardiani Commentarium in Aphthonii Progymnasmata* (Leipzig 1928); the commentary on Hermogenes is unpublished. For the author and his works, see Rabe's introduction, xvi-xx. The manual of Aphthonius was a standard textbook for primary education in the Byzantine period; imitations and commentaries on it were the typical productions of the age. For those, see the article *Aphthonios* by Brzoska in *RE* and K. Krumbacher, *Geschichte der Byzantinischen Literatur* (Munich 1897) 450-452. Krumbacher comments trenchantly on the literary and intellectual merit of the followers of Aphthonius and Hermogenes, calling their works the "langweiligsten Erzeugnisse der griechisch-byzantinischen Geistes," a remarkable distinction. For the importance of Hermogenes and Aphthonius in Byzantine education and literature, see Fr. Fuchs, *Die höheren Schulen von Konstantinopel im Mittelalter* (Leipzig 1926) 46f and G. L. Kustas, "The Function and Evolution of Byzantine Rhetoric," *Viator 1* (1970) 55-73. See also Nicephorus Blemmydes, *Curriculum vitae*, ed. A. Heisenberg (Leipzig 1896) 2, who studied Aphthonius and Hermogenes in the early thirteenth century; they are the only writers whom he mentions by name. For the nature of the work of Aphthonius, see D. L. Clark, *Rhetoric in Greco-Roman Education* (New York, 1957) 180-206 passim, with further references to the author's own works on the popularity of the treatise of Aphthonius in Europe through the seventeenth century.

29. For the patriarchal schools, see below, n.83 and for their imitations in the provinces, J. Darrouzès, *Recherches sur les officia de l'église byzantine* (Paris 1970) 75.

30. They have not been published; see Hans Georg Beck, *Kirche und Theologische Literatur im byzantinischen Reich* (Munich 1959) 510.

31. Vita Lazari, *AASS* Nov. III, 536 cap 90.

32. For Peter, see the standard works on Photius: J. Hergenröther, *Photios* (Regensburg, 1867-1869) and F. Dvornik, *The Photian Schism* (Cambridge, 1948). Most information about him derives from the *Vita Ignatii* by Nicetas of Paphlagonia in *PG* 105.488-574. The quotation is from Mansi XV.810.

33. Nicetas Paphlago, *Vita Ignatii, PG* 105.572; see that page and the following for Photius' arbitrary transfer of bishops and appointment of his own partisans.

34. *Vita Euthymii Patriarchae CP*, ed. P. Karlin-Hayter (Brussels, 1970) 116, 225.

35. J. Darrouzès, *Epistoliers byzantins du Xe siècle* (Paris 1960) 128f. Seal: V. Laurent, *La Collection Orghidan* (Paris 1952) no. 381.

36. Leo I: Darrouzès, *Epistoliers*, 67-71; R. Browning, "The Correspondence of a Tenth-Century Byzantine Scholar," *Byzantion* 24 (1954) 419, 429; W. Hörandner, "Leon Metropolit von Sardes und die Briefsammlung in Neap. III A 6," *Byz. Forschungen* 2 (1967) 227-237. Leo II: Darrouzès, *Epistoliers*, 174ff.; Germanos, *Melete*, 54. A Leo, metropolitan of Sardis, who cannot be more closely identified, was the author of an unpublished letter and of some verses on the Octoechus, one of the hymnbooks of the Byzantine Church; the verses were edited by L. Sternbach, "Analecta Byzantina," *Ceské Museum Filologické* 6 (1900) 305ff.

37. *Vita Euthymii* 116. For a similarly suspicious instance, compare the case of Nicephorus, metropolitan of Ephesus, who, when he was elected patriarch in 1260, arrived in Nicaea with a great deal of money which he had brought from Ephesus: Pachymeres I.118,126. That these were not isolated examples is suggested by the rule that a bishop must make an account of his property when he entered office and that his heirs might make claim to no higher amount after his demise: Beck, *Kirche*, 72.

38. For the origins of metropolitans of the period, see L. Bréhier, *Les institutions de l'empire byzantin* (Paris 1949) 511f., and, for the twelfth century, R. Browning, "The Patriarchal School at Constantinople in the Twelfth Century," *Byzantion* 32 (1962) 168: successful teachers in the school were frequently rewarded with promotion to a bishopric; these were, of course, men who had spent large parts of their lives in the cultural center of the empire. It is significant in this context that the metropolitans were not elected locally, but at Constantinople by the patriarch and a synod composed largely of other metropolitans: Darrouzès, *Officia*, 469-474.

39. The reluctance of metropolitans to leave the capital for their dioceses was a constant problem for the church. Justinian legislated extensively against it, ordaining that metropolitans might attend one synod a year in Constantinople but must otherwise not leave their sees without permission of the patriarch and in no case for more than one year. So many of them came to the capital and stayed there, however, that a special synod, the *endemousa*, was formed from them as early as the fourth century and persisted through the Byzantine period. See J. Pargoire, *L'église byzantine de 527 a 847* (Paris 1905) 55f. and Beck, *Kirche*, 43. On the reluctance of bishops to leave the capital and their rhetorical expressions

of misery when forced to do so, see Ihor Ševčenko, "The Capital and the Provinces," *DOPapers* (forthcoming).

40. For the chancelleries of the metropolitans see Darrouzès, *Officia*, 117-122, 282. They imitated the bureaucracy of the patriarchate on a smaller scale, and are best known for Smyrna in the thirteenth century, where the local church had an extensive and complex establishment: Ahrweiler, "L'histoire et la géographie de la région de Smyrne entre les deux occupations turques (1081-1317)," *Travaux et memoires* 1 (1965) 100-121.

41. *BASOR* 170 (1963) 33; 166 (1962) 38-40; 162 (1961) 33f, with the MS reports (n. 146 above).

42. See the MS reports cited above, chap II, n. 8.

43. For Chaka, the main source is Anna Comnena VII.8, VIII.3, IX.1,3, XI.5. For his career, see the sketches of I. Melikoff, *La geste de Melik Danişmend* (Paris 1960) 85-88 and H. Ahrweiler, *Byzance et la mer* (Paris 1967) 182-187, both with references and bibliography.

44. Ahrweiler, "Smyrne," 124f.

45. For Philadelphia as the capital of the Thracesian, see J. Darrouzès, *Georges et Dèmètrios Tornikès, Lettres et Discours* (Paris 1970) 148, 170, 172, letters written in 1155 and 1156 which conclusively show that the *dux* of the theme resided at Philadelphia, and appointed a representative in Ephesus. Other passages which state or imply this are: Anna Comnena XIV.3 (Gabras, 1111), Choniates 318f, 340-342 (John Comnenus Vatatzes, 1181-1182), ibid., 523f. (Basil Vatatzes, 1193), Ansbert, 73f (*a dux civitatis et regionis* at Philadelphia in 1190). The complex discussion of Mme. Ahrweiler, "Smyrne," 123-130, is thus to be revised. In the Chrysobull of Alexius III of 1198, a province of Philadelphia is mentioned (G. Tafel and A. Thomas, *Urkunden zur alteren Handels-und Staats-geschichte der Republik Venedig* [Vienna 1856] 271), as it is by Acropolites 12 dealing with events of 1208, and in some documents of 1235: Miklosich and Müller, *Acta et Diplomata* IV.5,18,19,179. The relation of this province to the Thracesian or others is by no means clear: Ahrweiler, "Smyrne," 137f, 163ff.

46. Attack of 1113: Anna Comnena XIV.1. Her narrative makes it clear that she is writing of the Hermus, although she calls it the Maeander and discourses on that river with her typical affectation of learning.

47. Coins at temple; *Sardis* XI, viii. The continuity here is in notable contrast to the long break on the Acropolis and elsewhere; see Bates, *Byzantine Coins*, 138f, where no coins from 1081 to 1185 are recorded. Although the occupation of Sardis by Chaka may explain a break in the archaeological record, the long hiatus in the coin sequence remains enigmatic.

48. *Sardis* I, 44f, 52, 64, 67, 95; *Sardis* II, 14; *BASOR* 162 (1961) 33. Gap in coin sequence: *Sardis* XI, vii.

49. Sardis VII, 176. On the peculiar form of *beta*, see C. Foss "Historical Note on the Church at Sige" in H. Buchwald, *The Church of the Archangels in Sige* (Vienna 1969) 67 n.21.

50. Houses: *Sardis* I, 95, 127. Cemetery: ibid., 94, 134. Building L: *BASOR* 154 (1959) 11, 30. Limekilns: *Sardis* I, 44, 67. Coins: *Sardis* XI, viii (temple area), Bates, *Byzantine Coins*, 150 (Bldg. L).

51. *BASOR* 166 (1962) 33; 162 (1961) 26, supplemented by MS report of M. del Chiaro 1960. Coins tabulated: Bates, *Byzantine Coins,* 150. The inscription, IN 61.23, was kindly read by Professor Ihor Ševčenko.

52. See above, chap. I, n. 118.

53. Coins: Bates, *Byzantine Coins,* 1112 (Leo VI from MTW), 1129 (Constantine VII from HOB).

54. Coins tabulated: Bates, *Byzantine Coins,* 149f. Earthquake: *BASOR* 162 (1961) 43 (cf. chap. II, n. 9 above). Habitation: *BASOR* 182 (1966) 32, 187 (1967) 53. Limekilns: *BASOR* 154 (1959) 16; 157 (1960) 36; 174 (1964) 29; 187 (1967) 57f. Furnaces: *BASOR* 199 (1970) 43. "West of West B": *BASOR* 191 (1968) 38. For the gap in the coin sequence cf. chap. II, n. 47 above.

55. IN 61.30, read and dated by Professor Ihor Ševčenko.

56. *BASOR* 154 (1959) 21f; 157 (1960) 40, 43; 162 (1961) 45 n.80; 199 (1970) 40; Sardis Report 1, chaps. 9 and 10. Bracelets: chap. I, n. 40 above.

57. Choniates 318f, 340-342. An inflated version of these events appears as the epic story of "Constantine Vatatzes" in the late life, written c.1370, of the emperor John Vatatzes, who was supposedly the grandson of the rebel: A. Heisenberg, "Kaiser Johannes Batatzes der Barmherzige," *BZ* 14 (1905) 160-233; for Constantine Vatatzes, see 199-205 and the editor's remarks in his introduction, 162-166. It is this source which mentions the adherence of Sardis. In fact, it would seem that the emperor Vatatzes was no relation of the rebel. For his family and ancestry, see D. Polemis, *The Doukai* (London 1968) 106f.

58. For Mangaphas, see M. Hendy, *Coinage and Money in the Byzantine Empire 1081-1261* (Washington 1969) 149, with reattribution of the coin found at Sardis and attributed to Mangaphas by Bell in *Sardis* XI, 104. For the third Crusade at Sardis, see Ansbert 73 and *Historia Peregrinorum* 154 in *MGH, Scriptores rer. germ.* V, ed. A. Chroust (Berlin 1928). Mangaphas subsequently appears as the leader of a Byzantine army which defeated the Latins of Constantinople at Adramyttium in 1210: Choniates 798.

59. Magnesia: Ahrweiler, "Smyrne," 44-47 and Hendy, *Coinage,* 149. Nymphaeum: Ahrweiler, "Smyrne," 42-44.

60. Buildings of Vatatzes in every town and village: Scutariotes *ap.* Acropolites, ed. Heisenberg, 285. Foundation of churches and monasteries: Heisenberg, "Kaiser Johannes Batatzes," 199, 207.

61. Scutariotes, *ap.* Acropolites, ed. Heisenberg, 295, adds the detail that the sultan and emperor proceeded from Sardis to Magnesia.

62. For the history of the period: C. Cahen, *Pre-Ottoman Turkey* (London 1968) 269-314, S. Vryonis, *Decline of Hellenism . . .* (Berkeley 1971) 133-142, 244-286, and the more specialized studies of I. Hakki Uzunçarşılı, *Anadolu Beylikleri* (Ankara 1969), P. Lemerle, *L'Emirat d'Aydin, Byzance et l'Occident* (Paris 1957), Himmet Akın, *Aydın Oğulları Tarihi hakkında bir Araştırma* (Ankara 1968), P. Wittek, *Das Fürstentum Menteşe* (Istanbul 1934) and *The Rise of the Ottoman Empire* (London 1938), and Ç. Uluçay and I. Gökçen, *Manisa Tarihi* (Istanbul 1939).

63. Acropolites 136f.

64. The leaders of the Turkish states founded on the borders of the Byzantine

Empire later called themselves *ghazis*, warriors of the faith, but the term seems not to have been used this early. The *ghazi* mentality, however, was present among the early Turkish invaders of Anatolia: see Vryonis, *Decline of Hellenism*, 171, 273, and for the later importance of the *ghazi* ideal, Wittek, *Rise of the Ottoman Empire*, passim.

65. For the emirate of Denizli and the origins of Germiyan, see Claude Cahen, "Notes pour l'histoire des turcomans d'Asie Mineure au XIIIe siècle," *Journal Asiatique*, 239 (1951) 335-354, and for the history of Germiyan see Uzunçarşılı, *Anadolu Beylikleri*, 39-54, and H. Inalcık, "The Emergence of the Ottomans" in *The Cambridge History of Islam* (Cambridge 1970) 265-269.

66. For the revolt of Philanthropenus, see Pachymeres II.210-229 and P. Schreiner, "Zur Geschichte Philadelphias im 14. Jahrhundert," *OCP* 35 (1969) 376-383. The ineffectual efforts of the government of Andronicus II to hold Asia Minor are surveyed by A. Laiou in *Constantinople and the Latins* (Cambridge, Mass. 1972) 76-93.

67. Pachymeres I.220,311,468. Magidion, also called Magedon, has not been securely located: see Ramsay, *Historical Geography*, 122, 211.

68. Pachymeres II.435.

69. Pachymeres II.433-435.

70. Pachymeres II.310-316.

71. Pachymeres II.433-435.

72. I. H. Uzunçarşılıoğlu, *Kütahya Şehri* (Istanbul 1932) 72f; Akın, *Aydın Oğulları*, 41. For the history of Philadelphia in this period, see Schreiner, "Geschichte Philadelphias," 375-431.

73. Pachymeres II.428.

74. Several bishops of Sardis are known; for the ecclesiastical history of the period, see below.

75. C. Greenewalt, MS report 1968. The wall, however, seems small and encloses too narrow an area for many people to inhabit.

76. Cistern: *Sardis* II, 14. Coins: *Sardis* XI, viii.

77. Building L: *BASOR* 154 (1959) 11,30 and G. M. A. Hanfmann 1968 MS report; coins tabulated: Bates, *Byzantine Coins*, 150.

78. Coins tabulated in Bates, *Byzantine Coins* 149f.

79. L. Vann, (forthcoming publication).

80. Church E: see provisionally *BASOR* 170 (1963) 15f; 174 (1964) 14-20; 211 (1973) 17-19. A final report is being prepared by Hans Buchwald.

81. Southwest Gate: *BASOR* 186 (1967) 28.

82. Council of 1191: *BZ* 11 (1902) 75, cited by V. Laurent, "A propos de l'Oriens Christianus," *EchO* 29 (1930) 190. The two epitaphs are published by S. G. Mercati, "Poesie giambiche di Niceforo Chrysoberges, metropolita di Sardi," *Collectanea Byzantina* (Bari, 1970) I, 587-589.

83. For the career of Nicephorus, see Mercati, "Niceforo Chrysoberges," 574-578, and R. Browning, "The Patriarchal School at Constantinople in the Twelfth Century," *Byz.* 32 (1962) 184-186. Three of the speeches are published by M. Treu, *Nicephori Chrysobergae ad Angelos orationes tres* (Breslau 1892). For the *maistor ton rhetoron* see Darrouzès, *Officia*, 69, 78 and Fuchs, *Höhere Schulen*,

36, 40f. The patriarchal school is discussed in detail by Browning, 167-202 and by Fuchs, 35-41; for a description of it in the thirteenth century, see Nicolaus Mesarites VII-XI, XLII: *Nicolaus Mesarites: Description of the Church of the Holy Apostles at Constantinople*, ed. G. Downey. *Trans. Amer. Phil. Soc.* 47 (1957) 855-924. The *Progymnasmata* of Nicephorus are published with translation and commentary by F. Widmann, *Die Progymnasmata des Nikephoros Chrysoberges*, BNJ 12 (1936) 12-41, 241-299.

84. In the attributions of his orations, Nicephorus is described as rhetor, not bishop, of Sardis; the last of them was given in 1204. For the synodic letter and Alexius, see Germanos, *Melete*, 55f. V. Laurent, "L'Oriens Christianus," 191, raised an apparent chronological problem relative to the career of Chrysoberges. If Galenos is to be identified with the Theodore who was bishop of Sardis in 1191, and if as his epitaph states, he presided for five years, how could Chrysoberges, who was *maistor ton rhetoron* as late as 1204, have been his direct successor? There are two possible solutions: either the Theodore of 1191 is not the same as Theodore Galenos, or Chrysoberges occupied two offices at the same time. It is not impossible that a metropolitan could occupy another high dignity concurrently with his episcopal title: see the discussion of Darrouzès, *Officia*, 79-86, "cumul et favoritisme," who, however, has no examples of metropolitans who were also rhetors. Laurent's objection that a metropolitan was obliged to reside in his see is invalid, since violations of this rule were common. R. Browning, "Patriarchal School," presumed that Chrysoberges was both metropolitan and rhetor. For the present, the chronological problem cannot be resolved.

85. For the schools of Asia Minor in the thirteenth century, see Fuchs, *Höhere Schulen*, 54f.

86. Mercati, "Niceforo Chrysoberges," 590f (text), 579-583. The poems are accompanied in the MS by another poem in honor of Gabriel, which was canceled. For Michael at Philadelphia, see "Kaiser Johannes Batatzes," ed. Heisenberg, 202.

87. For this embassy and its results in the context of Papal policy to the empire, see W. Norden, *Das Papsttum und Byzanz* (Berlin 1903) 359-378. It was at about this time that Andronicus received three surviving uninformative letters from Theodore Lascaris: *Theodori Ducae Lascaris Epistulae*, ed. N. Festa (Florence 1898) nos. 123-125.

88. Acropolites 179.

89. For the career of Andronicus, see the article "Andronic 4" of R. Aigrain in *Dictionnaire d'histoire et de géographie ecclésiastiques*, with the corrections of Germanos, *Melete* 56-60.

90. For Chalazas, see Pachymeres I.126,296, II.51 and, for the embassy, the letter of Peter of Aragon to Michael VIII in R. Lopez, *Genova Marinara nel Duecento: Benedetto Zaccaria* (Messina 1933) 256f. Since the ambassador is described only as bishop of Sardis, Lopez (pp. 66-69) identified him with the more famous Andronicus, who, however, at this time was still a monk under the name of Athanasius. For the political significance of the embassy, see D. J. Geanakoplos, *Emperor Michael Palaeologus and the West* (Cambridge, Mass. 1959) 375f.

91. Pachymeres II.50-52,65f.

92. Germanos, *Melete*, 60f.

93. Cyril is mentioned in the following letters of Athanasius: *Vat. Gr.* 2219, 12v, 49v, 61r, 132r, 158v. These are all unpublished. Through the courtesy of Professor David Mitten, summaries of these texts with commentary were supplied to me by Dr. Alice-Mary Talbot, who will shortly be publishing them under the title *The Correspondence of the Patriarch Athanasius I with the Emperor Andronicus II* (Dumbarton Oaks publications). In the meantime, Laiou, *Constantinople and the Latins*, 88, 334f, may be consulted for Athanasius, whose zeal to rid the capital of indolent prelates is described by Gregoras I.181f. For the grants of a second see *kata logon epidoseos* and the decline of the church in the fourteenth century, see the long and important discussion of S. Vryonis, *Decline of Hellenism*, 288-350.

94. For the diocese of Sardis from 1315 to 1369, see Germanos, *Melete*, 62f and for its suppression, see source 34.

III. Turkish Sardis

1. For the territory of Saruhan see Gregoras I.214 and Ducas 83. No critical history of the state exists, but useful sketches are provided by Uzunçarşılı, *Anadolu Beylikleri*, 84-91 and Uluçay and Gökçen, *Manisa Tarihi*, 20-43, and the article "Saruhan Ogulları" by Uluçay in *Islam Ansiklopedisi*.

2. For Magnesia and Nymphaeum in the thirteenth and fourteenth centuries, see Ahrweiler, "Smyrne," 42-47. After the conquest, Nymphaeum (called in Turkish Nif) became the seat of a separate principality ruled by Ali Pasha, the brother of Saruhan. It is described by Al-Umari (fourteenth century): *Al-Umari's Bericht über Anatolien*, ed. Fr. Taeschner (Leipzig 1929) 44f (Arabic text); trans. E. Quatremere, *Notices et extraits* 13 (1838) 367f (French translation; Nif mistakenly identified with Nicaea). The state seems soon to have been absorbed by Saruhan.

3. Pachymeres II.318f, 402,441f and Vryonis, *Decline of Hellenism*, 254.

4. The Acropolis will be discussed below. Village and cistern at temple: *Sardis* II, 14. Byzantine coins found at the temple continued through John V (1341-91); the Turkish coins were not published, but were perhaps used to determine the date of the abandonment of the cistern: *Sardis* VI, viii f.

5. *BASOR* 182 (1966) 31; 187 (1967) 53.

6. *BASOR* 174 (1964) 14; 177 (1965) 3; 182 (1966) 25.

7. *BASOR* 170 (1963) 14f; 174 (1964) 19.

8. On the campaign of Tamerlane and the prevalent notion that he was responsible for the demise of the city, see Appendix II.

9. For Junayd, see the article "Djunayd" by I. Melikoff in *Encyclopedia of Islam²*. I am preparing a detailed discussion of his career with particular attention to the chronological problems of the period.

10. Ducas 243.

11. For Sardis as part of the vilayet of Aydin in the Ottoman period, see below. The Byzantine sources cited above (chap. III, n. 1) make it clear that

Sardis had been included in the lands of Saruhan. This is confirmed by the numismatic evidence: of the Seljuk coins so far identified, 37 are of Saruhan and only 7 of Aydin. These coins will be published by Dr. George Miles in a forthcoming volume of this series; I am grateful to him for the kind communication of his preliminary results. According to Evliya Çelebi IX.55, Sardis was taken by Yıldırım Bayezid from the emirs of Aydin; this is no doubt an error due to his knowledge that the town was first taken by Bayezid and that it was in his own day included in the vilayet of Aydin.

12. *BASOR* 170 (1963) 33-35.

13. C. Greenewalt, MS report, 1971.

14. The reduced importance of Sardis after the fifteenth century is clearly illustrated by the quantities of Turkish coins found on the site. There were 111 Seljuk coins from the fourteenth and early fifteenth centuries, 211 Ottoman pieces from Murat I - Mehmet II (1362-1453), and only 164 from the late fifteenth century through the nineteenth, of which 55 were of the enormous issue of emergency coinage of Süleyman II (1687-1691).

15. The only piece of information I have found in a historical source concerns the immediate vicinity of Sardis, not the town itself. The plain of Sardis had the distinction, on May 26, 1566, of being the birthplace of the Sultan Mehmet III (1595-1603). His father, the future sultan Murat III, was then governor of the province of Saruhan: I. H. Danişment, *Izahlı Osmanlı Tarihi Kronolojisi* (Istanbul 1950) III, 142.

16. See, for example, the notice of a detailed register of village populations, revenues, and military holdings in the district of Sardis and other parts of the province of Aydin, dated 1529: Akın, *Aydın Oğulları*, 136.

17. For collections of such documents, see Ahmet Refik, *Anadoluda Türk Aşiretleri* (Istanbul 1930), M. Çağatay Uluçay, *Saruhanda Eşkiyalık ve Halk Hareketleri* (Istanbul 1944) and Ibrahim Gökçen, *Saruhanda Yürük ve Türkmenler* (Istanbul 1946). The latter two works are part of a valuable series on local history sponsored by the Manisa Halkevi in the 1930's and 1940's. Individual documents will be discussed below.

18. For these documents, see Akın, *Aydın Oğulları*, 136, 164f, 86f, 101f, 90, and for the Ottoman administrative system in general, H. A. R. Gibb and H. Bowen, *Islamic Society and the West* (London 1950) I, 137-173 and 153ff for the *kaza*.

19. Salihli: Paul Lucas, *Voyage du Sieur Paul Lucas* . . . (Paris 1712) I, 306; cf. F. V. J. Arundell, *A Visit to the Seven Churches of Asia* (London 1828) 176, where "Salickly" is stated to have 13 Greek houses and 35 Turkish. For a general account of the region in Ottoman times, see Foss and Hanfmann, "Regional Setting."

20. Akın, *Aydın Oğulları*, 102; with this expression might be compared the exactly parallel practice of the Byzantine ecclesiastical chancery which used the word *ētoi* to indicate the same kind of change.

21. Gökçen, *Yürük ve Türkmenler*, 73.

22. Evliya has a highly polished style, to the requirements of which he is well capable of sacrificing accuracy. He is not always reliable and included in his work descriptions of many places he never visited: see the article *Evliya Çelebi* by

J. H. Mordtmann and H. Duda in *Encyclopedia of Islam²*. Since Sardis was on main routes, it is probable that he visited it, but it is not necessary to take his stereotyped listing of mosques, markets, caravansarays, and baths as a literal description. Nor does it seem possible to determine whether his statement of the size of the town—700 houses, which might imply a population as large as 3500—is accurate. If so, it would suggest that Sardis had achieved considerable prosperity in the seventeenth century, an impression in direct contradiction to the contemporary reports of the travelers.

23. Earthquake: Uluçay and Gökçen, *Manisa Tarihi*, 52; for the popular revolts and other disturbances, which were particularly severe in the late sixteenth and early seventeenth century, see the detailed studies of Mustafa Akdağ, *Celali Isyanları* (Ankara 1963) and Uluçay, *Saruhanda Eşkiyalık*; the latter contains a large collection of documents.

24. For the remains of this village, see *BASOR* 170 (1963) 14f; 174 (1964) 14; 177 (1965) 3; 182 (1966) 25 and, for the coins, chap, III, n. 14, above.

25. Thomas Smith, *Remarks upon the Manners, Religion, and Government of the Turks, together with a Survey of the Seven Churches of Asia* . . . (London 1678) 235-239. The text of this and other travelers to Sardis will be published with commentary by Jane Scott in a future volume of this series; I am indebted to Mrs. Scott for most of the references which follow.

26. This text may be taken as the point of departure for a general discussion. With it may be compared the following accounts of contemporaries of Smith, from whom they may well have copied the little information they provide: Paul Ricaut, *The Present State of the Greek and Armenian Churches* (London 1679) 77; Jacob Spon, *Voyage en Italie et du Levant* (Amsterdam 1679) I, 264; George Wheler, *A Journey into Greece* (London 1682) 263.

27. Aşıkpaşazade cap. 56, 65, *Die Altosmanische Chronik des Aşıkpaşazade*, ed. F. Giese (Leipzig 1929) 56, 66.

28. Gökçen, *Yürük ve Türkmenler*, 24. For village names from the Saruhanid period, see M. Çağatay Uluçay, *Saruhanogulları ve Eserlerine dair Vesikalar* I (Istanbul 1940) 208-212 (index) and II (Istanbul 1946) 37-117 passim (documents referring to the Saruhanid period arranged by *kaza*); see also I, xvi, lists of village names taken from documents of 1628 and 1631. Note, however, that the immediate region of Sardis is not included in these documents, since it was a *kaza* of the province of Aydin, for which similar material has not yet been published.

29. For Ottoman efforts to settle the nomads and the influx of tribesmen into western Anatolia, see X. de Planhol "Geography, Politics and Nomadism in Anatolia," *International Social Science Journal* 11 (1959) 526-528, repeated with maps and some modifications in "L'évolution du nomadisme en Anatolie et en Iran," *Viehwirtschaft und Hirtenkultur*, ed. Laszlo Földes (Budapest 1969) 79-81, 84-87. My thanks to Mr. Rudi Lindner for these references.

30. See the list of village names of the region of Saruhan derived from tribes in Gökçen, *Yürük ve Türkmenler*, 24, and the list of tribes in F. W. Hasluck, *Christianity and Islam under the Sultans* (Oxford 1929) II, 475-482; this includes several tribes in Lydia. Also of considerable interest is the study of tribes and village names of the vilayet of Aydin in A. Gökbel and H. Sölen, *Aydın Ili Tarihi* (Aydin 1936) 225-245. The study of place names, with detailed lists, in F. Sümer,

Oğuzlar (Ankara 1967) 209-362, 412-449, is limited to toponyms derived from the names of the 24 tribes of the Oğuz Turks. In the vicinity of Sardis, the following village names are derived from tribes mentioned in the documents: Tatar (Tatarislam and Tatarocağı), Karayaşlı, Eldelek, Yağbasan, Tekeli, and Gılcanlar. Most others are probably of similar origin, since their formation resembles that of tribal names; only a few of the tribes which settled in the area are mentioned in the documents. For names formed from tribes, see also X. de Planhol, *De la plaine pamphylienne aux lacs pisidiens* (Paris 1958) 103-109. Such names include those formed from personal names with the suffix "-li," such as the main market towns of the region, Salihli, Ahmetli and Turgutlu: a tribe of Ahmetli is listed by Hasluck. *Christianity and Islam*, 475 as settled around Kula and Simav; Turgutlu may, however, be derived from the ancient town of Trocetta which stood nearby; such turcification of a foreign name is common in toponymy. For the formation of tribal names, see the important discussion of Hasluck, *Christianity and Islam*, 127ff, 135f, and 337-341; he shows that most tribes bear names of some real or imagined ancestral chief, with or without the suffix "-li." For that and other formations, with remarks on the derivation of village from tribal names in the European provinces, see M. Tayyib Gökbilgin, *Rumelide Yürükler, Tatarlar ve Evlâd-i Fâtihân* (Istanbul 1957) 99-108.

31. Refik, *Türk Aşiretleri*, 187f, a document of 1732.

32. Gökçen, *Yürük ve Türkmenler*, 75, 94f.

33. For the nomads, see: J. A. van Egmond and J. Heyman, *Travels through Part of Europe, Asia Minor . . . etc.* (London 1759) 148; Richard Chandler, *Travels in Asia Minor* (London 1817) 294; Felix Beaujour, *Voyage militaire dans l'empire ottoman* (Paris 1829) 169; and Charles MacFarlane, *Constantinople in 1828* (London 1829) 206, 211f. The desolation of the country is described by Edmond Boissier, *Lydie, Lycie, Carie . . .* , ed. W. Barbey (Lausanne 1890) 38 and Charles Fellows, *A Journal written during an Excursion in Asia Minor* (London 1839) 289.

34. For these events, see Uluçay, *Eşkiyalik*, 334, and Refik, *Türk Aşiretleri*, 98f, 118ff, 218.

35. Hanfmann, *Letters*, 125, 127 fig. 93, of which the caption treats the coin as an isolated piece, "perhaps lost by a traveler." Professor Hanfmann, however, has informed me that the piece was only one of a small hoard.

36. See the extremely useful study of F. W. Hasluck, "The Rise of Modern Smyrna," *BSA* 23 (1918-19) 139-147 and the remarks of Fr. Taeschner in "Die Verkehrslage und das Wegenetz Anatoliens in Wandel der Zeiten", *Petermanns Mitteilungen* 72 (1926) 202-206, and, for the roads which radiated from Smyrna in 1766, see C. Niebuhr, *Reisebeschreibung* (Hamburg 1837) III, 120-123.

37. *BASOR* 166 (1962) 45f, undated.

38. The location of the caravansaray is not specified by the travelers, who state only that it was on the main highway. It may possibly have been built into the substantial ruin called Building A.

39. Edmund Chishull, *Travels in Turkey* (London 1747) 15.

40. Smith, *Remarks*, 239; van Egmond, *Travels*, 148; Chandler, *Travels*, 294; Spon, *Voyage*, 264.

41. Boissier, *Lydie, Lycie, Carie*, 38; Beaujour, *Voyage militaire*, 169. It

would appear from the excavations that Sardis had some permanent inhabitants in addition to the nomads through the Ottoman period. Such evidence, however, is not altogether unambiguous, for nomads will use or restore houses in locations convenient for their pastures. I have observed this phenomenon among Kurdish nomads of the Hakkari district. MacFarlane's description, quoted below, also shows that nomads lived in houses; it is therefore possible that such settlements as that of PN were only fully occupied during the winter.

42. F.V.J. Arundell, *Seven Churches*, 184; Alvah Bond, *Memoir of the Reverend Pliny Fisk* (Boston 1828) 133. For the Greek colonization and the nature of the Greek settlements, see Karl Dieterich, *Hellenism in Asia Minor* (New York 1918) 35-55 and M. L. Smith, *Ionian Vision: Greece in Asia Minor 1919-1923* (New York 1973) 24-29 with further references. No comprehensive account seems to exist. This settlement affected the area of Sardis by the early nineteenth century; Arundell (*Seven Churches*, 176) noted that there were thirteen Greek houses in Salihli, and eight in Tatar Arab Cafe (between Salihli and Sardis), while the neighboring village of Tatar Dere was entirely Christian with nine houses, five mills, and a church. By the early twentieth century, there were considerable numbers of Greeks in the Hermus Valley; see the tabulations of populations of the towns of the ecclesiastical provinces of Magnesia and Philadelphia in *Xenophanes* 2 (1905) 428f and 3 (1905/6) 238f. See also Lampakis, *Efta Asteres*, 360f for the Greek community of Salihli and its churches in 1906, and 362f for the Christian village of Hiristiyan Tatar (to be identified with one of the villages mentioned by Arundell; now there is only one village, called Tatar Islam) an hour east of Sardis, with its new church of Saint John the Evangelist (illustrated, 363) which contained icons of the mid-nineteenth century. A similar phenomenon is to be observed with the Jewish population. Nothing is known of Jews in Lydia in the Byzantine period. As early as 1416, however, they are attested at Manisa, where their number grew rapidly after their expulsion from Spain. They began to settle in the smaller towns of the province with the construction of the railway. In Salihli, for example, there were only four Jews in 1882, but a sufficiently large community had been formed twenty years later that a synagogue was under construction. The Jewish settlements were visited in 1904 by Abraham Galanté, about the same time that Lampakis was investigating the Greek communities in the region. For details, see his work, *Histoire des juifs d'Anatolie* II (Istanbul 1939) 70-126 for the Jews of the vilayet of Manisa, and 110-112 for Salihli.

43. MacFarlane, *Constantinople in 1828*, 206-223.

44. Ibid., 208. Although he wrote that the village was at the southern end of the Acropolis, it is quite apparent that it was in fact on the north side of that hill.

45. Ibid., 212, 217f.

46. Richard Burgess, *Greece and the Levant* (London 1835) II, 97-100.

47. Abbé E. Le Camus, *Voyage aux sept églises de l'apocalypse* (Paris 1896) 219, 225. The account is of greatest interest for its photographs of the Turkish village, pp. 219 (blurry) and 228 (here fig. 37), the latter showing clearly the structure of the wattle-and-daub house with thatched roof, as well as the family posed before it. To judge by the photographs, the village was in Building A. The

cafe was below Church D (plan of site, p. 220), apparently on the site of the earlier mill. Whether the absence of inhabitants was due to the season (when transhumants might have left for the summer pastures) or to the lack of observation or interest of the Abbé is impossible to determine.

48. *Sardis* I, 16; the villages are shown on the plan, p. 30.

Plans

1. Gymnasium-Bath
2. Synagogue
3. Byzantine Shops
4. House of Bronzes
5. Upper and Middle Terraces (a,b)
6. Roman Bridge
7. Pactolus Industrial Area
8. Southwest Gate
9.1-9.34 Byzantine City Wall
10. Pactolus North
11. Churches E and E(A)
12. Peacock Tomb
13. Pactolus Cliff
14. Pyramid Tomb
15. Expedition Headquarters
16. Northeast Wadi
17. Temple of Artemis
18. Church M
19. Kâğırlık Tepe
20.1 Acropolis Top
20.2 Acropolis North
20.3 Acropolis South
21. Acropolis Tunnels

22. Western Ridge Fortification (Flying Towers)
23. Byzantine Fortress
24. Building A
25. Stadium
26. Theater
27. Hillside Chambers
28. Bath CG
29. Building D (Byzantine Church)
30. Building C (Roman Basilica)
31. Mill
32.1 Claudia Antonia Sabina Tomb
32.2 Painted Tomb
33. Brick Vaulted Tombs
34. Roman Chamber Tomb
35. Road under Mill
36. Road to Byzantine Fortress
37. Vaulted Substructure
38. Roman Agora
39. Rubble Walls east of Gymnasium

40. Odeion Area
41. Foundations
42. Hypocaust Building
43. Marble Foundation
44. Minor Roman Building
45. Rubble Wall
46. Wall
47. Brick Vaulted Tomb
48. Walls
49. Butler's House
50. Shear's Stoa
51. Lydian Walls (AcN)
52. Pre-Hellenistic Walls (AcS)
53. Holes in Acropolis Scarp
54. Şeytan Dere Cemetery
55. Hellenistic Steps
56. Hellenistic Tombs
57. Street of Pipes
58. HoB Colonnaded Street
59. Building R and Tetrapylon
60. East Road
61. West Road?
62. Conjectured Ancient Road

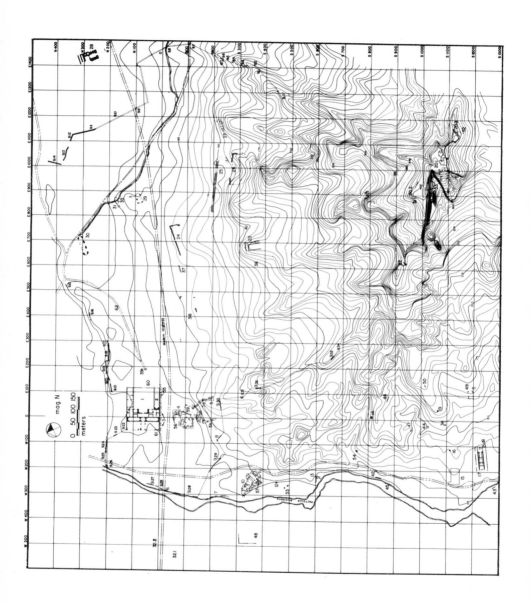

Plan I. Site plan with excavations and ruins of Sardis

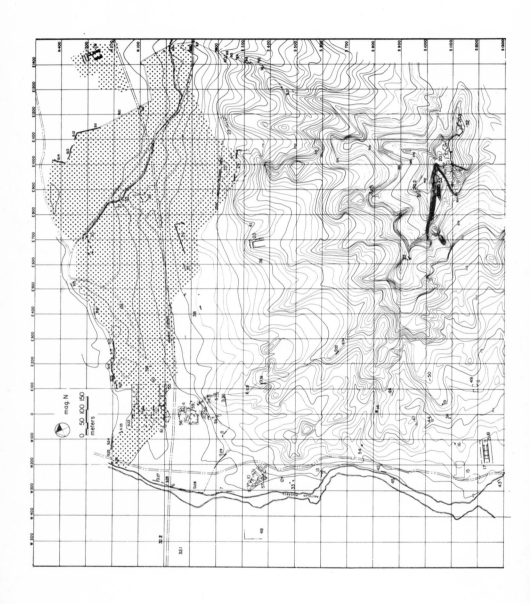

Plan II. Sardis ca. 300

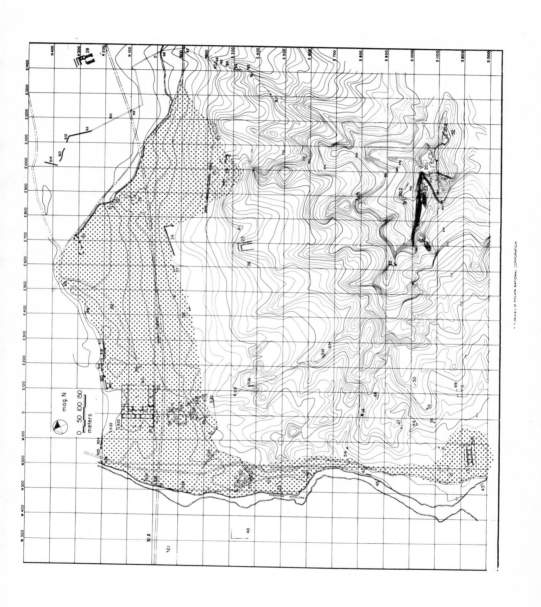

Plan III. Sardis ca. 600

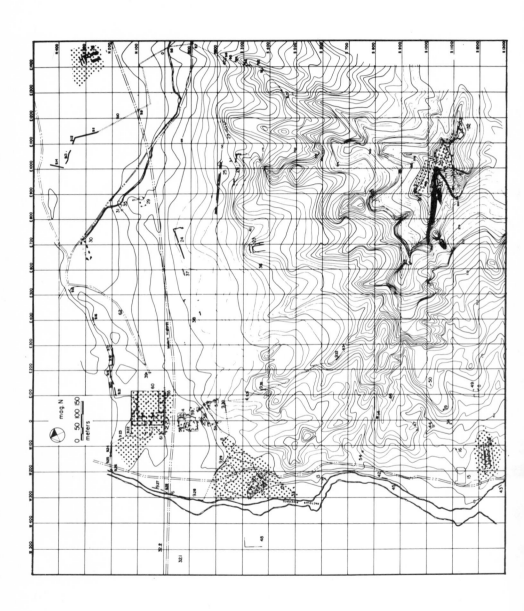

Plan IV. Sardis ca. 1200

Illustrations

ILLUSTRATIONS

Figure   1. Section of the late antique City Wall

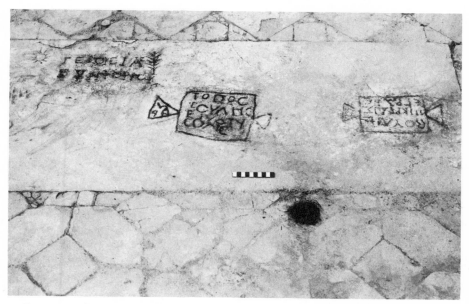

Figure 2. Inscriptions of the Gymnasium floor mentioning the *boule* and *gerousia* IN71.6 a-c

Figure 3.

Portrait head from the Gymnasium, late fifth century. S66.24

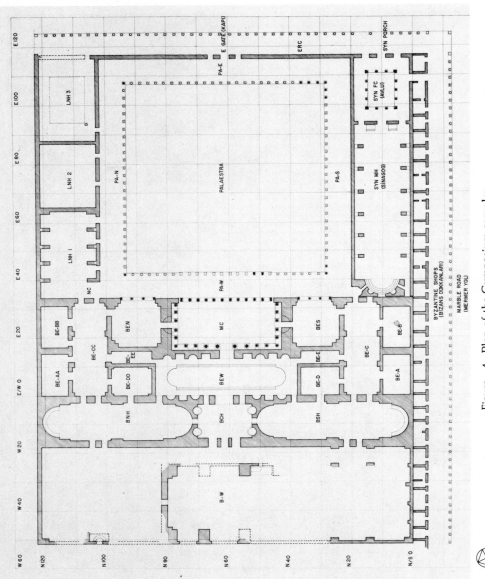

Figure 4. Plan of the Gymnasium complex

Figure 5. Gymnasium with Palaestra, Synagogue, Shops, and colonnaded highway viewed from the slopes of the Acropolis

Figure 6. The Marble Court, as restored. Photograph by Reha Günay

Figure   7. Central Sardis and the Hermus plain: on the left, in the middle distance, Basilica C; in the center, Building A; on the right, Basilica D

Figure   8. Eastern wall of Building A, west face

Figure 9. Plan of Artemis Temple and Precinct

1. Lydian Lion-Eagle monument
2. Vaulted tomb
3. Marble steps, Building U
4, 5. Terracotta wells
6. Stelai
7. Sarcophagus
8. Mortgage inscription on wall
9. Two small columns
10. Exedra monument

11-14. Vaulted tombs
15. Terracotta well
16. Concrete base
17. Sandstone base
18. Building LA, Lydian Altar
19. Perimeter structure
20, 21. Bases
22. Well

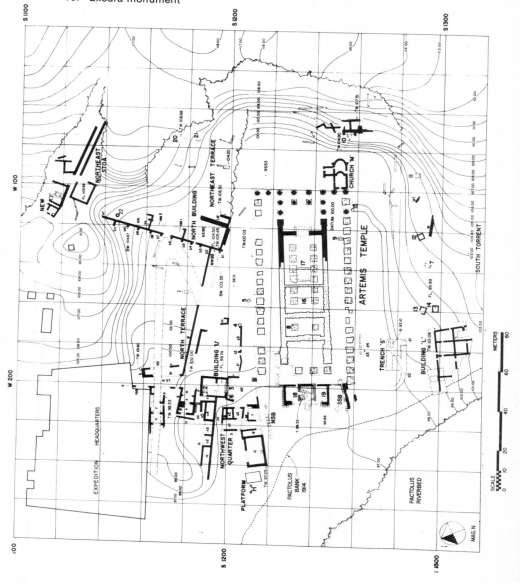

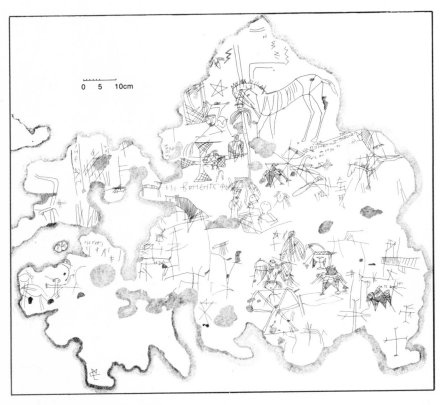

Figure 10. Graffiti on west wall of north diagonal passage leading to Synagogue apse

Figure 11. Surviving piers of the Justinianic Basilica D

Figure 12. Cut marble floor of the Marble Court, ca. 500

Figure 13. The Synagogue, looking southeast

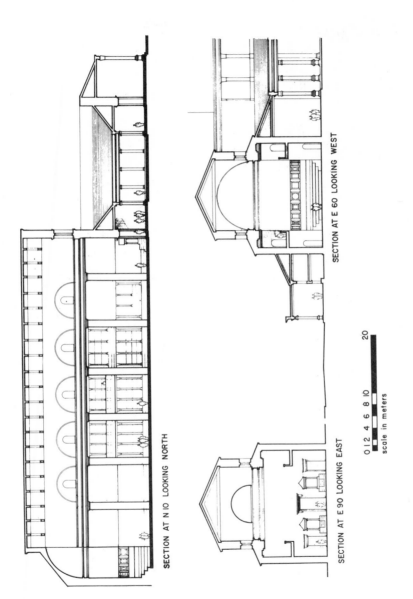

SECTION AT N 10 LOOKING NORTH

SECTION AT E 60 LOOKING WEST

SECTION AT E 90 LOOKING EAST

0 1 2 4 6 8 10   20

scale in meters

Figure 14. The Synagogue, possible restoration

Figure 15. The Synagogue, apse mosaic *in situ*

Figure 16. Mosaic of the Main Hall of the Synagogue

Figure 17. Forecourt of the Synagogue

Figure 18. Synagogue Forecourt: mosaic with donors' inscriptions

Figure 19. Marble-paved highway with colonnade. Shops and Gymnasium complex behind

Figure 20. Interior of one of the Byzantine Shops (E6). Synagogue wall on right

Figure 21. Objects from the House of Bronzes: a. censer; b. embers shovel; c. lamp holder. M58.31-33

Figure 22. Keystone of ruined structure, possibly the Tetrapylon

Figure 23. Section of the *embolos,* with terraced houses behind

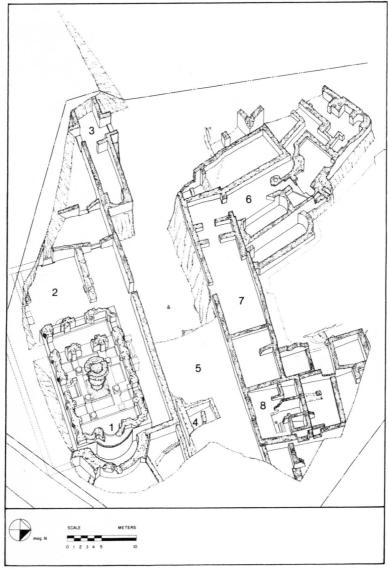

1. Church E
2. Church EA
3. North Chapel
4. Turkish Village House Wall
5. Roman Street
6. Late Antique Bath
7. Mosaic Suite
8. Roman Funerary Precinct

Figure 24. Pactolus North, late antique and Byzantine levels

Figure 25. "Eagle" mosaic floor of late antique villa at Pactolus North

Figure 26. "Dolphin" mosaic floor of late antique villa at Pactolus North

Figure 27. Apse of Basilica EA at Pactolus North with Byzantine Church E built inside it

Figure 28. Fresco from the Peacock Tomb, detail

Figure 29. Mosaic floor of the villa at Pactolus Cliff

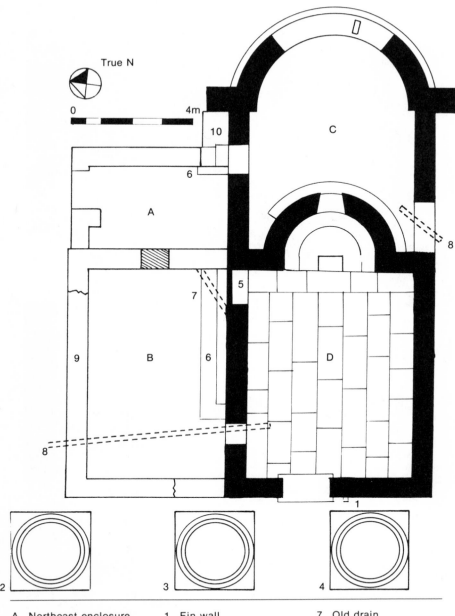

True N

0   4m

A

10

6

C

8

5

7

6

9   B   6   D

8

1

2   3   4

A. Northeast enclosure
B. Northwest enclosure
C. East Apse
D. West Apse

1. Fin wall
2-4. Southeast Artemis
    Temple column bases
5. Niche
6. New retaining wall

7. Old drain
8. New drains
9. Destroyed foundation
10. Probable doorstep

Figure 30. Plan of Church M at the Artemis Temple

Figure 31. Church M with columns of the Artemis Temple viewed from the east

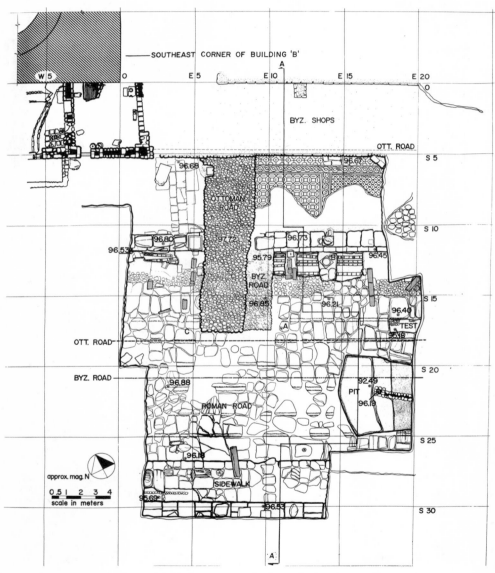

Figure 32a. Byzantine and Ottoman roads through the Gymnasium
complex: plan

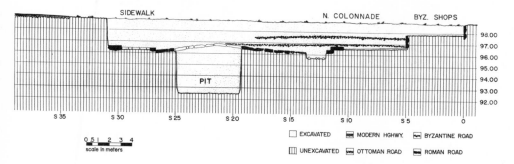

Figure 32b. Byzantine and Ottoman roads through the Gymnasium complex: Section A-A

Figure 33. Fortification wall on the south side of the Acropolis

Figure 34. Isolated western tower of the Acropolis fortification

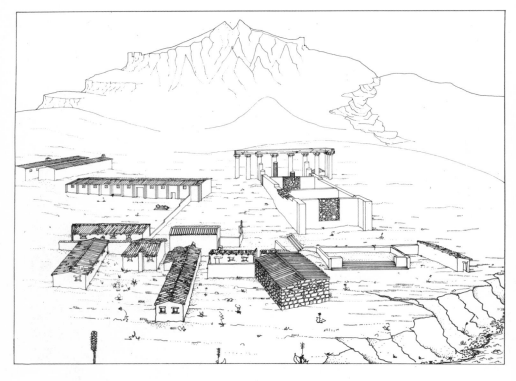

Figure 35. Reconstruction of the Middle Byzantine village at the Temple of
Artemis (highly hypothetical)

Figure 36. Pottery kiln in ruins of Gymnasium complex

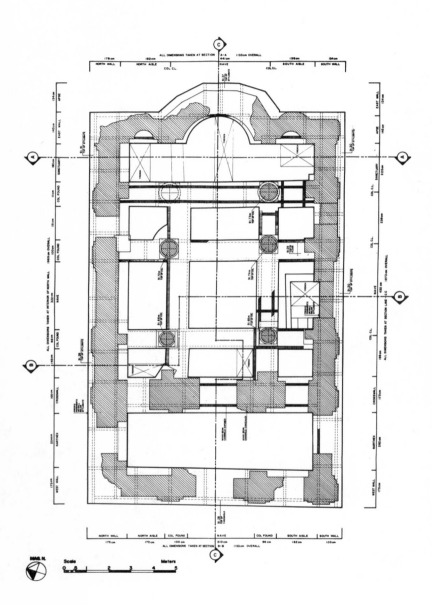

Figure 37. Plan of Church E at Pactolus North (thirteenth century?)

Figure 38. Remains of Church E at Pactolus North. Photograph by Alison Frantz

Figure 39. Turkish family and house of Sart village in Building A, 1896 (from Abbé Le Camus, *Voyage aux sept églises de l'Apocalypse*)

Index